African Christianity Thrives Under the Shadow of Traditional Beliefs

Reverend Henry Settimba

ISBN 978-1-905399-60-4

Cover Design by Duncan Bamford
http://www.insightillustration.co.uk

PERFECT PUBLISHERS LTD
23 Maitland Avenue
Cambridge
CB4 1TA
England
http://www.perfectpublishers.co.uk

CONTENTS

Preface

There is widespread fear of a resurgence of ritualistic human sacrifice in many parts of Africa and this situation looks as though it will continue to cause fierce doubt among rational thinkers. Most areas faced with this harrowing prospect are hurt and anxious and the disruption of relationships in these communities due to suspicion has affected the general population's well-being. It is argued that the ghosts of the 1930s have returned; in particular, the source of fear is attributed to the unfair abolition of traditional religious beliefs and freedom of expression that occurred at that time. The resurgence is said to spring from those groups that were disadvantaged and suppressed in this way.

When I was a child, I would set out on my bike early every morning and travel five miles from home to school. I had no protection, no mobile phone or water bottle. I spent the whole day without communicating with my parents. Now, as an adult, when I look back, I wonder how I survived my childhood. The good old days are long gone for most children and the carefree days of yesterday have been replaced by vigilant protection and surveillance to detect anyone who might cause harm to your child. The whole atmosphere has changed, away from the previous sense of community care for one another.

Today, in almost every community, there is a feeling of uncertainty, of uneasiness and of not being safe, which was never the case before. It is troubling and heartbreaking for parents to wake daily knowing that there may be a danger to their child. We need to address this problem that for too long has gone unspoken, because it is evident if nothing is done it will continue to cause many children to live under a cloud of fear and to struggle with anxiety.

Here we will pay attention to a different concept, a non racial one, which of Global Africa, meaning a special worldwide sense of reality, is spread between all those who recognise some link with continental Africa. It is not exactly ethnic, but it makes sense by acceptance of a cultural inheritance in a very specific way. Globalisation is characterised in contemporary discourse as a negation of universality or fundamental values, which increasingly perpetuates the marginalisation of poor countries. Yet, most disappointingly, two major development factors - easy access to information and increases in mobility - could have been the source of global harmonisation in theories and practices, including indigenous ideas.

This book will address the key issues relevant to this context systematically, such as the acceptability of corruption in cultural development, the impact of the deterioration in moral values and the problem of faking culture as an assumed means of success. Its aim is to trace the potential ways of developing a model of diagnostic tests of culture, to help society put in place restraints to reverse a system that seems to have gone in the opposite direction.

Different performance characteristics (such as drawbacks, false imaginings, validity across a variety of innovations), applied at different points of care, could inform appropriate treatment decisions. The impact of changes in society will also be analysed and considered as a question that should guide national developments in the global influence of commercialisation and fear. These are the twin realities of life in most African countries and have increased pressure in the modern way of life in its search for materialistic success.

It is important to recognise that we live in a society in which materialism is a necessity. A number of people who are largely either good or bad influence those who wish to be successful, like their colleagues, and in doing so are compelled to break moral principles that everyone must follow. This in fact endangers their material success, denying their own children access to the opportunity they deserve, and threatening the stability and security of the communities and the region. There is no indication that such incidents of insecurity are going to diminish, in societies where it is possible to have a degree of influences on the choices to be made. Whether it is the most recent search for materialistic success, the dictates of *haute couture* from the world of fashion or the latest in technical gadgets, we are enamoured with the idea that newer and different is better. This underlines the current pressures and contradictions in human thinking, and in a sense has accumulated pressure and put greater challenges on individuals to the extent of corrupting moral behaviour in the search for materialism, and could be argued to have worsened the position of those in less privileged, poor communities.

Furthermore, the unfortunate consequences of change have not been accompanied by sound moral values which have gradually moulded African people's behaviour and altered the way in which they thought and acted. A century ago, trust and confidence were underpinned by religious values; however, modern globalised society depends for its stability on the power of the human intellect to solve problems. In fact, the denial of the existence of moral values in some instances intentionally distorts the prevailing situation. In this case, the distortions are not supported by facts on the ground but are rather based on ideological assumptions about anything that previously made sense in African society to justify controversial decisions. This hinders the continuity that is essential to achieve community restraint in the successful implementation of moral values, and leads to a high and rising state of societal disintegration.

From the records of colonisers and missionaries it is clear that continuity was one factor that did not exist in their vocabulary, and in most cases they acted as if they were all agents of change. The view of change will be considered throughout this book, as it led to far-reaching consequences for African society. I will endeavour to show that it is a misconception that the old image of mission, as something taken from Europe to the rest of the world during the colonial period, is long gone, and that in fact the ghost of the past still lingers today in many African people's minds. It is essential to recognise this fact in order to understand the kind of the struggle people go through and the language or religious code that engages their minds. While the church is still caught up in missionary doctrines it negates what is real to people faced by daunting challenges, such as the rapid speed of the rise of materialism in the industrialised world, the emergence of religious pluralism, religious violence and the consequences of economic globalisation. All these have overstretched African society.

There is an overwhelming risk of creating short-sighted Christian teaching, which is representative of modern styles, obscuring the reality it represents, although the line of presentation inevitably places the latest developments to the fore in a historical context. In discussing normal perceptions and differences between societal changes, institutions and the deterioration of moral value, it is the central concern of this chapter that the church should be able to think about how to restore cultural values and traditions in order to create the context within which Christian teaching has to be done today.

As a matter of strategic priority, this means that the mission of the present church will tend to underemphasise certain aspects of context. For instance, a wave of outbursts has produced an explosion in media and public outcry related to rapid mobility and easy communication, which has facilitated human trafficking and ritualistic sacrifice. This is why there is a greater need to assess what has led to the tragic increase in ritual murder and examine its representation in press coverage.

The operative analysis will be based on a theory that seeks to establish whether there is any link between ritual murder and the historical, traditional religious beliefs that were abolished during the missionary period and are today argued by elderly respondents as being the source of the resurgence of ritual murder, related to suppressed beliefs and wider economic influences.

I believe that this book is a unique and valuable resource for the churches and for secular groups concerned with the way in which ritualistic beliefs are increasingly endangering human lives and have led to a worsening moral deterioration in society in general. It draws its argument from traditional religious groups, anthropological studies of wider societal myths and beliefs in ritual celebrations, tracing the history of human sacrifice from Jewish tradition to the European influence in Africa.

Although it may sound ridiculous and even illogical to start talking about missionary work in the 21st century, to gain an understanding of this most difficult historical area it is necessary to revisit past events to highlight how the process of conversion attempted to erase traditional African beliefs. At the same time, it is not necessarily traditional beliefs that are responsible for ritual sacrifices. It is the aim of this book to investigate and analyse how people's traditions and history undermined the role of culture and traditional religious representations of a community that still today serves as a locus for change, but the moral restraint of which seems to have disintegrated.

The intention of the analysis of traditional religious history is to address issues of concern around abolishing cultural and religious diversity, distortion and social cohesion. It will produce outcomes that will make a useful contribution to knowledge and will include items of interest to the wider academic community. The missionary process of converting Africans to Christianity amounted to gross injustice in both policy making and to the general public, including grievances such as abolishing traditional healers in favour of colonialist interests and providing support for missionary teaching, enabling society to learn from very rich and advanced cultures, yet with a hidden agenda and little known history in the colonies. For instance, Mahatma Gandhi observed that missionaries were doing a social service with the ulterior motive of conversion, which he considered offensive. He commented that if this situation continued in a free India, he would ask the foreign missionaries to leave the country (Cfr. Manufacturing Kufr: Reads Christian Missionaries in the Muslim World Amir 'Abdullaah Article ID: 825 | 4380).

I hope to revisit the missionary influence in conversion in relation to a number of issues and to take the reader on a fascinating tour to re-examine how cultures were forbidden. The fact that there has been a resurgence of the old in the new shows that what was forbidden is still alive in many people's minds in Africa. It not only casts some light on the present crisis, but poses a challenge to society. It also leads to the question of the intention of producing changes, not in the sense of development, but in people's religious beliefs, depending on whether you are looking at local or wider influences. This serves as a context for those interested in training for church ministry in Africa, those who work among communities, social workers, academics and new incoming missionaries, providing awareness to prevent the repetition of past mistakes.

It is important to find the source of the resurgence of past beliefs to be able to eradicate the seemingly instoppable rise of (Abafere) fake traditional healers or the exploitation of religious pastors. The new culture of faking will be analysed in order to highlight how wider economic influences have ramifications for rich and poor societies alike. For instance, consider the recent reports of a convicted fraudster who agreed to repay nearly £600,000 gained from faking the death of her husband (http://www.timesonline.co.uk/tol/news/uk/articles6912213.ece).

The question is, what drives people to such behaviour? In my view, it is not only a challenge to civic leaders, but society at large. In the case of Africa, it should be traceable purely as a process of weakening social integration through the violation of local religious beliefs, which intrinsically entails resistance to prolong its existence, despite the external forces aimed at converting anyone to Christian beliefs. This is why this should be a wake-up call to the Christian church leadership and theologians, to listen to the grievances of the practitioners of traditional beliefs.

Henry Settimba, February 2010

Introduction

I will start by arguing that to change people's concepts, beliefs and behaviour, you need to live among them in order to understand what you are changing and whether it is valuable or not. Therefore, this book is an attempt to explore the intersections of the source of what has been happening among African countries since the advent of colonialism and missionary influence in the past and how it has led to recent human sacrifices, which poses a serious threat to African society. This is to acknowledge that there is no going back, but that the present has to negotiate with the beliefs of the past, which remain a challenge in the resurgence of ritualistic sacrifice.

This is a fact that the church and society at large in Africa need not only to accept, but to face with understanding, imagination and commitment, in order to examine whether present economic pressures are related to human trafficking. To do so, the church and civic leadership will need to grasp clearly the causes and nature of changes and to appreciate deeply the effects of those changes on society as a whole, especially in so far as they have a bearing on religious beliefs or on how the abolition and suppression of beliefs are conceptualised and contextualised.

In this process of trying to investigate the source of the resurgence of human sacrifice, however, the main effort will be put into the analysis of information drawn from instances of attempted child abduction, kidnapping, human trafficking and the discovery of human remains by the police or the public. I will analyse the previous work in the general area, including theoretical work (local and wider academic debates), polemical work (for example from individual traditional healers), empirical work from research reported in journals/academic books and official and unofficial sources. I will move beyond providing narrative incidents to analyse the narrative itself and how theoretical accounts offer differing schools of thought which characterise the changes in society.

I will also explore the conclusions to which such analysis may lead, as well as pursuing a comparative study to assess which countries may provide signs of a corrupt fake culture. The pattern that has emerged establishes that human ritualistic sacrifices are not taking place spontaneously, but rather seem to be well planned. There is evidence pointing to certain actors, but definite conclusions will be reached based on a scientific process of investigation, data collection, analysis and deductions.

The book starts with a critical assessment of the workings of the unquestioned banking loan system, the massive loans offered, which in my view seem to have partly contributed to the perpetration of human sacrifice. Since loan transactions and the maintenance of loan repayments could show the changing nature of accumulated pressures arising out of beliefs surrounding the ritualistic sacrifice as protection, this invariably might illustrate the historical factors that need to be analysed to validate whether this is true or not. And if it is true, I wonder if this kind of grievance, the feeling that someone has directly ignored your culture, experience and beliefs, must compel the church to adopt a critical approach to issues of culture and traditional beliefs in society that are still regarded as areas of grievance. The purpose is to achieve and disseminate cultural and religious representations based on the original body of primary press and oral history source materials that address the analysis of the deplorable question outlined above.

We live in a time when people have not only lost faith in God, but also in each other. Consider the following incident where a 20-year-old Ugandan woman, Rita Nansamba, was nearly strangled for human sacrifice. Her ordeal started when a man only identified as Alex and a resident of

Nyendo convinced her grandmother, Maria Asaba, to release her for a job in Kampala. She said the man hired a taxi that took them to one of the Kampala taxi parks, from where they took another taxi to Kyebando. She lived with Alex's relatives from Friday to Tuesday evening, when he came with other men in a small car.

"After discussing with the men, Alex told me to go with them so they could give me a job," she said. No sooner had she entered the car than the killers gagged her with a piece of cloth and bound her hands.

"They took me to a storeyed building and were joined by more men who inspected me," she related. (New Vision, "Woman survives ritual murder", Thursday, 19th March, 2009).

The suspects agreed she was not the right candidate, but decided to kill her out of fear that she would report them if they let her go free. There were other missing people, both men and women. Arrested for the attempted kidnap was Ronald Kagugube, a resident of Kata village, Matugga in Wakiso district.

I will mainly use a sociological and theological approach to investigate the history of the church and the background of ritualistic celebrations in various countries. In the process, putting colonialist and sociological concerns to one side, a basic functionality should also apply to the teaching involved in missionary conversion. For instance, I will endeavour to assess what took place during the early period when cultural values were on the verge of extinction and missionaries' classical social theories introduced new ideas in an effort to replace them. The beliefs of Christianity wrapped in European culture, values and colonial ideological interests so often surfaced in the conversion teachings for the new Christian faith.

It is argued that by imparting Christianity as a body of influence through knowledge, missionaries combined it with their own cultures and contributed to the institutionalisation of society in the Christian discipline. In particular, there is a need to trace how traditional beliefs and practices were endangered, which should throw a great deal of light on how the current crisis has developed. The analysis will involve hidden activities such human trafficking and many other problems that are not related to cases of human sacrifice, but also examine critically the explanations that have been used in relation to traditional ritual practices, to try to develop a coherent, unified social theory of how the process has developed.

Also, I have attempted to see how traditional believers, the church, the government and society at large, are reacting to the current crisis and whether those reactions are appropriate or not, because I do believe that any social theory has to say something about human action, whether it is individual or collective and about social structure and the organisation of society. This is to analyse the human interactional point of view, taking rationality as a standard by which society can be judged as good or bad, in order to assess how the development of human sacrifice enters into the economic life of the people as a source of aggravating factors, which has led to a change in the way people have adopted sacrifice rituals in a search for wealth. (New Vision, "Woman survives ritual murder", Thursday, 19th March 2009).

Max Gluckman has observed that the practice of ritual involves highly conventionalised performances through which people believe that they can help, by mystical means outside of sensory observations and control, to protect, purify or enrich the participants and their group. He has asserted that ritual celebrations give expression to the relationship that is supposed to exist between people in their environment and the world (Cf. Gluckman, Max, 1966: "Politics, Law, And Ritual In Tribal Society", p.224).

Again, the crucial question is to assess the reasons behind these sacrificial rituals. According to Chris

Kiwawulo, ritual killers have changed tactics and started killing more adults than children. For instance, in one month, seven people were killed in suspected ritual murders and another 45 went missing in Uganda. Those killed were three male adults, two female adults and two children. They were killed in Kampala, Kamuli, Ntungamo Mubende, Soroti and Bushenyi. Nine people were arrested and four were charged. Traditional healers have found that there is a lucrative business dealing in human heads and body parts as a source of amassing quick wealth (Chris Kiwawulo, article, "Ritual Killers change tactics", Monitor, March 2009).

I will therefore trace how the church in African society can approach this crisis to advance the fundamental role of the Christian church and subsequently address the underlying issues of concern especially, but not exclusively, those who are excluded and demonised just for following traditional beliefs. There is a need to find long-lasting solutions to religious tensions and provide pastoral care to offer a Christian example in society.

For more than a hundred years the church has been very good at visiting church members, but it does not appear to have taken time to analyse the source of the current crisis. Some people seem to be convinced that the resurgence of the belief in rituals suggests that missionaries could be right to describe this as black magic, although as we shall see later on, not all ritualistic magic was evil. However, the current request for these powers is increasingly turning modern civilised men and women back almost into savages. This appears to accord with the view that some people have drive, some have skills and others don't, but do have ability, yet others have the enthusiasm for evil innovations.

The book will also assess the political and economic situation, in which it seems true that society is ever changing, either forward or backward, for good or for worse. In other words, it is argued that what appears today as if it were something new is in fact not. Greater attention needs to be paid to issues of the historical and cultural ritualistic context, especially in how actively different ritualistic rites across various continents are interpreted. The evidence shows that human history is littered with wicked acts of human sacrifice going back at least 5000 years in the early agricultural societies of Europe, which will be described below, and readers are left to draw their own opinions and conclusions.

Probably the earliest case in the world is that of two girls found at Sigersdal near Copenhagen, killed about 3500 BC. One was about 16 and the other, who was about 18, still had a cord around her neck. Danish farmers sacrificed human offerings, but also stone axes and flint tools, amber jewellery and food, by depositing them in pots in bogs. Likewise, in Africa farmers are more likely to be inclined to such practices as a means for asking either for rain or a good harvest, which is all related to a survival culture. Another type of sacrifice was that of fertility rites among the Sukuma/Nyamwezi, performed by elders to take care of the fertility of the land of their people. ("Sunday News", 26th April 1970, T.N). To discover more about ancient Africa, one needs to read Mama's article:
(http://www.mamaafrica.com/article/articleone.php/16/9/2009).

French archaeologists in Sudan uncovered the oldest proof of human sacrifice in Africa, the tomb of a 5,500-year-old man surrounded by three sacrificed humans, two dogs and exquisite ceramics exhumed north of Khartoum (http://news.yahoo.com/s/afp/20080215/sc_afp/sudanfrance archaeology_080215201642;_ylt=AsVyfwTgpxINUkUEsR wE._xFeQoB).

Mass human sacrifices were particularly a feature of ancient states whose dead leaders required their courtiers and followers to accompany them into the afterworld. Each of the tombs of the first dynasty of Egyptian pharaohs (3100-2890 BC) was surrounded by the graves of their courtiers. (http://www.bbc.co.uk/history/ancient/bri). In the royal tombs of ancient Mesopotamia the courtiers – guards, musicians, handmaidens and grooms – died at their posts in the tomb, having taken a lethal draught of poison. Some of the largest mass sacrifices accompanying dead rulers can be seen at the royal tombs of the African kingdom of Kerma, around 1500 BC, where 500 people at a time were buried in huge grave pits next to the dead king and covered by a large mound. Around the same date, the royal tombs of the Shang Dynasty at Anyang in China were similarly provided with sacrificed bodies. In the second century BC, workers and soldiers were buried in the tomb of the first Chinese emperor and, in addition, he was provided with an other-worldly army of terracotta substitute soldiers. (http://www.bbc.co.uk/history/ancient/bri).

The ancient civilisations of the Americas are also well known for their human sacrifices. Within the Inca Empire of South America, children and teenagers were sacrificed to the sun god, bestowing considerable prestige on the child's parents and on their local community:
(www.bbc.co.uk/history/ancient/bri).

Mike Parker-Pearson describes how the bodies discovered were garrotted, their throats slit or they were bludgeoned to death. The evidence for human sacrifice in the Iron Age is most prolific in Denmark, Germany and Holland, where many bodies have been found completely preserved in peat bogs:
(http://www.bbc.co.uk/history/ancient/bri).

In an attempt to provide external perspectives on the reality of what is happening locally, I will refer to anthropological findings to try to observe indirectly what is almost impossible to see directly. In this way, findings and the discussion of findings are merged into one entity, rather than being separate elements. Thus, a key reform tries to erode indigenous practices by distinguishing bad elements related to the practice of witchcraft. In indigenous African traditional religion, otherwise called African Traditional Religion (ATR), the culture of the people and the religious traditions are intertwined. Issues relating to the rise of ritualistic beliefs and sacrifices seen from the perspective of traditional beliefs will explore how environmental stimuli interacting in the daily lives of the people might or might not be having an impact in society currently.

Accordingly, I wish to clarify from the start that the discussion will limit itself to the question of the relevance of converting Africans where a totally different version of the revelation of God was deliberately created to reject the African concept of God. I will raise various voices from different academic persuasions that represent the catholic, protestant and world religious views, both traditional and evangelical, with added interpretation simply to highlight what has been argued elsewhere.

This analysis recognises the missionaries' process of converting Africans to Christianity as a distortion and generalisation of religious activities (ATR beliefs and practices) as a result of diverse cultural and racial structures. Therefore, it is arguable that indigenous beliefs provide room for people to utilise their potential both within and outside the formal religious setting and that formal religious affairs and rituals played complementary roles within society. This is why, in the first instance, if the missionary church had used local knowledge, there was a need for it to be selective in the words used in the conversion process to assess what methods were used to highlight after conversion to Christianity.

In fact, the methods missionaries employed to convert colonies to Christianity were dubious and indefensible. But they still persisted with rough and ready methods of conversion in the knowledge that though the first generation of converts were likely to be superficial Christians, their descendants would become devout Christians in the course of time. As a Christian I find these past methods of conversion to Christianity very disturbing and it is hard to believe that Christians could ever do this to other humans.

I have decided to revisit the early period of conversion to verify the reasons why today there is a resurgence of ritualistic murder. The spiritual quest for guidance of those searching elsewhere for help could be the source of the crisis, resulting from the missionary teachings. This argument seems to agree that the church has not even provided theological inclusiveness to develop traditional and cultural values as a ground on which people can unite.

Therefore, everything seems to be conspiring against normalising social values and provides compelling reasons to distinguish these past failures of missionary conversion, in addition disseminating biblical messages of Christian values, which would become a means of salvation to each society, rather than demanding that everything should change. The emphasis will then be on the question of change in society to assess how Church can reform to develop theological strategic measures and help church members how to handle the resurgence of ritualistic sacrifice.

I will examine the role of schools, hospitals and employment in the conversion process, to highlight all the tactics employed and the impact on society. I will even go further to inquire into the reasons why Christianity in Africa ignored local cultures, traditions and beliefs and show whether people just gave up the culture, tradition and beliefs that had given them protection and spiritual guidance as a form of security in an unsafe environment.

William Bascom and Melville Herskovits rightly argue that there is no African culture that was not affected in some way by European contact, and there is none that has entirely given way before it (William Bascom and Melville Herskovits, (1963). p.3).

I will, moreover, try to raise the argument that for an African to be fully converted to Christianity, the converters needed to consider that people's beliefs were not allowed to be practised in openness, which was a tragic and unnecessary experience, changing African culture and tradition for ever. The reason for raising this concern is that the Christian conversion exercise looks like a dramatic repeat of colonial policies. Therefore, this substantially discriminatory policy increased the dominance of the colonisers at the expense of a realistic possibility of obtaining consensus and voicing objections about the conditions that accompanied Christian conversion and the mutually consistent colonial framework of brutal rule.

Besides the Christian values it promoted, the colonial perception often diverted the church of Christ from fulfilling its real mandate, which consisted of serving and enabling God's people to experience life in all its fullness. Consequently, the rationalisation of conversion became a major platform of missionary influence and was effectively used by colonialism to implement policies for changing society. It would have been possible to apply a range of other policies other than abolishing the existing arrangements.

Societies are like houses of cards; fragile constructions built on tentative assumptions about shared values and understandings, liable to collapse under any of the contradictory situations that abolished the cultural and religious life that has been known and useful within that society. It is seen as a valid argument that when people's culture and tradition become less important, the Christian message also becomes less relevant. In evaluating the way people's tradition and culture were ignored, there seem to be two possibilities: first, that the missionaries were right; second, that this approach was deficient and had a hidden agenda. If the first possibility is acceptable, whether by faith or by reason or by a combination thereof, it is arguable that the question of the cultural sensitivity of the approach could have been settled. However, in relation to the second possibility, it is still debatable how could it be objectively verified as truthful or deceitful.

For the convenience of presentation, it may be useful to see whether the assumption of the possibility of faking traditional healing can be substantiated. If it were true, it only becomes a fact when Christian behaviours increasingly are contradicting Christian principles, which mean that the church's teaching is still hanging in the air. It is worth investigating the revelation of God in the African context to highlight African knowledge of God and what people say God has done for them in the past, the present and the future. This is in jeopardy if society doesn't act now, as the struggle will stretch to the generations to come.

The main reason for this book is to discover what has happened to society, because I believe that the increase in ritual murder can't just come out of the blue. It is an attempt to look back at the last hundred years and trace the questions surrounding African society, to establish the source of the situation that has led to this crisis.

In fact, it is argued that corruption was unheard of in African history, which suggests that it was a cultural importation. Since customary laws forbid lying, cheating and forgery, corruption was heavily punished, to the extent that the punishment includes the entire family. However, now African society appears to be full of corruption, even to the extent of fake church preachers; in fact, some pastors have been accused of enriching themselves by asking their followers to sow (donate money) in order to reap (have miracles performed). Pentecostal pastors in particular have been embroiled in a bitter fight over followers, with some accusing others of witchcraft (New Vision, April 2009).

In addition, there has been a great increase in fictitious traditional healer's revisionism of the interpretation of human sacrifice, representing the opposite of this principle.

What has inevitably and progressively become a culture full of bribery has led almost the entire population of Africa to do anything for material gain, to the extent of murdering fellow human beings for wealthy ambitions. I will therefore attempt to put forward proposals for action so that the fears of society can be reduced, to determine the issues that have led society to this crisis and to see what part, if any, Christians in Africa might play in continuing pastoral care and support to victims who have lost their beloved ones in this tragedy of human sacrifice.

On the other hand, to an extent there is a justified difference between risk taking as part of the Christian calling and perhaps what we may call the risk taking of the Christian faith; or even arguably that when operating on Christian principles you need to travel a spiritual journey by faith, in which case Christian spirituality is increasingly becoming irrelevant. However, no matter who is involved in this situation, what one needs is to be aware that true faith is often tested. When the priests carried the ark into the river Jordan at the flood, there was a risk they could lose the ark to the river. But this is not what happened. If we glance at Josh we read, "As soon as the priests who carried the ark, the Lord of all the earth set foot in the Jordan, its waters flowing downstream will be cut off and stand up in a heap." (Josh 3:13).

It is under such a situation likewise that the Israelites required believers to follow God where God wants them to change and made it possible to walk across without the pressure of wading through the powerful water only when they took the first step. Risk means that there is a potential for loss. However, when God leads us to take a risk, then He is there whether we succeed or fail. He is there in the success and He is there in the failure. If God leads people to take a risk, it may not always succeed in the way we think. In fact, it could even fail. The only true failure is when we fail to take the risk when God is leading us to do so.

Sometimes the fear of failure is a greater obstacle than the risk itself. In complicated and sensitive situations, discernment is seen as the difficulty in understanding how human beings can degrade fellow human beings to the extent of trading each other as nothing but objects of offering for sacrifice to fake traditional healers or witches.

This is a view that springs from personal conviction and the belief that when studying people's behaviour, it is necessary to take into consideration what they believe and value in their lives as the most important factor in their social, political, religious and economic life. The intention is to examine society's views about human sacrifice. Human trafficking is outlawed under UN Protocol (The New Times, Rwanda, 9th September 2009). Nevertheless, it is a common phenomenon that has been in effect for a long time, and stories of human trafficking have been heard in almost all areas. Tragically, the most vulnerable children are targeted in deprived areas and families, which has brought into play various viewpoints and movements in an attempt to streamline the control of this diverse phenomenon.

Chief Supt Elias Kabera from the Rwandan National Police, who is also an officer with Interpol, attributes the increase in human trafficking to reasons such as tourism and the Internet, saying that the income that is generated from human trafficking almost surpasses that of drugs. On a global scale, the human trafficking industry earns US$32 billion per year. The Rwandan government recently received two boys from the Ugandan authorities; one of them had been on the human trafficking market for 23 million shillings, around Frw8 Million (The New Times, Rwanda, 9th September 2009).

There is a need to understand the priorities of leaders and how society can bring ritualistic practices under control, within a perspective linked to the contradictions that are relevant in societal institutions such as Christianity in Africa, community authorities, police and policy makers.

Since human trafficking has been known to be connected to the sickening industry of child sex tourism in the past few years, it has been reported in various places as the exploitation of young girls in prostitution. After the liberation of South Africa, there were rumours of a great increase of witchcraft and traditional religious practices in the villages and poor suburbs of South Africa. From the outset, let me make it clear that it is important to examine the historical wide use of human sacrifice, to relate the current resurgence with the way in which traditional beliefs were forced to operate underground because of their abolition under colonial rule.

In the next chapter, I will concentrate on the dangers of suppressing traditional beliefs and relate it to the question of how the concept of social change became embedded in society and had an effect on the deterioration of human behaviour. Arguably, as a theoretical model, moral causation distinguishes the grounds on which the motivation for human sacrifice lies in a quest for mob justice, or lynching suspects as culprits, through revenge or fear. It is therefore a key chapter and the most substantial, because it needs to give more details of how these problems came about in society.

Chapter One

1.1 The Background to Ritualistic Murder

The purpose of this chapter is to examine the two interpretations of the source of the current human sacrifice crisis in some places, especially currently in East African countries. First of all, this is an attempt to provide an interpretation of traditional beliefs that are never mentioned, since fear of the ritual murder act tends to overshadow how the belief in human sacrifice has come about. Therefore, the source of the crisis is traceable in the way people conduct their daily commercial dealings and business transactions, which suggests that there are various contributing factors to the fact that ritualistic human murder in the guise of traditional religious sacrifice has dramatically increased.

During the investigations for this book, I asked about the general views of traditional healers and they kindly shared their experiences and what they thought to have been the source of the rise in ritualistic human murder. The starting point was also all the information from various news reports and societal agencies.

The whole source of the rise seems to have been exacerbated by a loss of moral value and the degradation of life that gradually develop during civil wars, when there is an increase in the military use of force, rape, robberies and murder for monetary gain. This is argued as gradually drifting into various avenues of corruption and the quick innovation of many dubious means of acquiring wealth, which eventually embed in society the fake theory of ritualistic human sacrifice. The long-term genesis of this practice started with so-called traditional healers who had migrated from various African countries to South Africa and West Africa, particularly immigrants who went to

Nigeria for economic reasons due to the great demand for traditional healing services there. However, a second theory claims that ritualistic murder is not related to traditional healers. Some of my interviewees argued that magicians from countries such as West Africa, Tanzania and Congo travel to different locations in Africa to make money with their trade.

People have lost moral responsibility towards each other and materialism has come to be more important than human life. People who are willing to use any means to become rich, and those who dismiss objective values on immoral grounds, seem to me to be vulnerable to fake ritualistic sacrifices, cheats (okufera), skimmers (okulembeka) or other innovations of the crisis, seen as symptoms of deteriorating behaviour, which does not value human life. In fact, the rise of this culture has been exacerbated by the increasing fear created by fake healers. There is a whole illegal culture in which people are searching for riches, competing in business, showing rivalry in dealings, jealousy, dishonouring agreements in business deals, competing for the same lover or under threat of repossession of one's property. Those who acquire wealth characterise successful people as heroes, while honest people are considered as losers (Cf. New Vision, Saturday, 25th April 2009).

How does human sacrifice start? According to information gathered from various sources, the human sacrifice crisis is a social problem that may start either as a family issue or from ill health. Articulating the trajectory of the destructive impulse, in the new culture of global structures for financial innovations, problems faced by those in poor communities may start as normal business, but due to various business factors begin to build up. Often under such circumstances when one is trying to eradicate poverty, people unknowingly get entangled in banking bureaucracy and get caught up in loans that suffer high interest rates. In fact, while they are trying all available means to sort themselves out, they get caught in more serious problems.

What is equally important is that the explanation for the current resurgence of human sacrifice in Africa is also a subject that now requires research. What must be investigated is the particular dynamics, the globalisation of society and the homogenisation of cultures, which might have caused both smaller and wider-scale influences.

Readers might not be aware that the economic poverty crisis in poor societies has been identified as having played a major role in the rise of what is labelled the 'new behaviourism of fakers', which explains why the crisis has the nature of corruption. What follows will therefore be of interest to a lot of readers. Incidents of witchcraft are also reported as being on the increase. For instance, New Vision reported that residents of Kijjomanyi village in Kalungu sub-county, Masaka district, attacked a man whom they accused of practising witchcraft. The residents also accused Felix Ssali of killing his enemies just by pointing at them. They claimed, "If he pointed at you saying he would 'light you up', you would not take two weeks before you are dead." (The New Vision, Uganda, 12 November 2009), which is also related to human trafficking.

For instance, six Sri Lankan nationals in Uganda were rescued from the hands of suspected human traffickers, who were purporting to offer them jobs. Police sources, who preferred anonymity because they aren't authorised to talk to the press on behalf of the force, identified the suspected human sacrifice victims who were rescued from an unfinished building in Ngombe 'B' Zone, Makindye Ssabagabo Sub-county. "They have been living in a terrible situation because they didn't even have beds, they were sleeping on mats," a CID source said. The two suspected traffickers, who were on the run, were believed to be of Asian origin. But investigations revealed that they were collaborating with some Ugandans to execute their plans.

This is the fourth time in two years the police have rescued victims of Asian origin from traffickers in the country (Daily Monitor, 2009). According to a Ugandan police annual report for 2008, a total of 25 cases of ritual murder where children were the main victims were reported. Of these, 19 were males and 6 were females. Twenty of these cases were successfully investigated and the suspects charged in court. An anti-human sacrifice/trafficking task force was formed to:

1. Monitor, coordinate and spearhead intelligence, investigations and public sensitisation on the handling of reports of alleged human trafficking and sacrifice all over the country.
2. Prevent human trafficking and sacrifice through enhanced timely detection, public sensitisation and effective investigations (Uganda Police Crime Report, 2008).

Other incidents of witchcraft were reported in Rwanda, with three identified as Francois Nsoro, 49 (a witchdoctor), Marie Jose Kayitesi, 37, and 42-year-old Francine Mukaneza. Supt. Morris Muligo, the Head of Serious Crime Investigations at the CID, said that Nsoro, the key suspect in some serial murders, had previously been jailed for unsuccessfully attempting to steal a baby gorilla. During an interview with *The New Times,* Muligo said that the police had discovered a number of dead bodies before they were able to link the murders to Nsoro, who eventually confessed. Police spokesperson John Uwamungu warned the public against involvement in witchcraft (The New Times, police report in Rwanda, Monday 11th May 2009). So far, local explanations show three categories of victims of human sacrifice:

1. The first category are those seeking wealth who are willing to sacrifice their own children to become richer. I was told a story of one person whose son's voice keeps telling him to wake up and go to work when he is trying to sleep. This person is always on the run day and night, driving around from one night club to another until he drops down as if he were dead in order to catch some sleep.

2. The second category are those seeking protection for their wealth from either ill wishers who are threatening their advancement, or bankers or private money lenders who terrorise individuals by taking their property after lending them a small amount of money. Often complaints are heard from small traders who pay exorbitant interest rates charged by loan sharks.

3. The third category falls into two subgroups:

(a) Those suffering from undiagnosable diseases, not treatable by modern medicine, who are often advised by medical practitioners to go home to die.

(b) Those suffering from mysterious attachments to family members who are possessed and talk in unknown voices, or the known voice of someone who died long ago, classified as related to family spiritual matters that need settlement, while others are attacked by bad spirits sent by their enemies or ill wishers who are jealous of their success. (Interviews at Seeta, Kyaggwe and Kiwoko, Bulemezi Uganda, February 2009).

In traditional beliefs, "force" is identical to "spirit", "being" and/or "existence", so that it comprises all human-perceived reality. According to Karade, the concept of "force" or "spirit" is also iterated by Karade Niger-Congo peoples. Karade holds that, in the Yoruba tradition of Nigeria, "force" is called "ashe". He asserts that the task of a Yoruba practitioner is to contemplate and/or ceremonially embody the various deities and/or ancestral energies in ways analogous to how *chakras* are contemplated in *kundalini* yoga (Karade, B. The Handbook of Yoruba Religious Concepts, page 21). Similarly, Samuel Weiser cited accounts suggesting the same experience in reference to the Sudan (i.e. areas west of Cameroon and south of the Sahara). (Samuel Weiser Inc, 1994).

Extensive life history interviews were conducted with local people (most of whom were elderly or middle aged) and recorded on analogue recording equipment from early 2009 to September 2009. This was originally connected with immigrants returning from either West Africa or Southern African countries, or under the influence of Nigerian films, as some had claimed. Furthermore, there were unconfirmed reports that among Ugandans who responded to the booming market in South Africa, these migrants included fake healers. However, after riots in South Africa, riots migrant workers were expelled and there were other reports in the media, which began to speculate that in Tanzania there was a high demand on the market for buying human organs from traditional healers. This was later followed by numerous reports in Tanzania that traditional healers were sacrificing albinos in the belief that individuals who performed that ritual would become richer.

A recent report (Insight in Sunday Monitor, Uganda 20 Sept, 2009) stated that to obtain body parts, performers of the dark arts kill people in order to harvest specific organs for use in the occult. Ritual killings have been reported in Mozambique, where the country's Human Rights League has blamed them on the proliferation of witchdoctors from Western Africa. A report revealed that during the early 2000s, there were widespread cases of people being killed and skinned in the Mbeya region of Tanzania and the Mwiki outskirts of Nairobi. In an effort to raise awareness about the trade in human skin, Tanzania's chief government chemist's office kicked up a storm at an international business fair in Dar es Salaam by displaying skin and other human body parts.

Nigeria has the highest number of occult killings in the continent (Sunday Monitor, Article, “Insight”, 20th September 2009). The 2001 murder in London of a Nigerian boy, whom British police named “Boy Adam” for lack of positive identification, brought Nigeria’s ritual killings to international attention. A confidential report by the police afterwards established that children were being trafficked into the UK from Africa and used for human sacrifice. Although in 2008 alone more than 300 cases of ritual murder were reported to the police, only 18 of them made it to the courts (Sunday Monitor, Article, “Insight”, 20th September 2009).

In rural areas, people have been known to sacrifice their own children. Believed to have magical powers to attract wealth in a short time, albino body parts are a hot commodity for sorcery and witchcraft in that country. The case of Elizabeth Hussein, a 13-year-old girl from Shinyanga, is a testimony to the plight of albinos. Official reports in Tanzania indicate that 35 albinos were murdered in 2008, mostly women and children, but leaders in the Tanzanian albinism community believe that the number of deaths could be higher. The growth of mining and fishing activities in the Lake Victoria regions of Mwanza, Shinyanga and Mara has led to a sudden rise in demand for albino body parts. Besides these three regions that are known for witchcraft, some miners and fishermen believe that albino body parts cause instant success. Reports also indicate that albino body parts harvested in Tanzania are being exported to neighbouring countries where they fetch higher prices.

4 May is National Albino Day in Tanzania and draws representatives with albinism from Ghana, Kenya, Malawi, Senegal, South Africa and the United Kingdom. During the

2009 Albino Day forum in Dar, the Albino Association of Kenya chairman, Alex Munyere, urged Tanzanian authorities to stop the killings before they spread to Kenya. However, albinos in Burundi, affected by the wave of killings in Tanzania, got a moral boost when eight men charged with killing albinos in the town of Ruyigi were sentenced to life imprisonment. "I think it will reduce the amount of attacks on albinos in our country," Mr Kazungu Kassim, spokesman for Burundi albinos, told journalists (Sunday Monitor, Article, "Insight", 20th September 2009).

It was claimed that albino bones, freshly mixed with certain herbs, work as "medicine" to improve romantic relationships and businesses. Fake witchcraft doctors, who are earning a lot of money, get cattle, houses and wives from their activities. The Tanzanian government intervened to end these practices, but this did not end them elsewhere. It was also alleged in Uganda that after South Africa expelled immigrant workers, those who returned to Uganda brought with them a belief that human sacrifice was related to wealth and this was the period when there was an increase in reports of people going missing.

I also aim to look at the wider influence of sacrificial murder and identify a multitude of factors or circumstances, ranging from lack of educational attainment to wider implications. The aim is to assess the information gathered from what has been happening recently and identify what may have contributed to such behaviour. The book also highlights how technological advancement has contributed globally to an increased ability to fly to various places within a few hours, which in a way raises new concerns related to human trafficking, whether or not it is associated with human sacrifice. The book will concentrate the discussion on human sacrifice in Africa and in particular will focus on the churches. Illustrations of the human problem of ritual sacrifice will particularly concentrate on

Uganda for two reasons: it seems that these beliefs have found more fertile ground in Uganda than elsewhere in East Africa; and Uganda as a country has a habit of openness.

As a matter of fact, it will be remembered that Uganda, among many countries in Africa, was the first to admit to the HIV/Aids crisis in the early 1990s. In the wake of the major ongoing problem of ritualistic murder, (the shocking statistic was 22 ritualistic child murders from 2008–2009), the government, churches and civic leadership have all come out to condemn and oppose these barbaric acts, whatever the diversity of interpretation. The church leadership has to recognise that community or traditional beliefs are not simply going to go away, however much it would like to pretend they will. People who hold these beliefs are not just going to be defeated and silenced. For the foreseeable future, they are going to be there, recognisably doing something like the church is doing.

There are a number of factors by which the latest demands of ritualistic sacrifice have spread not only corruption, but a dangerous culture of murder for economic gain, which has to worry the continent. To start with, there are still huge public constraints, which are confusing because people do not know where to turn for help or support. However, the first question to ask is why colonial and missionary influences were advanced in the demand to convert to Christianity and even to an extreme European lifestyle. Was it not possible for missionaries to relate their Christian messages to people's culture or history?

The police, politicians and religious leaders seem to be still gathering information on how to respond appropriately to the human sacrifice crisis. Generally, the public reaction is condemnation for these acts. In the light of their persistence, it is argued that condemning these horrible acts is right, but often authorities overreact on reported incidents, which in some cases has caused embarrassments to the authorities. For instance, there was a girl in Mukono who for her own reasons decided to hide from her parents for weeks. After a long search without finding her, the mother convinced the police and other relevant authorities that she heard her daughter's voice telling her where she was buried. The police were led to a newly constructed property where the mother of the missing girl presumed she had been sacrificed and buried. But a few weeks later the girl reappeared safe and sound and revealed that she was hiding from her family for her own reasons.

Concerns are still voiced in society about how people's behaviour has deteriorated with an obsession for self-enrichment at the expense of others. This has increasingly led to murder, abortion, road carnage, shoddy work on buildings, burning of schools and business premises. I think a connection can be made between this type of obsession and the desire for materialist success, which leads to a skewed interpretation of "traditional healers" in fakery.

I am a realist, of course: human greed and ruthlessness are partly to blame, plus the increase in mobility has made it easier for child trafficking to occur. A lack of moral development has seriously affected parents and allowed human traffickers to convince them that they will find jobs for their sons and daughters, so that they will surrender their children to them. It is under these circumstances that they either sell them for sacrificial rituals or to those who use them for sex.

Indeed, these developments have a tremendous effect on people's behaviours and this is extremely worrying for society, because the deterioration of morals has not only created fear, but also affected people's ability to withstand temptation and inducement of all sorts. For instance, there was an example of a woman from Rwanda who was caught with a young boy trying to sell him for sacrifice in Masaka in Uganda. The boy explained that he had come with the woman, who had promised to find him a job. The main question here is to analyse the situation that seems to have created these acts by trying to trace them in the African historical background, within cultures that are marked by a persistent and deep commitment to traditional religious beliefs. However, the persistence of traditional practices in the long run seems to have been appropriated by greedy, self-seeking groups who have turned these practices into a commercial healing industry.

In the view of what was happening during the missionary period, it is argued that to take a fair and logical approach to other people's history, beliefs and cultures does not leave any room for doubt of any ulterior motive. Since then, the major cause of violence has been a struggle to maintain people's existence at all costs, which has led to fake groups exploiting traditional genuine religious beliefs.

It has been recently reported by Charles Jjuuko that the Mengo kingdom stopped traditional healers in Kayunga district from carrying out rituals on the River Musamya, which connects the district to Mukono. The Bugerere county representative on the Buganda Lukiiko, Ssevume Musoke, stopped the gathering of cattle and chicken to be slaughtered so as to appease the misambwa (spirits) on the river, which the traditional healers said were causing misfortune to the community. Musoke said that the people who pioneered the cultural rituals were Basoga and knew nothing about Bugandan rituals that should be performed on the river.

What I find most interesting about this development is that none of the sides seems to be mutually exclusive and none of the rituals were complete in themselves, yet they cannot somehow be added together into a total ceremony. Each area's ritual celebrations reveal uniqueness, but are not far from each other and the disagreement only comes in trying to give priority to one form of explanation or another

("Ritual Killers Change Tactics", Friday March, Monitor, 2009).

What emerges out of all this is a need to assess whether societal institutions such as various faith groups and governments in African society agree with the idea of regularisation by putting in place guideline policies observed by all traditional healing practitioners. Therefore, this book aims to discuss various views from a variety of voices that express concerns. Evidence reveals some groups who are committed to traditional beliefs and practices and others who raise their voices against the existence of traditional beliefs in society. For instance, recent reports assert that a spokesperson of the cultural leadership in Uganda said the spirits needed to be appeased. Further complications will emerge, as quoted by the Buganda spokesperson who said, "We will comply with the kingdom directive, but it was the spirits who told us through in dreams to do the sacrifice."

However, interestingly, there is always commonality in African tribal legendary claims of sacrificial narratives. These narratives have been depicted in the press and in the individual and collective memory of communities. This book looks at examples of the recurrent and changing narratives and rhetorical tropes of difference over the years from the missionaries' arrival until the religious and social changes of the 1960s, which had far-reaching consequences. The new law recognised the existence of the supernatural and effectively legitimised many practices of traditional healers, but only if they are used for good.

1.2 The Drive for Change in Social Structures and Beliefs

In many African traditional religions, there is a belief in the cyclical nature of the revelation of God's reality; the living stand between their ancestors and the unborn. Like various other traditional religions, African traditional religions embrace natural phenomena; ebb and tide, waxing and waning moon, rain and drought and the rhythmic pattern of agriculture. These religions are also not static, not even within their consciousness of natural rhythms. They incorporate the ever-changing actual experience. For example, Sango, the Yoruba god of lightning, assumes responsibility for modern electrical processes. In Africa as a continent, there is a belief in the "Supreme Being", for instance among the Banyarwanda (Imandwa), that the "Eternal God" (Imana) was the state religion, which is referred to as traditional religion (ATR).

A central feature of traditional religious beliefs is a sense of cultural grievance. The concern for locals is that if these issues surrounding people's belief have not been addressed, they are likely to be a source of wider grievances in African society, despite the use of power to silence people. On the other hand, it can be argued that it is short-sighted to imagine that silence will make society move away from traditional religion in favour of the new teaching in Christianity. The silence merely allowed the deterioration of human values to exploit the community of nations. The world has paid dearly for its complicity with and silence about the corrupt policies of the last decades, which have culminated in the deepest and most dangerous ritual; human sacrifice. Thus, it is argued that if you want to change the spiritual climate of society, you must address the principles that rule that society. Such was the case for the apostle Paul when he went to the city of Ephesus. The people of Ephesus worshipped Diana of the Ephesians (also known by her Greek name, Artemis). The people gave money to this false god, which strongly influenced the economy. The city was also a centre for magic and the occult (Jer. 7:18).

It was wrong for missionaries to choose simply to replace all that had been believed for centuries. New African identities were developed around consumption patterns of a new culture, which is today criticised by locals as a transition that weakened or lessened unity in the community context. Of course, this is an exaggeration of the past: Dalby reminds us that the pre-Bantu were already a people of mixed composition. Where the Bantu came they mixed further with aboriginals. They further mixed with Bushmen, Hottentots and Neolithic people. It is argued that Christianity should have been marked by love and unity within itself. The contrast with what took place demonstrates why it is now necessary to integrate the old into the new.

In order to widen theological development and encompass the recent surge in ritualistic murder, the answer seems to be that the reformed theology needs to be able to take the initiative and come up with creative solutions in the broader evangelical context. How did Africa move from multicultural independence to colonialism? This question isn't simply answered by the desire to have more land. The fact is that there were a number of things that led up to what is now called the "Scramble for Africa". (http://www.mamaafrica.com/article/articleone.php/16/9/2009).

Essentially, there are natural signs that what society seems to be asking is for a dialogue between imported cultures, Christianity and African traditional beliefs, rather than maintaining the atmosphere of estrangement between the new and the old. Similarly, the church in Africa should be curious about its heritage, because there are more and more African-American churchmen who are embracing it, while those who need it most wait for help to come from outside Africa.

However, a misconception seems to have originated from the previous Christian concept of mission, which was that it was Jesus Christ's own command to go out and preach the Gospel to the world and change it. This was interpreted to mean that the sacred task of missionaries was to spread the good news to non-Christians and turn them into followers of Christ, which was partly true, but the added emphasis of change is the source of contentious concern for many in previous missionary churches today.

Does theology have anything to say in this situation to help the church in Africa as it tries to respond to the worries about ritualistic murder in society? In any case, the priority of the church is particularly important in the contextual aspect that the African church leadership should demonstrate its impartiality, independence and competence to create an open forum for pluralistic theological debate. The argument of African Christianity to embrace local beliefs underscores the fact that, in a culture of pluralism, the chief virtue is toleration to the exclusion of the truth and the church aspect of theological integration or communion, significant in the New Testament, was communion as sharing one another's burdens. This was never complete; there was always a search to enter more deeply into identity with one another. To say that communion was not a simple yes-or-no matter was not, therefore, "to shrug one's shoulders" and be satisfied with the current situation. It was a journey that offered further sharing.

Dialogue seeks to repair broken bridges and to restore the lost culture, unity and identity. For so long people in society have been asking for the freedom and restoration of all that was stigmatised by missionaries as evil. This is the kind of situation that Bishop Sheppard describes: "To go to such an area from Europe, imagining that you know everything and that the people there can't help themselves, would destroy the value of going." (Sheppard, D., 1983, p.22).

Certainly, during the period of colonial rule, the missionaries in particular failed to slow the political drive of rapid change. Ian Corrine Brown adds, “No culture or custom is odd to the people who practise it.” (Brown, I. C., (1963, pp. 14 - 15*)*. The point being made is that individuals live within institutions. If these institutions are traditionally structured, they will produce individuals with a consciousness of the societal values that are dictated by their daily lives.

To an extent, anything that was not European was distorted as devilish and was falsified. Such beliefs minimise traditional religious achievements in society, which underlines the importance of the need for the African church to revisit the past missionary conversion of Christians in Africa. Despite the long-term criticism expressed and agreement among various academic sources that the culture was imported and the Christian belief strained local norms and values, the missionary churches seems to ignore these criticisms to the present day. So far, the lack of church action is embedded in conversion as an important early Christian doctrine in missionary work in Africa. Ideological factors facilitated the legitimatisation of colonialism and the missionaries’ dominance to abolish traditional beliefs and establish Christianity. European culture and Christian influences were legitimised without accommodating local cultures and people’s beliefs. Furthermore, Christianity subsequently established itself on a new identity, on which the changes of beliefs, culture and social structures were founded, based on European interests.

If Christian conversion had used a neutral approach, there should have been a slow process of liminal periods to give space to allow old beliefs and traditional religious structures to be integrated gradually into the new and to pass away what was important to people without using repression or abolishment. The main criticism here was that missionaries abolished what they did not understand and the relationship was characterised by a profound ignorance of the other. This is especially the case where there was imprisonment of those who were opposed to change in the new beliefs and social order. In fact, to be suddenly thrust into a requirement to change to another religion that was not previously known is likely to be difficult to take on board; therefore, the criticism of opposition is justifiable, because the best way of changing must come from an inner desire to be better.

At this stage conversion had not yet taken shape, so in such a period to belong is to be "in transit". The teething problems should have been anticipated as arising from not understanding how the other religion and cultures worked, but the trouble was the lack of the logical, ethical or Christian principle of tolerance on the side of missionaries, which was one of the great moral wrongs of the early Christian conversion approach in the colonies. That is the reason why Christian missionaries were often seen as colonial collaborators in the colonial period.

In addition, the conversion doctrine used escalated fear of damnation or punishment in hell for those who were traditional believers (worshipped the devil). In this case, the devil referred to traditional beliefs. Furthermore, the doctrine preached identified Christianity as "the only way and the truth for salvation". (Cf. John 14:6).

Elderly people interviewed claimed that before the missionaries' arrival in Africa, they had worshipped the true God, like Jews and millions of other religious believers all over the world who do not subscribe to Jesus Christ, to an extent where one wonders whether the God talked about is the same God revealed in Christ incarnate. In this context there arises Christ's theme of the Kingdom of God, calling in Africa to be universal (catholic), reaching across all human divisions through the mystery of incarnation. This leads me to argue that there was a divisive bias to African beliefs and culture.

Not only was there bias, it was contrary to Christian teaching, which precisely portrays Christ as not just a Man but the Man par excellence who came for all mankind; the Man in whom we are all to be united in a universal brotherhood, in whom all diversities can exist in unison. Moreover, in Christ is God, the God of all through a new beginning is an end to the old order in an act of God incarnate, ushering God much nearer to humankind for our salvation. There were also two other important virtues of God's love: first, the dramatic act of Christ's accomplishing the final act of sacrifice on the Cross, which symbolised a bridge and a new order of salvation for all to reach out to God. Second, Christ's sacrifice symbolised the end of the old tradition or tribal sacrifices.

The compelling illusionism of this period rested heavily on the dual pivots of changing societal perspectives, which led to an insistence on abolishing old traditions, which were not given a chance to advance. Interestingly, the parallels being drawn about the wave of suspected ritual murders are stark, as are those with murders in specific areas of economic deprivation. People interviewed asked why all of a sudden traditional healers have stopped prescribing medicine and demanding a human head as a sacrifice. People linked with, or accused of, witchcraft are representative of both poor and rich communities, which is interpreted as showing that fake healers do have a manipulative culture of both poorer and the so-called rich out of greed.

Working with two interpretative theories has created a cultural system of moral guilt, especially about traditional mediums and out of public anger traditional healers are victimised. However, the supposed witch can also be the opposite of a loser. He or she may be someone too beautiful, too clever and too successful in business. There is usually a great fear of displaying one's ability to build a remarkable house, dress smartly or do well in school. In addition, reports of research by students in the Lands Institute of Dar-es-Salaam showed that witchcraft beliefs were an obstacle to development in the northern district of Handeni in Tanzania.

Henry Ibanda was right to question whether there could be a connection to the moral panic over human sacrifice. In the process, critical questions were raised in order to ascertain whether or not the increase in human sacrifice is a problem linked to the accessibility of Nigerian-made films (locally known as Bi-Nigeria). It is presumed that the majority of Bi-Nigeria is associated with witchcraft and human murder. It remains a notable subject of concern in the media that characterises African public discourses of religious and official societal problems. This could be the case with Nigerian films. I am not against those making a business out of the film industry, but am more concerned about what such movies could be contributing to the increasing levels of child sacrifice.

The research based on modern slavery reveals that whereas previously what was commonly reported was trafficking of young people, who are employed to work as house girls, mistreated and not paid for their service or labour (Ibanda, H., Programmes officer Jinja NGO Network, New Vision, Saturday, 7th March 2009), most of the recent human trafficking that has been featured in reports is the facilitatation of young children for sacrifice, so that individuals who sacrifice other humans are either protected from their enemies or get richer. One of the incidents already mentioned above occurred in London, when parts of human organs were discovered in the river Thames and Scotland Yard police traced the incident to

Nigeria. They wanted to find out whether in Nigeria there was any family who were missing a child and to establish whether the human organs they had found could be related to ritual sacrifice or not.

I have done my best to compile ritual incidents, to analyse the situation and to present the context in the best possible light. Ali Mazrui rightly observed that Africa has been a home to three major influences, namely Islam, Christianity and the indigenous African traditions. He argued in *The Africans: A Triple Heritage* that Christianity had failed to fend off African traditions. Most people felt anger and a sense of astonishment that those who claim to be practising Christianity or Islam implied that there could be some dangerous and serious repercussions for those involved. Therefore, it is argued that fake healers could be misleading society to wage war against completely innocent traditional healers.

However, what do these incidents tell us about how what has happened in society has led to the practice of human sacrifice? Society is obviously asking questions to explore the source of the deplorable acts. However, this type of crime seems to have developed as a way of life in communities where opportunities for economic advancement are blocked. This means that there is a connection between rapid social changes and a loss of manipulation of vulnerable people and environmental degradation and instability.

Therefore, let me make it clear from the outset that I do not oppose Christianity as a doctrine or as a religious discipline. I do argue that Christian conversion was a conspiracy against the vexing issue of transitions in Africa, and that the continent continues to suffer a dilemma as it seeks to replace the old order with a new order in a process that has not really produced the desired outcomes after abolishing traditional beliefs, practices and culture. As we shall see later, African religious beliefs were not antagonistic to Christianity. I have chosen to concentrate the search on the topic of the recent rise of human murder in order to examine why in the past ritualistic practice include human murder was not conducted on such a scale. On the other hand, I also want to assess claims that before European influence ritual celebrations played a major role in African society.

In the context of the debate about how to avoid buying into the politics of bias against traditional beliefs, true Christian and true African traditional religious beliefs can co-exist and pursue the worship of one God. But there is confusion among those who are self-interested and try to depict their own righteousness instead of the righteousness of God. History (facts), matched with faith, lead us to the truth. The debate that goes on in such situations identifies a number of key factors that have emerged as central to the latter crisis. Anthropologists describe rituals as having many functions, both at the level of individuals and of groups or societies. They can channel and express emotions, guide and reinforce forms of behaviour, support or subvert the status quo, bring about change, or restore harmony and balance. Rituals also have a very important role in healing. They may be used to maintain the life force and fertility of the earth, and to ensure right relationships with the unseen, whether of spirits, ancestors' deities or other supernatural forces (Bowie, F. [2000]. "Ritual Theory, rites of passage and ritual violence". The Anthropology of Religion, Oxford: Basil Blackwell, 151-85. ISBN 0631 208488, p.150).

I will therefore trace how history has led to the current resurgence of human sacrifice through the use of a combination of two methods, mainly desk research and inquiry focused on journalistically reported incidents in various areas concerning human sacrifices.

This raises the question of historical factors articulated in the process of social change in Christianity and comparison with recent reports assessing the positive and negative effects. Sociologically, African traditional religion can be described as having played both a religious and a social organisational role in the maintenance of order and as being a custodian of people's beliefs in the reason of their existence and reverence for God. This is why it is argued that the Christian church in Africa should have preserved the cohesion of society, rather than neutralising perceptions and values which had provided an overall framework for explaining both spiritual and other things happening within society.

So far nothing has been mentioned about the range of human experience, which is commonly called the appreciation of other people's values. Similarly, the African concept of God, like any history of revelation, espouses pure rationalism through human experiences and mythological ideas, on which I believe that the Christian faith deduces the Christian truth. Christianity appears to ignore the African revelation of God.

In order to develop the mythology of the revelation of God's existence that reduces the opportunity for scepticism, based on the testimony of miracles, there is a need to have a natural explanation of how the African revelation of God was deliberately dismissed, not on the ground of validity but on the source of those in authority. However, the historicity of all revelations has a similar base, which is that human experience has revealed the nature of God to humankind. The argument arises here that if the revelation is through human experience then the where and who received the revelation is immaterial, and then the revelation is merely a case for either God's providence or second-order causation.

What we will be focusing on here is first-order causation, where a miracle is any event such that the natural conditions for the said event were not present. If it were true that the African concept of God were fabricated and untrue, then two sub-possibilities may present themselves: that missionaries might have misunderstood or ignored it, because there has never been any attempt made to find out whether the traditional religious claim was a fabrication or not.

The missionary failure to stoop down to see beneath African beliefs is argued as deliberate negligence, as care should have been taken to examine what Africans believe rather than going ahead with their own interests. The missionaries' mistakes were to throw out the baby with the bathwater and not to be willing to care enough to do something about the concept of self as subject. What was at stake was how the Christian control could be exercised within conversion, which ideally means beginning with an understanding of the controlling context.

Most frequently, conversion is interpreted as control, either knowingly or unknowingly, (though they might have done it unconsciously), but physically and mentally treating converts as savages who dwelt in the Dark Continent and the missionary mission as saving these heathens. Considering such an attitude, it seems that Africans were all victims it of a political correctness that insists we ignore physical differences. But we are good at ignoring unpleasant truths in polite society.

In this case, colonisers and missionaries allegedly imprisoned and punished traditional religious practitioners. It is even right to ask how they could be saving Africans as often as they claimed. In fact, at this period it was becoming harder and harder for missionaries morally to justify their concern over local issues, which became worse when they abolished what glued communities together.

What people saw were constant changes against their beliefs and their culture, which the missionary procedure insisted on doing. Ironically, rather than the claimed concern for locals, the motive seems to have been to fulfil their mission, but not as they claimed, to care for others.

Local voices argued that even the education and medication that was introduced had hidden implications, not aimed at local interests but at the missionaries' long-term interests. It was impolite to ask whether local people agreed with decisions or not, where all the evidence contradicted the claims of care, and it is arguable that if one is concerned for others, then one must be willing to listen to what they are saying and to learn what sort of help they need. The fault was taking this for granted, which raises the question of operating out of a preconceived mindset, unwilling to bend, or from an evangelical zeal for converting heathens, but without empathy with the people thus converted to Christianity.

Therefore, the dominant control is argued as an instrumental construction of contradictions, like other patterns of human innovation, to meet the satisfaction of human needs. As there is no other way to argue why missionaries chose to ignore African revelation, this allows criticism as a deliberate purpose, because it was not designed in the European concept and that is why it was ignored at this stage.

Almost all research done on various missionary activities in paradigm shifts pursued during colonialism, in various countries at different times, is conclusive on the significant correlation between colonialist control and the influence of Christian conversion on society. Therefore, I feel rather resentful at having to prompt and indicate key data to repeat precisely the context in which the Christian mission feasibility study was required as mandatory. Namely, I want to establish precise criteria of how it was appropriate to introduce Christianity in a society that had its own beliefs about pastoral visibility, so that both Christianity and traditional beliefs would have been enabled to work out some reasonable integrative process, religious definitions of what was acceptable and not and a mission with realistic and achievable goals.

Simply ignoring traditional beliefs could have been a motive caused by a hidden agenda linked to power and domination of colonies, which is where the imaginary realm joins with, and supports, ideology.

Dhiru Shah argues that in the early days of Christianity, those who refused to believe in Jesus were first branded as heretics and witches and were then killed or burnt at the stake. In the name of holy wars, military missions were sent, which resulted in millions of people being massacred in South America. To perpetuate the forces of imperialism in Asia and Africa, the Western powers fit like a hand in glove with the missionaries, (Dhiru Shah, Mother Teresa's Hidden Mission in India: Conversion to Christianity).

In the *Washington Post*, the CIA even admitted a "controversial loophole" that permits the agency to "employ clerics and missionaries for clandestine work overseas". "During famines, you will find them swarming to our lands under the cloak of 'aid' or 'relief' work. They will bring aid and relief but it isn't given to the Muslims for free - it does have a price." (Manufacturing Kufr: Reads Christian Missionaries in the Muslim World Amir 'Abdullaah Article ID: 825 I 4380).

It is this latter question that will be explored in some detail throughout this book to analyse the data collected from newspapers and magazines in relation to specific events, which have raised the issue of ritualistic sacrifice in African society. Sociological analysis of the modes of representation employed within the area of conversion that seemed to have uprooted Africans from their environment, argues that instead Christian conversion could have assisted Africans to work out their salvation within their environment.

To explore the question of what went wrong, it would be helpful to clarify the methodology that will be followed. Targeted interviews were conducted with elderly people in the local area and then collated and analysed. Detailed analysis was also undertaken of selected oral history "insider" narratives from those who participated in discussions among communities from emerging research results. As yet, inside investigation shows that there is still no unanimity on the actual source of the alleged traditional healers' ritualistic sacrifices, resulting in what investigators are linking to the claims of organised fake healers. By using these selected interviews, the analysis reveals a catalogue of things that were a distortion of the usage of the word "religion", which is an intellectual deception.

Values identified by elderly people as being targeted, gave birth to one of the most astonishing sagas in the history of Christian conversion in Africa and shows how Africa was thrown into religious contradictions which moved moral restraints backward rather than forward, representing the moral deterioration in African society today.

I soon discovered in discussions that what has happened recently in communities is emerging from a distortion of past beliefs and practices. African indigenous religions, or African tribal religions, is a term referring to a variety of religions indigenous to the continent of Africa. African traditional religious beliefs are always described as tribal religions from other parts of the world, which is incorrect. African religious traditions are also claimed to be narrowed largely on tribal boundaries, which is also not true, as we shall see later that the African concept of God was beyond tribal lines. Therefore, it is illogical to ignore people's religions, beliefs and experiences that have moulded them from childhood and for decades, involving teachings, practices and rituals that lend meaning to structural institutions and to daily activities and people's lives.

As a matter of respect, these traditional beliefs also played a large part in the cultural understanding and awareness of the people in their environment. This is the kind of the situation Bishop Sheppard describes: "To go to such an area from Europe, imagining that you know everything and that the people there can't help themselves, would destroy the value of going." (Sheppard, D., [1983]. Bias to the Poor, London: Hodder and Stoughton, p. 22).

The whole argument of this book will rely on evidenced sources drawn from press materials held by various agencies and interviews with trusted elderly witnesses. I will therefore undertake a comparative analysis of the modes of representation employed within the missionaries' and "insider" narratives produced in the communities' discussions and conclusions from individuals and community groups.

1.3 Domination, Movers and Innovators

It was in this period of domination, movers and innovators in which climatic change delineated African culture, when there was a loss of power in rituals and traditional institutions, which were treated as primitive practices that had no place in Christianity or modern society. That was not actually the case, but even if it had been, the beliefs could have been respected as part of the legitimate pride that people take in their society. This is the argument that will be concentrated on in later chapters to discover some answers to the question of tradition and culture. Adrian Hastings notes that missionaries considered themselves to be messengers of change. (Hastings, A.,

[1979], p. 22). However, Welbourn argues that missionaries brought with them not only the Christian gospel, but also an attitude that was more characteristic of nineteenth-century scientific rationalism. (Welbourn, F. B., [1965], p. 37).

1.4 Distortion of African Traditional Religion

The distortion also pointed out a number of inconsistencies in the missionary teaching and conversion process. One example is giving exaggerated meaning to traditional religious beliefs, in spite of an erroneous and centuries-old misapplied and improperly conceived Christianity that developed rather shortly (a couple of hundred years) after the missionary misinterpretation of part of the Bible to suite ideological mission in colonies.

This points to the grass-roots level work of theological discernment that goes on in African communities and the role the Bible plays in this task; because it is so different, the top-down structures are threatened by its success. They did not understand that true power is liberated through equality, dignity of the individual and freedom of expression. They view traditional religious beliefs as revolutionary and ultimately self-destructive because of a lack of authority vested in a dictatorial head. In my prophetic view, this dissemination of authority is precisely in the traditional religious beliefs which, whether allowed or not, will succeed in prevailing and surviving and will eventually lead the way to Christianity.

That is why traditional religious beliefs will continue courageously to seek to manifest the Truth as shown by Christ Jesus, not necessarily the way presented by the church as a corrupt institution, which instrumentally implements advocacy for the twisted truth.

Analysis of missionary activities is often preceded by the use of analogies and each analogy presents possibilities of clarification as well as problems of distortion. But the piece-by-piece distortion method employed was how traditional beliefs and ritualistic celebrations became distorted, in the sense that if little or no fairness was observed by those converted, it created doubts among church members. After Christian conversion, everything in society faced a strong challenge from the church. Missionary ventures followed in the footsteps of the colonisers, so it is arguable whether missionaries were inclined to admit their actions in the process of persuasive teaching and conversion, which mixed biblical interpretation with Western culture and was aimed at changing Africans, not only spiritually, but in both culture and lifestyle. (Cf. Bournique, J. [1867], p.92).

The changes and effects of missionary initiatives are evaluated through the missionary penetration of African society through Christian teachings as the moral authority of the dominant strata, to the extent of trying to extinguish the local culture and customary rituals. However, before the widespread missionaries' influence, which ignored native customary law, customs naturally had a tremendous effect on an individual's reconnection with their social obligation in communities. Therefore, there is a fundamental grievance where the Bible as the Word of God cannot accept people's identity, beliefs and practice; in this view the church was advancing that God never allows for situational ethics. However, the denial of people's cultural values was narrowing the Word of God as simply employed to privilege the messenger of change from the superstructure, simply to use the privilege of being messengers and restricting the interpretation of the Word of God to talk to people in their own environment.

It is important to point out, however, that there are many essential differences that further refute the missionary thesis. On the other hand, an intriguing puzzle unfolds as the present reveals the fragmentary recollections that oscillate between what the missionaries in Africa and the colonisers thought and did about traditional beliefs. This might have been to do with the colonial philosophy that emerged from the 1870s to 1960s, in which colonial advancement was a transfer of knowledge to determine what was evil and what was not in the colonies.

Therefore, for clarity, some of the ethical issues that led missionary movements to convert to Christianity in as many ways as possible, can be argued as certainly having employed bad methods in the process of conversion; they distinguished converts' needs from their own home experiences, which could have instead created a boundary in the understanding of local needs. But this should not be regarded as discrediting the whole mission as having been bad, as sometimes missionaries do feel hurt by African criticism, as if nothing good came out of the entire mission.

However, the reasons for all this criticism are simply to correct past misconceptions, because if they are not corrected Christianity will remain in conflict with traditional beliefs and practices. The church's insistence on defending the missionary condemnation and abolishing what was African in many ways can be argued as ignorance of the fact that Africa as a whole was disregarded in its beliefs, tradition, identity, thoughts and culture.

This is why criticism of the conversion to Christianity attributes the problems of contradictions that distorted traditional religious beliefs in Africa as significantly related to colonialism and Christian missions, in which their messages varied in various ways. It was certainly unfair to ignore a wide spectrum of issues of African traditional religious theological similarities with Christianity, including the concept of God, origin of sin, the necessity of blood sacrifice and atonement for one's sin by someone else.

Christians are well aware that all men are sinful, a basic Christian doctrine, so the sins of the missionaries do not discount the truth of African sacrificial dogma. In other words, the church teaching lacks the understanding of real human dilemmas and the situation has led many people to search for a source of help outside the church. The state of confusion prevails when these horrible acts of human murder perhaps are linked to the past abolition of traditional religious practices. Therefore, ritual sacrifice has be traced further, right back to the poor methodological conversion to Christianity during the early days. It is a serious contradiction of the missionary proclamation of truth when love is withheld in fellowship, when in theory the so-called common identity of Christian faith and baptism was portrayed to be of less importance in action than colour and kith and kinship.

On the other hand, the world outside can see clearly that the church is not living up to its own professed identity. I know committed church members might disagree with the analysis, but the church's failure stems from its social setting of the past, and perhaps may be due to missionaries deliberate ignoring anything that was unknown or being blind or short-sighted about the long-term mission, or even to the fact that many missionaries also live double lives. There is a contradiction to the world between Christian conversion and the gospel. The early situation of the church after conversion can still be regarded as initially a problem that arose from religious instructions and worship in which converts found missionary messages inapplicable and contradictory to their social setting and daily lives, particularly where some missionaries evangelise the "locals" during the week, but on Sunday revert to their own space to share and associate with their fellow countrymen (colonisers). In reality, this highlighted how difficult it was to relate easily with the converts, whom they perceived as different either in colour or in culture. The critique of the change argues how Christian conversion varied between missionary groups and countries of origin and depended on each Christian's denomination; genuine Christian teaching was persuasive in some places, while in other places it seems to have bought the ideas of colonialism, whose impact varied.

The benefit of African traditional values, beliefs and cultures is that they provide insights, according to which it makes sense for the church to eradicate past influences that were fashionable in the 1960s and have continued to endanger local beliefs and to deny them existence. Instead of condemning what they did not understand, findings suggest that society needs to understand that the exposure of a variety of evil deeds seems to arise from the fact that secret traditional healing practices were denied to public view. To religious enlightenment and colonial ideological critics this dialogue is expected to resolve the outstanding disagreement between the centre and theorists, who have made much of the deterioration of local community values and argued that this is a source of human sacrifices today.

On the other hand, evidence reveals that these beliefs are important and the extent to which unscrupulous, immoral innovators have used traditional ritualistic sacrifices as forces to weaken people's morals. Rather than being a reactionary response in the wake of the recent crisis, this represents a total failure to recognise the extent to which such inhibition of traditional beliefs has led to all sorts of immorality in society, such as the recent development of open mob justice. In fact, the indirect colonial policy of past colonial ideologies means that after independence traditional beliefs continued to be denied any room for freedom in public, as a result of which various innovations are likely to remain hidden while the church's role remains on the level of condemnation, assuming that they will disappear.

So far, studies over several decades reveal that church condemnation has no effect and it can be argued as a greater mistake to have overlooked the importance of the integration of traditional religion into Christianity. There is a need to consider both the theological and anthropological dimensions and to urge the church to see others differently. Through dialogue and solidarity, traditional believers hope that the church will be able to accommodate them in the Christian church.

In fact, the absence of freedom of practice confirms the failure of the church's teaching in society to eradicate hidden areas of reported human sacrifice. Historically, behavioural pressure has been built on the level of hidden practices in communities. In recent years, however, secret healing practices have also been on the upswing. Wherever Christianity spread, it took the place of local ideologies and religious beliefs. It was extremely intolerant of other religions and fought them with unrelenting malice. Louise Pirouet, in their defence, argued that most missionaries were from secular states in which people were free to follow their conscience in matters of religion. (Cf. Pirouet, Louise, [1989], p.4).

Nothing better illustrates the colonial mentality characterised in the Christian mission, especially in the old Portuguese colonies, where missionaries existed on sufferance and the government of Portugal took the most active measures to prevent the Pope from sending to Africa missionaries who were not under Portuguese control. (Cf. Oliver, R., & Fage, J.D., [1962], p.135).

The crux of the matter is that the process of missionary conversion disregarded the African revelation of God and discounted traditional beliefs and culture. This lack of consideration is irrational and unacceptable and mostly obscured or denied the development of an African revelation of God and their heritage. However, in response to the question of lack of development, the next step has to assess historical events drawing on the missionaries' perspective that was the hallmark of the conversion messages, to explain how perhaps missionaries' tinted lenses failed to let them see the essentials of local traditional beliefs and culture and instead replicated their own social world.

However, a few quotations from the Bible and from African experience were not essentially different to each other and possibly the only difference was that one was from a book (Bible), whereas the other was experiential, lived and practised daily in African religiosity. It is further argued that missionaries seemed to forget that the world they had in their minds was irrelevant unless the recipient of the message was taken into consideration. I believe that traditional religious healing will play a complementary role in reawakening and reforming the spiritual vitality of Christianity in African society, returning Africa to its former, morally integrated vision, ways and principles.

It is amazing today to think about how much these beliefs are still as active as ever underneath society, just imprisoned by the past, which forbids their practice and development. This is this reason why it is argued that African Christian spirituality is still finding its way in society and thriving under the shadow of secretive traditional religious ritualistic practices. This is all linked with missionary teachings, which were not done out of only one intention or because of a strategic calling to save perishing souls.

In a very real sense, more than one interest was officially enshrined in the "ideological manipulative" policy, which continued to operate even after independence. Ismael Kasooha in New Vision, Uganda resonated as WESTERN religion was still used to colonise Africa. Owobusobozi Desteo Bisaka, a cult leader in Uganda's south-western district of Kibaale, has said, "How can we boast of independence when we still cherish religions brought by foreigners? We are now shunning our indigenous religions, considering them to be Satanic." (Kasooha Ismael, the New Vision, Uganda, 22nd December 2009).

On the negative side, there was a significant manipulative ideological policy, which offered short-term incentives in the improvement of living standards for people, which explains how Christianity was embraced during colonial period. However, without realising it there was a hidden economic and religious dimension that had an influence in terms of major long-term control and wreaked moral damage on local communities, which was argued as having contributed to the current crisis.

A variety of economic and political interests are portrayed in the dominant theories of economic policies in colonies. According to Mama Africa, one of the things that led to the idea of colonising the whole of Africa was the fact that due to the industrial revolution that occurred in the nineteenth century, Europe was in need of raw materials. Considering Africa's abundance in natural resources, it was natural for Europe to look south in order to expand its industrial growth.
(http://www.mamaafrica.com/article/articleone.php/16/9/2009).

To this effect, both colonialism and Christianity introduced racial policies and legalised repressive measures of control and dominating codes of conduct, governing what to do and what not to do and what to believe in various African countries for the purpose of control. C. R. Boxer observed that both the Catholics and Protestants in

Europe readily accepted the principle that the ruler and the ruled should belong to the same faith, which is expressed in Latin as follows: "cujus regio illius religio". (C. R. Boxer, The Portuguese Seaborne Empire 1415-1825), (London Hutchison, p. 28).

All of this is argued as dominated by economics and the power to control the real motive that served the interests of a secular entity, which typically highlights the European conspiracy during the advent of Christianity in colonialism. There is a historical basis for this suspicion; for example, the militantly secularist French Third Republic (1870-1940) encouraged the missions as de facto French outposts and agents of influence in the colonies. This business was based essentially on economic interests, whereas in other places missionaries acted as forerunner agents (John Baptist typology) for softening the colonial ground of operation. T

The political and the religious became intertwined to generate an endless repetition of empowerment of some, and the exclusion from power of others. Kofi Asare Opuku in the Baobab Tree of Truth: Reflections of Religious Pluralism in Africa argues that truth is like a baobab tree; one person's arms cannot embrace it. (Kofi Asare Opuku in the Baobab Tree of Truth: Reflections of Religious Pluralism in Africa, 2000 world council of churches).

All of that changed forever on 15 November 1884 when the Berlin Conference was organised by German chancellor Otto von Bismarck at the request of the European nation of Portugal. The conference was intended to settle some of the questions and disputes over expansion and control of territory on the African continent by various European powers. In an attempt to increase their strength and power, European countries were moving further and further out of their boundaries to conquer new lands. Africa's proximity to Europe made it a common sense solution to many. (http://www.mamaafrica.com/article/articleone.php/16/9/2009).

The conference lasted three months, until the Treaty of Berlin was signed. This spelled out that the Congo River and Niger River would remain neutral territory and the parties bickered over which boundaries would be used to split the continent up into sections, which they could divide among themselves. There was no attention paid to the natural boundaries formed by the language, religion or ethnicity of the African people. Other issues that were addressed at the conference were suppressing the internal slave trade and ensuring a European monopoly of the gun trade by outlawing the importation of firearms into Africa. (http://www.mamaafrica.com/article/articleone.php/16/9/2009).

Protagonists of religious traditions, which lay exclusive claim to divine revelation, have tended to regard Africa as a blankly barren land, waiting to be planted and watered with the heavenly seeds of truth that are found in their particular religious traditions. This assumption fuelled the Christian missionary enterprise in the past two centuries and continues, unabated, to this day. (Kofi Asare Opuku in the Baobab Tree of Truth: Reflections of Religious Pluralism in Africa, 2000 world council of churches).

The attitude of softening is argued as the way the missionaries used persuasion through conversion to Christianity, which attracted vulnerable young people looking for a better future and to live the modern European lifestyle and gradually led many to abandon their tradition and the observance of community obligations, which gradually weakened traditional and cultural values in communities and yet did not cease to exist. In fact, traditions, beliefs and norms are based on clans. Even if traditional institutions were abolished, it was simply a myth as norms and culture will remain because they are deeply entrenched in people's daily life.

Chapter Two

Sweeping Changes Through Christian Conversion

2.1 The Past Changes Seen as Grievances

This chapter attempts to map out the recent wider network of counterfeit production and cultural changes through analysing the history and reflecting on the rise of corruption and an excessive obsession for success, which have introduced a fake superstitious culture into traditional beliefs. This is arguable as a point of departure from traditional norms, which glued communities together to resist any bad influence, which helps to explain why societies need to sober up because of what has gone wrong in the last fifty years. Therefore, it is wise to ask what has gone wrong and what factors are involved in people's moral deterioration in society today. Does a departure from African culture count? This can be answered through the analysis of factors influencing the origin of the bad influence, which has led society to a new form of fake, corrupt culture, which is disseminating the resurgence of traditional beliefs.

It is extremely important in this chapter to map out the recent development of co-dependence in ongoing (re)innovative "fake claims" and exploitation of "traditional healers". What is argued as "fake culture" is the most imaginative and eloquent impersonation and yet it is by far the deadliest. It is no longer a mere difference between real traditional healing and fake claims in the new culture, but is dangerously entrenched in "fake corrupt culture", which means "counterfeiting" as well as "appropriating". (In superstitious magic, both "fake" and "innovative" culture exploits traditional healing means.) That is, counterfeiting highlights the level of societal power of fake corruption and disseminates the seriousness of culture itself.

Take, for example, the case of Uganda. When reports of ghost soldiers first emerged and stories started breaking about troops being fed on rotten rations and their medicines being diverted by corrupt officers and sold to private clinics and pharmacies, it was tough to believe. Therefore, the "fake healing culture" is the "dark corruption cultural flow within society", which has created the new culture of corruption. It counterfeits and appropriates the fake culture of so-called magician healers, repetitively reduplicating and desecrating traditional beliefs, which are subject to the cultural imagination and the obsession with materialism and have developed through the influence of long-term moral deterioration.

This is argued as caused by the mistake of having abolished what was valuable for society in the name of conversion to Christianity in Africa. This is still a huge controversy and a source of social disintegration, which now and then rises in various forms, argued as a failure on the part of missionaries to realise the long-term repercussions to society. However, two reasons suggest what would be more appropriate, but was ignored: the first is African traditional beliefs in the rites and customs of initiation of infants into the community (conversion and baptism), which would have been familiar to anthropologists as the rite de passage, a ritual carried out to mark the transition from one state in life to another (for example); the transition from one state in life to another was not something missionaries dared to assess.

The second reason is the church's role of support and care to mothers who have given birth to babies who were once regarded as barren women. Infant baptism is wholeheartedly received by Africans, because it is seen as welcoming the member (baby) into the community and purifying him or her in baptism, which symbolises protection from any harm or danger. On the other hand, baptism is regarded as a practice of thanksgiving, which generally in African tradition is appropriate, since initiation and purification both traditionally and in Christian practice share a similar view, where in Christianity is cleansing the original sin while in African tradition is purification. Therefore, the water used in baptism is interpreted in an African sense as a symbol of life.

What Africa holds as dishonest is the mindset of evangelical seekers for converts to an unmodified form of Christian domination, which prevents the truth from admitting the divine source of African traditional religious beliefs. European missionaries did not use a rational cultural encounter to rationalise African religious beliefs, those of literate societies that were as yet untouched by European influence or national endeavour. In this case, it is argued that to use this approach it is not necessary to worship the devil, but this was ignored because European missionaries viewed themselves as the pinnacle of civilisation and Africans as unsophisticated barbarians.

Critics argue that the Christianity that was imported into Africa was not far from colonialism. Christianity, post-Reformation and post-Luther, with its teaching of a direct, personal, two-way link between the individual and God, unmediated by the collective and insubordinate to any other human being, smashes straight through the philosophical/spiritual framework. It offers something to hold on to, to those anxious to cast off a crushing tribal groupthink, while the other needs to be more than to people who were uprooted spiritually from their environment long ago.

This is an area of contentious argument to the present day and that is why it needs to be liberated. In other words, to be fairer with such assertions, we need to look at the mission teaching, which had the double purpose to convert Africans to Christianity for salvation to change them and to see whether the methods that were used ignored what could have made sense to people. For instance, the failure to adapt approaches similar to the rite of passage (Gennep, 1960), with its three stages of separation, liminal transition and reintegration, might have helped if they were translated into Christian conversion and baptism.

Bournique concedes that missionary conversion was foolish to begin talking about God or Christ before the way had been paved for such notions, before the possible recipient of the Good Tidings has been sufficiently moved to interest by fundamental problems, questions or calamities. (Bournique, J., in Good Tidings, July-October, [1967], p.92, East Africa Institute Manila). Therefore, the notion of past beliefs being closer to people and the sense of coherence, can be likened to other forms of imaginary closeness to the familiar and various critics have proposed a number of analogies in recent years.

It is argued that realistic analogies similar to Christian conversion could have reduced misconceptions and misunderstandings and minimised differences, where an emphasis on likeness was primarily needed to allow converts to be subsumed within the discourse. Perhaps this could have assisted converts in transiting the process and integration (structuralism or psychoanalysis) takes traditional ritualistic practices into Christian worship, since Christ's death as a sacrifice bears some resemblance to a risk of lapsing into reductionism.

Also, rites of passage are another aspect of African traditional religious beliefs that are widely practised, for example in the Akan and other parts of the continent. In African belief, life is a cycle; for instance, birth, puberty, marriage, death and the hereafter. No one can stay in one state forever, but must move on to the next.

(Cf. http://colanmc.siu.edu/BAS495/students/chris/ghweb.html).

If, therefore, Christianity had seen this aspect, it is argued that missionaries should have had a similar approach, adapting African converts in the context of their culture and tradition, as happened for instance in China. Frédéric Mantienne said that at one point the Jesuits even started to wear the gown of Buddhist monks, before adopting the more prestigious silk gown of Chinese literati. (Mantienne, Frédéric 1999 Monsignor Pigneau de Béhaine, Editions Eglises d'Asie, 128 Rue du Bac, Paris, ISSN 12756865 ISBN 2914402201).

It is therefore plausible to know whether those who resisted Christian conversion doubted Christianity on the basis of its truthfulness, or were simply committed traditional religious worshippers, since Christian conversion also contained contradictions that could have been eliminated at the early stage of conversion. It was not exceptional to see conflicting views from both sides, since each belief represented totally different cultures and human experience during this early period of transition to Christianity. Since then, Igbo people, for example, have tended to start monogamous courtships and create nuclear families, mainly because of Western influence. (Okeke-Ihejirika, Philomina Ezeagbor (2004). Negotiating Power and Privilege: Igbo Career Women in Contemporary Nigeria. Ohio University Press, p. 34).

They have also adopted Western marriage customs, such as weddings in church, but this is sometimes supplanted by a traditional ritualistic wedding (African families at the turn of the 21st century. Greenwood Publishing Group. p.161). Rites of passage could have played an integrative role for both traditional religious development and Christian conversion. This suggests that if missionaries had translated Christian baptism and marriage into rites of passage, it would have been easily received by society as a transition from an old order to the newness of life in Christ. (Cf. http://colanmc.siu.edu/BAS495/students/chris/ghweb.html).

This argues that converts to Christianity were supposed to acquire a new (Christian) identity and lost their former identity, but the criticism was the neglect of considering the question of identity. In some cases, the past condemnation of traditional beliefs, cultural and traditional structures is argued as having served as an obstacle to the development of a theology of inclusiveness of the traditional beliefs and cultural values of society. Missionary Western theology formulated as Christian missionary doctrine became a more complex process, but also a more politicised process, which was likely to become gradually more contradictory, with sharp differences between traditional religious beliefs and the missionary process of conversion to Christianity.

In order to understand the previous applicable and integrative religious networks, the proposed methodology requires the formulation of new and improved modelling of the assimilation of African traditional religious theological worship as a tool for Christianity in the African church. This is a necessary prerequisite, because the existing Christian model of worship and theological messages are not relevant and are not rooted in the spiritual environmental context, but are rather in superficial, social club type of gatherings without human simulation procedures offering protection, healing or nurturing in moral guidance and growth.

Therefore, for correct analysis, the future debate should be about trust, respect, compromise, working together in a flexible and an actively controlled, spiritually powered church that is capable of supplying healing with a high penetration of teaching and worship distributed through the generations, and the application of highly efficient, intelligent and automated motivation, protection and communication infrastructures.

According to empirical analysis of the early missionary approach, the church today needs to be revitalised and the situation begs for a restorative form of church ministerial care. One of the implications of the previous process is that converts were faced with the question of whether to live in fear or by faith. Of course, the implication of fear has the deceptive ability to influence and affect converts' daily living and the way people live according to double standards.

It seemed like a perfect candidate for hypocrisy, because deep inside fear led to a desire to please and agree with missionary-imposed conditions and demands for separation from an unofficial wife and their children. In my view, this was to hard to accept for many, but the majority of converts in the real sense never separated. This was why a central question of conversion to Christianity was blamed when the framework (of the conversion rules) disunited families rather than receiving them as they were.

I will be quick to argue that the church policy, which was needed at this period, was to encourage weak members and to discourage them from taking a second wife. In fact, for what is often referred to as the institution of marriage to operate, requires a number of skills such as tolerance, negotiation, wisdom and agreeing to disagree. Therefore, the appropriate approach for Christian conversion should have been tolerance of both polygamy and customary marriage, rather than using unrealistic rules to force families to separate.

The forced separation was, indeed, unrealistic to accept for many families, as from the African traditional point of view there was no institution that could be considered more important to Africans than the family. Men considered that they must have children, in order to ensure continuity with the ancestors. In traditional thought, this meant that marrying a second wife might become necessary in order to ensure the birth of children, particularly if the first wife proved to be barren. In this case, the western world's perception of polygamous marriage was largely contradictory to the African concept of polygamy, since the former considered polygamous marriage to be an affront to women and strongly condemned the practice as evil, which was often used as an argument to buttress the negative stereotypes of African polygamy.

The Holy Matrimonial Guide of the church of the Aladura offers the procedures that members should take to find partners. The instructions in the guide forbid members from marrying strangers. However, the epithet stranger does not apply to those of different nationalities, tribe, or spiritual and moral standard. Any member planning to get married, and especially church leaders, is supposed to consult the church authorities for guidance. Thus, referring to the Aladura movement as a model of the African church's approach to conversion, the church has never dismissed polygamists, nor has it encouraged monogamists to marry more, nor do they ask bachelors to marry.

Therefore, the reasons for divorce, suggested in the covenant of marriage by Primate J.O. Oshitelu, seem to have developed in the movement later, probably due to the developing situation after one partner was converted, but another partner failed to be. This is where one could justify his or her actions by using the Pauline doctrine of an unbelieving partner to get married again.

Nevertheless, the interpretation of polygamy is still a matter of whose interpretation to rely on from one society to another, and as a result different interpretations are most likely to obscure the true picture of endemic polygamous relationships. In conclusion therefore, please do not assume that the morality grass is necessarily "greener" across the neighbour's fence. Further, it is arguable that even in modern society polygamy still exists in many and different forms. For instance, there is "serial polygamy", which seems to be a trend in modern society where a change is made from one spouse to another, as opposed to many spouses at one time. The practice of polygamy is harder to justify when the same man is married to different women at different times. It can be questioned as morally justifiable that one man with a stable relationship is allowed to conclude that polygamy poses a problem in every way in society, whether Christian or not, and marriage breakdown in Europe is very significant.

On this note, whether the European Christian moral principle of monogamy is admitted or not, this seems to have been a serious fault that has failed terribly from its inception in Africa and is still a problem in Europe. Moreover, there is evidence to suggest that there are many people who are married for years, but are living a very unhappy life, where love or companionship has long since gone. Some are even in an abusive relationship, but are hanging on, for the sake of the children.

From an African point of view, the role that customary marriage played was vital and should have been seriously considered. It is even logical to argue that God does not operate in vacuum, but uses people; in the African society God had to use them, like He had used those in the Old Testament. In this case, it can further be argued that it was necessary for missionaries to stop and reason about people's culture, in order to have sufficient reasons why society arranged marriage in this way. It was therefore not convincing on the basis of conversion to separate couples who had lived together for years, happily or not, but who had children and others with grandchildren and it was probably at this moment when the meaning of conversion lost meaning. In contrast, Christian matrimony with its old beliefs seems to keep repeating itself, in general from our great-grandparents' era. It is often said, why put up with it;

why not leave? But on the other hand, the partners may feel as if it is too late, having had to put up with it for all these years.

The truth is that marriage is something that needs to be worked on daily by those involved to settle their differences, whether in monogamy or polygamy. There is always a degree of being brave enough! There are twenty-eight verses in the Bible in which God revealed His plan for human sexuality and the centrality of the marriage relationship between man and woman. In this context the New Testament represents the European cultural marriage and the Old Testament resembles the African relationship; therefore arguing about the church's teaching was to a large extent inconsiderate of society, which is also worth noting.

Whether the church is aware or not, there is still increasingly a moral grievance deepening the crisis in this area of Africa's past, negating the traditional religious point of view. The contradictions in society in the area of marriage are still a concern for many in society. In fact, in the New Vision (14th December 2009) has reported that Mityana Anglican Diocese Bishop, Samuel Stephen Kazimba, has established a scheme to reward youth who get married when they are still virgins. A prize of Ushs 100,000 has been put forward for any girls that fulfil the condition. He is said to have cited the example of the Virgin Mary who, he said, led a model life that others should emulate. The aim is to protect youth from HIV infection and from other sexually transmitted infections.

The prize is certainly well-intentioned and there is every reason to encourage youth to keep their virginity 'til marriage. It would appear, though, that there is a big patriarchal ring around this prize, as it targets girls, not boys. There is also the small practical problem of a girl having to prove her virginity. Will they institute virginity tests or get the girl to provide a medical certificate of some kind to prove she was a virgin before the wedding day? And another matter; where does that leave the girls who lose their hymen, not from sexual encounter, but through some other activity, such as sports or cycling? And where does that leave those otherwise chaste girls who might have had suffered the unfortunate experience of rape or defilement?

Lastly, the emulation of the Virgin Mary is interesting, considering that she got pregnant before marriage. Are we domesticating or adapting Mary to our own cultural traditions? Moves such as this one, might appear commendable under the present circumstances, but they have a down side and lead towards a slippery alley. This requires the church to be equipped with the ability to handle and resolve the long and overdue question of religious freedom and the denial of equal rights in an honest and healthy way. It is argued that it is hardly plausible to see Christian missionaries, whose own faith is based on the same divine revelation, deny and dismiss the justifiable claims of African. Perhaps it would have been plausible if the denial of the African revelation of God and the truthfulness of the concept was from atheists, since in the view of the missionaries, the African divine revelation was all about demons and superstitions.

Furthermore, there are unresolved grievances, which need to be addressed urgently within African religious communities, to assist people to recognise that a contextual theological revelation will resolve past missionary misconceptions or bias. In a sense, the process will require the theologically restorative aspects of traditional African elements to be assessed, especially from the start of the process of conversion to Christianity, which distorted anything related to traditional beliefs. This is trying to recognise that the cause of the grievances stems from abolishing these religious beliefs, leading to a lack of the community discipline that would have assisted individuals to kick their bad habits as an alternative. In fact, the nearest resemblance to the threat is found to be committed by society, such as the so-called acceptable murdering (hanging) of offenders in the name of punishment.

On the other hand, before advancing the argument, I am quite aware how many will object to the restorative theory of animal sacrifice as being too soft to paganism, which is why in my defence I argue that it does not rule out the fact that society has to do something and probably to reconsider the social strain of anomie. Merton's theory of crime deterrence in the prevalent context of the deplorable killing of innocent people is often argued in some communities as being due to the belief that it will lead to acquiring wealth or riches (Merton 1938). Animal sacrifice, then, cannot be innately sinful.

From the traditional observation, domestic animal sacrifice cannot be evil, but human sacrifice must be forbidden and corrected. That is the way to prevent the structural functionalist theory of collisions and contests leading to unanticipated consequences of purposive social action, including deterrence, when the sin of human sacrifice creeps into the equation (Cf. Merton, R., [1936], in American Sociological Review 1, pp.894-904); (Althusser), structuralism (Levi-Struss, C., [1949]; The Elementary Structures of Kinship Boston: Beacon Press); World-systems analysis (Wallerstein) and some variants of conflict theory (Dahrendorf, R., [1956], in Transactions of the Third World Congress of Sociology, 3).

The conversion to Christianity was received differently by people in various places in Africa. Some responded positively to the Christian teaching, whereas others had mixed feelings for both spiritual and materialistic reasons. Some wanted to look like missionaries, to be educated, to become rich and to be able to save themselves from poverty, whilst others were following a Christian search for salvation and spiritual renewal and were genuinely responding to the Christian message out of the conviction that they need to be changed by accepting Christ as their personal saviour.

I will agree that this emotional experience gave truth and reality to converts and that from the aspect of communication, missionaries spoke in a way that ordinary people understood. To some they offered an emotional experience of conversion, which cleared people's minds of the repressed realisation of their sins and feelings of guilt.

During this period of Christian conversion, this doubtlessly made a revolution in their personal experiences and moral lives possible. In some areas there were Revivalist missionaries who believed that, in a very particular sense, they were "saved by the blood of Christ". (Cf. Kolini, Emmanuel, [1995]). "Towards Reconciliation in Rwanda", Transformation, Vol. 12, No2, April/June, p. 13).

The Revivalist missionaries and their converts, known as "Balokole", lived a strictly disciplined life of daily devotion. Their members were able to quote the exact date of their conversion to give testimony to their faith. Revivalist converts bear witness to the power of "Jesus on the cross", where they were freed from their sins to walk in light. The movement definitely touched individuals in all churches, but seemingly did not reach society as a whole, because it broke cultural taboos. (Kolini, Emmanuel, [1995]. "Towards Reconciliation in Rwanda", Transformation, Vol. 12, No2, April/June, p. 13).

Among other things was the exaggerated Christianity identity of brotherhood and sisterhood embedded in the conversion message, which means that a Christian identity was asking converts to think the opposite way, to see themselves as a community saved from the traditional worship and sins of ritual practices. (Cf. Baghramian, M. Relativism, [2004], p. 2).

As mentioned above, the respect for African identity is argued as important, even though the missionaries' conversion was proclaiming a message whose emphasis was to introduce a radical change for every convert. Thus, the error made on these points was on a large scale in the establishment of independent churches.

Christ was proclaimed to the Africans as the answer to questions that Europeans missionaries would ask and the fulfilment of needs felt by the Europeans. It can be argued that missionaries did not see beyond their own needs and that the situation created variations in and across cultural differences where Africans became inferior and subject to ethnic distinctions, but their inability to separate out the essential principles of Christianity is argued as stemming from the colonial ideological influence and from their cultural background, which caused serious misconceptions among converts. The Christian conversion seems to have contained the validity of a completely different universe and system of thought. Also, these points were in a sense linked with missionary preaching of the Word and the Catechism, which often was extremely superficial. It did not touch on many facets of the life or the struggle of converts.

In most cases, converts seemed to have perceived that to be a Christian was to embrace European culture and lifestyles. As outlined above, I will explain in a later chapter a little bit more about the effects on identity and also endeavour to show that misconceptions about Christian identify could be called a form of Christian identification, which in my view was the key issue why the emphasis of Christianity's "truth" claims and teachings as the only religion holds the truth for salvation (John 14:6). At the same time, I appreciate that some developments undoubtedly lie at the heart of modern society, in terms of how and where people live their lives. Is truth a property of sentences, (which are linguistic entities in some language or other), or is truth a property of propositions (non-linguistic, abstract and timeless entities)?

We have come now to the most difficult point. In order to scrutinise how global and local social economic climate conditions have psychologically prepared individuals in how to get hooked on ideas of wealth accumulation after propaganda from the media, Donald Shriver rightly observed that during World War II, rhetoric was mobilised for war. (Shriver, W.E.D., Woodstock Report, March 1996, No. 45). This time the obsession for wealth creation has created a climate in which the number of victims has been doubled, as we shall see later. Aaron had been mentored by his brother Moses. However, we learn that Aaron still has vestiges of Egypt residing in him (Ex 32:21-24). Did you notice Aaron's explanation? Out came this calf! Aaron attempted to deceive Moses. Aaron failed to fulfil his role as a strong, Godly leader. He allowed "mixture" (Ex 32:21-24).

Indeed there are valid reasons for everyone to detest the action of sacrificing human lives. Nevertheless, the crisis has been caused by the current sacrifice of innocent children and adults in the context of so much that devalues human lives. But on the other hand, if assessed in a wide scope, this may highlight some general features that are helpful in understanding the various sides of human sacrifice. In fact, whether the sacrifice is for war, religion, wealth or power, it is all the same evil; it devalues human dignity and the victims pay the highest price. By sending people to wars that are not worth fighting for in the name of world peace, or in the interests of controlling order, in a very real sense this is sacrificing to protect political power and wealth.

However, under the current worry about the resurgence of ritualistic sacrifice, the findings in society indicate that a significant number of traditional healing practitioners still offer hope to a large number of individuals in society. One anonymous medium traditional healer interviewed in the study said that he would assist any client who sought help, even if he or she held a Christian religious belief that forbade them from following traditional practices. Another traditional healer said that clients who frequently visit searching for help in fertility were very unhappy about their church and wished that the church understood the reason. I just now want to raise awareness among church leaders that they should not shy away from understanding the challenging situations people are faced with in society. Therefore, such situations beg religious leaders and the state to find a solution to incorporate traditional beliefs and practices.

The challenge now is to discover how best to respond to help people adjust to their situation, to value them as people and show them the best alternative way to seek healing or resolve spiritual forces. One way is for modern Western medical practitioners, religious leaders and society at large to educate the public and avoid prejudice. Ignorance of the other did cause problems and lead to prejudice, but the real issue was often one of power; the power held by colonialism.

The missionaries were often criticised as interfering with traditional institutions to deny them freedom of existence, which led to the abolition of cultural institutions. Thus it is an issue of racism and a Christian failure to modernise the traditional beliefs and practices, which could be turned into something useful once the rough edges were removed and the practices purified to integrate them into Christian worship.

Religious tolerance and integration is a prerequisite to truth and you should not settle for less - even if it takes time. The goal remains visible and sacramental communion: something more than rediscovering shared history and more than the existing parallel structures of church life. It is similar to the present Christian churches' ecumenical dialogue landscape as a kind of "receptive ecumenism", a transitional period in which there must be a deepening communion between the two churches. A focus on spiritual ecumenism over doctrinal convergence is needed.

As a result of abolishing traditional beliefs, practices that correspond with the growth of fake healers were driven underground. In contrast, a gradual approach was appropriate, which suggests that the church in Africa should adapt the approach of Messianic Judaism, a Christian movement that began in the 1970s, combining a mixture of Jewish ritual and Christianity (http://www.messiahtruth.com/response.html).

There are a vast and growing number of these groups and they differ in how much Jewish ritual is mixed with conventional Christian belief. One end of the spectrum is represented by Jews For Jesus, who simply target Jews for conversion to Christianity using imitations of Jewish ritual solely as a ruse for attracting potential Jewish converts. On the other end are those who don't stress the divinity of Jesus, but present him as the Messiah.

If the church continues to ignore the question of integration, it is argued as offering a hiding place of fakers, who have become thief makers rather than healers (http://www.messiahtruth.com/response.html). This is the prototype that has created the resurgence in traditional beliefs and is part of ongoing corruption of culture for survival and gradually has turned the unemployed to the activism of fake healers. For example, Kimbowa gave evidence stating that in fact he had never been a traditional healer, but had become a fake healer in 1988 and pleaded for mercy that he had no money and job and was forced to become a fake healer out of desperation (Bukedde, Sunday 26 July 2009).

The process of wealth accumulation led many down the slippery road of further victimisation of other unrelated victims through the wave of conmen and women who pretend to be traditional healers and employ various tricks to fleece money out of their clients. The General Inspector of Police in Uganda reported that the police were working with international experts to examine the situation and added, "What is clear in all cases we have handled is that these are conmen disguising themselves as traditional healers, after conning businessmen who are struggling or whose wives could not conceive in pregnancy, and contract killers." (New Vision report on 25th July 2009). He pointed out an increasing "underworld" activity in Kampala, with people who resume their life at night in top city bars and clubs, yet they are not known to work anywhere.

The human psyche is being prepared for evil. Another consequence has been that human trafficking has been made easier and quicker by the modernisation of travel, which has opened up avenues of rapid mobility to enable people to move from one continent to another in a matter of hours. Modern means of communication have served the interests of greedy individuals who have exploited ways to subvert international immigration rules. Though when trying to create a hypothesis about how individuals drift into a belief in human sacrifice, it is a little harder to pinpoint exactly how all this happens. Among those who were reportedly fleeced was Edward Ssekyanzi, who in pursuit of riches lost sh15m, while Dorothy Nanyonjo was conned out of sh22m as she sought charms to catch robbers who had attacked her home. Dan Mazzi lost sh27m as he frantically sought employment (see New Vision, 27th July 2009).

To exemplify the interrelationship of past colonial events and the wider corruption culture of "get rich quick", the colonial system introduced and embedded the corrupt culture in society. People don't seem to understand that it is politicians have to end the culture, because corruption is a systematic part of social functioning. It is not necessarily something that Christian teaching can beat. It is, rather, a culture that politicians have created and used to reach where they are and have maintained to keep them in power. In this case, the corrupt culture has a major influence under which the poorest in society are more likely to be attracted by ideas of wealth accumulation, but instead be subject to an unstable situation in which they have ups and downs.

According to New Vision, Uganda, when his business transactions started deteriorating, a businessman sought help from a fake ritualistic, who convinced him he was being bewitched by jealous colleagues. The fake ritualistic demanded sh300,000 to settle the problem, but he reportedly failed to improve the client's business. "I later took sh5.2m and a motorcycle. He demanded sh1.2m to buy bulls and chicken for ritual cleansing," the client said. He added that when he demanded his money back, the fake ritualistic became furious and threatened to kill him if he revealed the matter to anyone. He said the fake ritualistic later asked for three lactating camels to be sacrificed to appease the spirits (New Vision Newspaper, Sunday, 16th August 2009).

Because of their hidden religious nature, traditional religious practices are not easily accessible and are partially invisible to outsiders. Due to past missionary influences and distorted teaching in the process of conversion to Christianity, they often appear to have been suppressed by the church. A major cause of lack of development and engagement led active practitioners in the opposite direction from known traditional quality values of community care and towards immoral prohibited measures within the traditional structural setting. A new methodology is required for any practitioners wanting to take action to promote the successful integration of reliability, power, quality, security and other relevant aspects of the quality of religious reform in an all-inclusive procedure, which requires inclusive assessment of both system and end-user performance.

Also essential is a willingness to take the trouble to read the evaluative, prevalent corrupt culture attributed to a combination of forces. This suggests that if nothing is done seriously in society by politicians, then this fits the arguments concerning the future along the lines of the more you build unfounded big "ups", you get big "downs". This raises a facile argument that is ordinary and commonsensical that all these are climatic influences linked to ritualistic sacrifice and a corrupt culture born out of the need to accumulate wealth for an easy life and comfort in this world. This is seen as the current source that builds pressure on people through a normal process and it is important to try to find out what all this is supposed to be and what the implications are in reality. In a long narrative it is where the ideal intended outcomes do not always find their realisation. One may then go on to inquire if there are indications of materialistic motives behind the culture of corruption, which indicate links to a pattern of ritualistic murder.

For instance, the approach of a bank may stem from an honest spirit of allowing access to money for many from poverty-stricken areas and may be interpreted as merely exploiting the freedom to make the greatest profit. However, things may start to go wrong, since the more loans are available, the more financial burdens accumulate, influenced by a “success syndrome” that drives individuals and business groups to acquire more and more loans in aspirations of becoming richer.

The reality though is that lenders take into account a whole host of complex factors when looking at lending out to clients. These include the underlying cost of interest, the cost of structuring each product, the cost of matching the maturity of what they are lending to the maturity of the funding, the cost of administering each loan, the cost of holding the capital against the lending being done and the cost of any risk associated with the loan. In other words, what banks do not reveal is that some customers are unable to understand terms and conditions and that some are not even able to realise the implications until the loan interest begins to bite. They may be crippled by debt and face worse excess surcharges and the process of repayment to the banks becomes a real problem. If this is a common problem, I think African parliaments, having heard the evidence, should be forced to intervene and to introduce regulating controls to protect unsophisticated borrowers from the burden of unfair charges.

Of course, it can be argued, as it usually is, that the bank lending system has also added pressure on people trying to escape from poverty traps; this is indeed not an easy situation. The reality is that when people are increasingly under pressure they tend to add more problems by taking every Tom, Dick and Harry’s advice. In a way it would be less trouble if their own lending systems were not so opaque and subject to constant change, but there is always a need to find a decent scapegoat in times of trouble.

The remarkable recent development is how individuals from poor backgrounds with no professional qualifications have acquired wealth from nowhere in just a short period. Of course, when they apply for massive loans to open up businesses or build tower blocks, this symbolises their power and freedom from poverty. This influences more people to apply for loans or mortgages, but when the repayments start biting, what was once was 3 to 7 years increases to 30 years, even 50 years or more.

To take this even further, if you dissect the word "mortgage", do you know what you get? Well, taken back to its root in old French, "mort" means "death", and "gage" means "pledge", so effectively a mortgage is a "death pledge". For many people it really is at least a "pledge until death" (Integrity UK).

It should be noted that high lending rates dampen a country's financial sector development. It may also be argued that the driving force for desperate individuals looking to become rich is observable in social and political mechanisms in the abstract. This has elements of both psychology and corrupt culture, so it often does not provide exemplary leadership and people never learn from the failure of others or from history.

On the other hand, the current trend towards a materialistic culture trend involves individual personal morality. The consideration of what morality is descriptively refers to a code of conduct put forward by a society, or some other group such as a religion, or accepted by an individual for their own behaviour, or normatively refers to a code of conduct that, given specified conditions, would be put forward by all rational people.

I shall look at morality from a normative point of view as a code of conduct put forward by all rational people to enhance good cultural values. When "morality" is used in its universal normative sense, it need not have either of the two features that are essential to moralities referred to by the original descriptive sense: that it is a code of conduct put forward by a society and that it is accepted as a guide to behaviour by the members of that society. However, there are still doubts about whether there is any immediate possibility of changing hearts and minds. If you think that the government can end corruption in society by simply talking tough, the logical question is: Why haven't they done that already?

Over the years, scandal after scandal has shown that waste, fraud and abuse are rampant in hospitals and government institutions such as the police, revenue offices and ministries. Why would anyone imagine that a new government medical programme, for example, will do what existing governments' programmes have clearly failed to do? The main cause of doubt about the immediate end of corruption is mainly out of concern that before no one ever expected priests and pastors to steal God's collection. Nevertheless, they do. We never thought lecturers and teachers would ask for sex in return for marks. Nevertheless, they do. We have seen money for soldiers' boots and uniforms diverted and the men sent to battle half-naked and barefoot. This is all evidence that the public should have noticed a long time ago.

It is very easy to point fingers at media, celebrities, divorced or single parents, working mothers, and "liberal" attitudes toward things like sex, drugs and alcohol and the fact that caring responsibilities are increasingly diminishing. However, whatever view society may hold, it is increasingly true that very few people would engage in personal enterprises or owning properties if they were not able to borrow from banks. However, I don't think that anyone goes into a loan agreement thinking that it is likely to take much longer than 30 years to actually pay it off and to go about it this way would even be unethical. In this case, it fits the analogy of marriage, since no one goes into marriage thinking about divorce. What this means is that everything is about risk. If an individual enters into an agreement, then even before receiving the money, the agreement is already binding. This type of arrangement can be argued as a device of legal jargon whose implications are never quite clear to individuals, but which legitimates a strange transitional reality.

As said earlier, many people's intentions may be to look for capital to conduct business in the idea of gaining freedom from poverty, so they consent to the terms proposed by the other party. Consumerism has rapidly become the culture of everyone and in many situations consumers will move around assuming everything was right and yet living in a mess with confused minds and disorganised, as are African urban commercial spaces. So often what the public sees is quite different from the reality; the reality of debt results in a situation when individuals are under pressure from banks, which has led many to wrong decision making. Thus, borrowers enter into these agreements innocently with little awareness of the concept of variable interest rates. In most cases, the borrower and bankers both have an interest in the deal and their main focus is on securing the finance.

To my mind it is hard to imagine that all agreements can be analysed into a form that fits snugly into the offer or judgements made by borrowers. Often the contrary is realised when it becomes too difficult to service or repay the loans and the true interest of bankers turns essentially into extracting repayment from borrowers using demands, which is a euphemism for making things too difficult for individuals. But when the situation is hard for some there is professional assistance or an offer put in place, to help them realise when the risk overrides the rewards. What is really happening is that loans were often made to borrowers who were desperate for money, which leads to a dilemma for individuals in poor countries where there are no professional debt advisers. The only option for some distressed borrowers is either to end their own lives or to harm others, including their family members.

There is clearly an urgent need for a collective voice and coordinated pressure on a society whose conduct has gone wrong, to ensure that both the relatives of victims and the suspected culprits are protected. Another point that must be remembered is that in most cases the idea of human sacrifice is not necessarily the initiative of, or involves one person; rather, a coordinated conspiracy is formed by greedy individuals in the aim of protecting bank borrowers when they desperately need help, which fits the argument that desperate situations call for desperate measures.

Although the traditional churches struggle to help victims through a supportive process, much more is still needed. In my view, if the church was more trusted and not judgemental of people's failures, but was willing to treat neutrally those seeking help, it would greatly help to heal minds under threat from either private lenders or repossession of their properties by the banks. To some extent the Roman Catholic Church does help through the traditional use of penitence. However, if individuals searching for help fall into the hands of fake healers posing as traditional healers, then the trappers of victims and the buyers of victims are the supposedly wealthier clients.

So far the diagnosis is that a situation of chronic corruption has turned into an endemic condition under which asking fake healers for protection has potentially become associated with human sacrifice. This means that those who do accept the services of fake healers run the risk of becoming the source of human sacrifice. It is evident that the tragedy of human sacrifice lies in the very success of the human quest for wealth. Modernity has apparently misused this and has not developed in the best way. We are presently failing to meet diverse needs and to prevent people from believing in witchcraft and makers of charms or amulets. The situation is particularly acute among entrepreneurs, who appear to have little professional guidance or counselling services. It is said that a drowning man can cling onto anything – even a crocodile.

Some people resort to faith healing or traditional medicine because of the difficulty of accessing conventional treatments that medical doctors can offer. It is alleged that those in search for protection are seen as vulnerable to all sorts of innovations that have led them to be conned or hoodwinked and that so-called traditional healing has created a culture of ritualistic murder in society. A false faking culture will need much consideration in order for society to be aware of how effectively these beliefs have gradually developed into ritualistic human sacrifice.

The modern day culture of "more, more and more" has overstretched the yearning for more wealth. The weakening of community values has affected both culture and tradition anchored in local social structures. Behaviour is instead constructed by the global mass media images that bombard people. People are no longer acting under the restraints of their communities or local cultural norms.

The disintegration of communities is likely to change for the worse, if nothing is done to collect tangible evidence against the perpetrators. People in communities are no longer what their cultural social structures and norms make them. For instance, according to one report suspects wanted to bury a sacrificial victim in Mr Waibi's new grinding mill. A police spokesman said that Mr Waibi had previously taken the deceased to his home and introduced her as his second wife (Daily Monitor, 16th Monday 2009).

Similar incidents have occurred elsewhere, which justify the assertion that people almost always act the same when faced with a mental or psychological crisis. For instance, during the credit crunch in the US, people in a state of psychological confusion chose to take their own lives and sometimes their families' lives as well. They go into a state of mental torture in a crisis and cannot handle the situation without professional help. Nevertheless, in certain circumstances where there are alternatives, these desperate individuals who could kill even their own family are willing to pay money to anyone who can save them from losing their properties.

In theory, those who are obsessed with accumulating more will go on looking for magic protection. This stems from the belief in the sovereignty of God and not in other forces and in the belief that they will protect themselves from the vulnerability of falling back into the poverty trap. According to a report by Insight, for example, in Swaziland, a country weighed down by intricate traditions and superstitions, police and the press have reported an upswing in ritual murders during electioneering periods. "It's a form of sympathetic magic where the life force of the victim is sacrificed to give power to the recipient," said Dr Thandie Malepe, director of the National Psychiatric Centre in Manzini, the country's commercial capital (Sunday Monitor, Article, "Insight", 20th September 2009).

On the other hand, society must stop and ask about the role of the media which specialises in advertising witchdoctors. For example, adverts for witch doctors from Tanzania claim that they can cure all diseases as well as give people luck. Through their evil spells, the harmful influences that are working against someone will allegedly be destroyed and the negative energy that is circulating around someone will be eliminated once and for all. When this important work is finished, the recipient's luck with money will be so surprising they'll probably have to make an appointment to see their bank manager!

Looking at the whole situation teaches us how to avoid the effects of the obsession with wealth accumulation and calls for moral therapy. It is a situation that conveys a particularly relevant idea of human decision making when their circumstances go wrong and begs other human beings to consider whether ritualistic sacrifice necessarily relates to a culture of corruption, or whether there is alternative to ease the pressure of the obsession with the accumulation of wealth. There is also another encroaching problem of lynching suspects in incidents of human sacrifice, thieves, robbers and any other suspected criminal wrongdoers. The emphasis must be put on the rule of law rather than allowing individuals or the mob to take the law into their own hands.

If this situation is not apprehended at an early stage, it will never go away easily. Once a society decides on an eye for an eye and a tooth for tooth – or in this case, a death for a death – it is drifting into a deeper crisis. It is argued that society must assess the long-term implications of lynching suspects. Yet the immediate concern for society has to be to consider that lynching may create another dangerous culture of mob justice.

There are those who may argue that a person gives up his or her rights when committing a crime. However, it is arguable that the person is no less human because he or she has committed a crime. How can a hypothetical consideration be the basis for taking a person's life? Moreover, it is completely wrong to kill a person on the mere grounds of being a suspect, for it has future political implications, as we shall see later.

If the people and crafty politicians sit silently and ignore a matter that would have been otherwise resolved under the rule of law, they will not prevent it turning into another national crisis. It is therefore argued that if nothing is done to control the lynching, it will confirm that killing is right in the hands of mob justice. One can understand that the fear of crime leads to a climate of mob justice, but unless there is a desire to place the protection of the public at the top of the law and order agenda, eventually mob justice will drift into a wider crisis. In the same way, in the near future, it could reappear as a political crisis, similar to the militia (Inteharamwe) groups of Rwanda.

Chapter Three

3.1 Sources of the Resurgence of Ritualistic Murder

To understand what happened during the Christian conversion in Africa requires analysis of how the European missionary methodology was used. Cultural attachment was an important part of the major issues instrumental in changing society and should include consideration of the deterioration of African's fundamental community values. This takes into account the rapid change in society that was brought about by colonial occupation, as well as by the missionaries who seemed to have worked hand in hand with the colonisers. Further, there is a need to examine why newly converted Christians would refuse to obey the traditional authority and why missionaries would side with them. Local voices also need to be examined, as so often they are heard to say that, during the missionary conversion of Africans to Christianity, it was as if the vision of the missionaries was to take over authority from traditional leaders and to demolish anything had existed as the establishment.

I will attempt to enquire whether the church was taking sides on Christian matters to see whether they acted in favour of protecting their members, or was simply in support of colonialism, disliking anything that hindered their mission and provoking the abolition of traditional leadership and local beliefs. The purpose of this assessment is to reach a possible conclusion as to whether a combination of two forces did or did not create uncalled-for change, especially in the way cohesion was implied in that change. The changes introduced unfortunately seem to have created a long-term blanket treatment of traditional ritualistic celebrations as devilish and endangering Africa.

One needs to take the stance of Jesus, who asked Herod: "Are you asking me because you know me, or is it because others have told you?" So much is unknown about African traditional religion, especially by those who preach against it. Much is distorted and crushed under bias and bigotry and misinformation. What people seem to overlook is how much it is still treasured, even today, after it has long been forbidden. It is argued that as a result people were forced to exercise their beliefs in hiding, which is why ritualistic sacrifices are practised secretly.

This snapshot from the societal point of view highlights the anguished cycle of killings practised due to these long-hidden practices, though recently officially permitted. It may be seen to show that secular institutions have a greater humanitarian approach, but of course traditional religious practices are still hidden as they have not been assisted financially. Therefore, they are not operating on high streets or funded for modernisation, which has partly led to some of the different interpretations of the abuse of traditional healing. The church's negative attitude has also not changed. This is why we should consider the question of abolition as the fundamental problem in generating a poisonous atmosphere, which both colonials and missionaries exploited to satisfy the needs and aspiration of creating long-lasting exploitative structures. It was totally wrong to disregard the usefulness of traditional beliefs and sacred places, to oppose cultural behaviours and to abolish societal arrangements or traditional religious rights and obligations.

In reference to the past and the way humans see and punctuate their experience and attribute meanings to phenomena, a narrative explanation provides an ideological approach and enables us to appreciate that it was simply folly for missionaries not to realise the contradictions and conflict they were creating between Christianity and traditional religion. It was unnecessary for them to expose people to such difficulties in the long run. Because the approaches used in the past were closer to ideology than religious doctrine, I seek to highlight the contradictions and suggest models for action in the present, not the past, even though the church leadership may use the past to do so. If this is linked to narrative events and myths in creating "a conceptual model of Christian conversion in Africa", it may explain nothing else, rather than understanding that people located in a complex social situation did not take significant actions to create social relationships. As such, the means of change determined the events and it was argued that the past ends justified the means, although they led to distortions, misrepresentations, demonising and half truths, as well as the suppression of existing revelations, beliefs, knowledge and wisdom.

This doubting of Africans' revelation, integrity or truthfulness is, in this view, criticised as a deliberate intention of the missionaries, because it did not account for people's views, beliefs and experience. The self-interests of past events return us to the question of missionaries' desire to change and control. There was a failure to appreciate and recognise the difficulties, or to imagine how the traditional religious manifestations could survive under these conditions, because for centuries people had used their traditional known culture to reflect on and homogenise or reassert their traditional identity as a resistance to dangerous forces. In this sense, the myth of change explains the resurgence of religious contradictions in Africa.

Some Africans hesitated to convert when they saw their beliefs, traditions and culture under threat when missionaries exacted what they believed to be a duty, such as self-sacrifice for something they considered to be their heritage, which could not be possibly be compromised into conformity with the ultimate Christian demands. The criticism of the teaching was very unfortunately seen as abolishing people's identity by promoting individuality, which was regarded by far-sighted Africans as dangerous to community stability. Among Africans, the collective mind was the system God had used to reveal Himself and immanent in the total interconnected social system of an ordered world. However, in the course of conversion it was necessary for action to distinguish the religious values on which people acted.

What missionaries seem to have taken lightly was that they were not employing a liminal conversion form of familiar African cultures and history, which could have turned into fertile soil in which to sow the seeds of the gospel. Instead, missionaries acted to the contrary to abolish traditional religious beliefs, which sowed the "mustard seed" of the neverending soil of conflict. In fact, the soil of conflict that was sowed also included the suppression of traditional beliefs, which they thought would simply disappear.

This idea of disappearance reinforces another point: that wherever there is abolition, there are several basic kinds of repression. Today's belief that traditional beliefs no longer live on under church repression is a dangerously inaccurate one. Traditional shrines are allowed to remain in practice, but are still severely negated by the church, which restricts their freedom of operation and speech. In defending free expression, we cannot pick and choose.

Some may find traditional practices evil or offensive to Christian values, but presumably the church doesn't favour censorship of religious practices. We either allow everyone to have their say, as sickening and as biased as their views may be, or we have politicians deciding what is sound doctrine or too offensive. I would prefer the former option, because as long as a church consists of negating the beliefs of, and not reaching out to, traditional believers, society is more likely to perceive them as a secretive culture. There is indeed the feeling that African religious tradition and culture are still under suppression. In other words, to be free they had to develop a culture of resistance, which passes tradition and ritualistic practice from one generation to another.

Christianity is thus thriving under the shadow of beliefs lingering through being poisoned by meanness, being remembered as benevolent memories of divine providence. The memory is linked to aromatisation images of past ritualistic exoticism in the form of the community discursive context in which “insider” collective memory has been articulated. This is when the younger generation was fed on inside knowledge of the forces of magic seen and unseen, in which magicians, witches and sorcerers are said to have the skills to bring about or manipulate relations between the two worlds.

It is therefore arguable that a Catch 22 situation keeps those under the influence of fakery looking back to the past. This is according to media images and individual collective memories of terrifying incidents mixed with narrated stories of the hopeless state of poverty in poor communities, which have recently been exacerbated by the culture of quick riches that has led many people to use fake claims of magic and powers of traditional protecting or healing. All these latest developments so far represent individuals who are muddled or frustrated and accumulate all sorts of dubious ritualistic practices out of frustration, or pressure from flawed business dealings.

Thus, in a corrupt environment where businesses dealings are part of the corrupt culture, the behaviour of those struggling to survive has led to a belief that one’s success has to be complemented by ritualistic means as an alternative in overstretched situations where people are faced with a threat to their livelihood. Therefore, it can be argued that this crisis seems to have been caused partly due to the lack of a base of the former community values, which had worked as restraints and that now people are likely to look for help from anywhere. In this way, individuals are misled by fakers who claim to have a solution to all problems, which is obviously just an exaggerated hyper-experience of human innovation. They promise those who are trapped that they will be able to move forward on the road of happiness and that they will help them to avoid pitfalls and open the right doors at the right time, making the right decisions without ever running the risk of being wrong.

The justified criticism it is that whatever Africans always did seemed to be wrong; they could not win and their life did not conform to what they were told they should and shouldn't eat or do. This was based on the missionary approach, whose theory of colonialism failed to take seriously the actions that African people deemed worth doing for their own cultural sake or traditional duty. Missionary advancement assumed the imposition of Christian teaching and European culture, which would eventually wipe out local culture and traditional beliefs. To begin with, it was surely obvious that missionaries transgressed their proper boundaries when they purported to deal with objective qualities, human values or moral principles and that past mistake still haunts African society, which exists at the final limit of destructive human experience. This is why it is argued that it was a mistake on the part of the missionaries not to have known that the failure to respect local values would be resented, and not to examine the implications of abolishing beliefs, which had a deeper meaning to people than the unfortunate categorising them of mere superstitions.

The greatest failure was to realise the reason for the likelihood of resistance to the abolition of traditional religious beliefs, because meanings and human values are always embedded and bounded in the location of people's social structure and institutions, which determine people's way of thinking and doing things. The spirituality referred to in African theology provides the basis for a whole sociological idea of a pluralist cultural concept, which so often appears daunting.

But the fact is that spirituality, which has to encompass all that seems difficult for the church, is in itself significant. It is argued that African theology has to be slightly different from that of South Africa or Latin America due to the fact that people in Africa have their own unique experiences and cultural needs. The first thing required is for collective civil and religious institutions to develop strategic measures that will address all sorts of innovative cultures. This innovation started right from colonial days, when separating people from their tradition and their culture left them defenceless against the destructive powers that imprison people's true humanity.

People need to understand their place and potential in society. This is more than a narrow preoccupation with material rewards, which is somehow linked with obsessional patterns of shifting behaviour regarding personal gain in every sphere of daily activity, including in the job market. This process of accelerating the influence of materialistic culture has strong effects on people's thinking and behaviour, when people are taught to despise their own culture, customs, values and beliefs as backward.

The main task here for the church is argued as engaging in the contextual theology in a similar way to the case of South Africa's "Ubuntu" notion and to analyse the process under which Christianity in Africa was misconceived for years, as well as the way it operated and still hangs on to the past misconception of distorted missionary teachings. The main objective is to deal with apartheid or racial segregation. Self-segregation, driven by fear of others, is a belief that this is the only way to promote, retain and protect self-interest, power and identity. In a way it is a cultural consciousness of community values that is the body of knowledge that enabled African people to know social life from the inside. Understandably, religious meanings in African people are often better understood when articulated in relation to people's experiences.

I wish to argue that the problem is that people have had to live with missionary Christian teaching during conversion. The difficulty is that missionary teaching exposed society to the sheer illusion, if not domination, of supposing that people can escape from their own environment to accept fully the futility of evangelism divorced from people's reality, which has turned out today as a challenge to society. As W.R. Sorley rightly once observed, "Understanding must be from within, not from without. People are part of the universe, or factors of it, and an outside view of it is impossible." (Sorley, W. R., Moral Values and the Idea of God, p.22).

The view that has been advanced is that the starting point of the approach was the dictum of evangelism that expectation must seek the ground for change from within. The source of long-term conflict that has emerged today in the church is a lack of the ability to maintain an open mind to societal traditional beliefs without prejudice. A more sensitive approach was required to develop an open mind to help to deliver the Christian message of diverse cultures, whereas the European cultural impact focused more on European structural functionalism and people abandoning their traditions altogether, which left some people wondering whether Christian conversion at the period was ultimately for them.

One may appreciate the contributions of Christianity to diversity, but it does seem to have led to elusive, unsatisfied aspirations and a denial of freedom of expression. This missionary approach continued for decades to have its effect on the course of social and political developments and it is to this that the moral deterioration in society is traceable. In the process, there was an absence of community values and a failure to admit societal differences, whilst at the same time the neglect of these beliefs and values waxed and waned. Therefore, it is argued that it is under these circumstances that unethical issues were perceived as leading those facing numerous problems to deviate from group norms. There is evidence of contradictory examples, as when people are overwhelmed with forms of change in their daily life and begin to look back to the past.

All such developments are interpreted today as historical developments manifesting unrealistic expectations. This of course exemplifies the negativity of misinterpretations and the fact that a distinction has to be drawn between intrinsic and extrinsic African social values and beliefs. This is why consideration should be given by the church to the following: what was previously esteemed as of worth by African society for its own sake; why the method of conversion was inappropriate and how development has been disadvantaged by the variety of limitations or biases embedded in colonial policies.

For the sake of clarity, it is arguable that the effect of a lack of African culture and of development of the traditional religion is seen as an injustice contained within the bias of colonial values against local beliefs and cultural ideas, which led to conflicting interests in society. This was perhaps inevitable, but was by no means acceptable as a proposed model for a society, which was far less harmonious. The distortion seen in policies was associated far more with colonial arrangements and was a Christian offshoot of conversion expectations in keeping with the turbulence of the 1960s. For local people, this time did not only directly correlate with colonial economic interests, which it is impossible to separate from the spiritual, but also had major repercussions in the way political policies were executed and decisions were made that disadvantaged society.

My experience of working as a parish priest in both developing and developed European inner cities has offered me knowledge of what bias means to the weaker members of societies and especially to the poor, which is the most central force that has led me to this conclusion.

These misconceptions have continued to imprison African people in a constant search for wealth as the means of their freedom or salvation and yet, in the process, many people seem to have been led into terrifying beliefs and unethical ritualistic practices. The driving force has been the corruption of society, mistrust and the devaluing of human life so that people are terrified of each other. The fear of this new phenomenon has led to acts of human sacrifice, which surprisingly have included a number of church members. It is therefore the intention of this study to provide an up-to-date overview of Christianity in African society and to propose that Christians in Africa should take seriously people's views and what they say and believe to have despoiled moral and human behaviour in society today.

The reality also is that borrowers are caught up in an undeclared loan repayment war over extortionate interest rates. The fact is that totally innocent people who have nothing to do with the borrowed money are sacrificed, while fake magicians play on minds and create a state of moral panic for victims of circumstance, who look for help from wherever it comes. Bank lenders seem to assume that the current crisis does relate to loan pressure and in fact that such pressure does not exist, that borrowers are happy and at peace.

Fake healers can be regarded widely as conmen who simply exploit the confusion to convince desperate individuals that they can either protect them from their pursuers by providing a remedy, or stop the loan crisis by misleading their desperate clients that spirits demand human organs for sacrifice. The technique of fake healers elicits stimuli that prompt the undesirable behaviour used in a manipulative culture of human sacrifice. This is exactly what has come to pass, inevitably perhaps; witness the results when African mystical celebrations were treated as if they were magic, curses and witchcraft, an attitude that is found offensive and hurtful by Africans. In the past years, society has experienced the depths of the distortion and extinction of this society's values.

This approach raises the question of unethical principles that ignored the rules of evidence in people's experience, beliefs in general being argued as the problem of "moral hazard", which claimed that converts were exposed to excessive risks if they do not expect to bear fully the consequences of their actions. This is commonly cited as one-sided, which contained the inherent disadvantages of reductionism for African society. It was doubtless wrong to deduce from imperatives or vice versa, but imperatives are based on factual judgements; when people choose to treat others with contempt, or decide to ignore their experiences and feelings, then it becomes unrealistic to suggest that these were Christian decisions.

In contrast, the analogy of missionaries as agents of change stresses the paradigm of descriptive criticism and the possibilities of a distorted interpretation of the traditional (Ryangombe) ritual in Rwanda, particularly since the process of change was soon exaggerated and politicised as the Hutus' submission to the King of the

Tutsi. It is this rationalisation that is seen as discounted by Desouter's study of the traditional Ryangombe ritual, which is based on the mythical story of a man of that name. From his findings, he stated that it played an important role in the understanding and celebration of the unity of the African population. Though this is not directly related to ritualistic beliefs, the bias towards traditional beliefs and practice was observed by Louise Pirouet as perhaps a hidden ethnocentric sense of superiority. At this period, racism did not allow missionaries to see the true role of the Ryangombe ritual (Pirouet, L., [1989], p.168).

This shows that mystical celebrations were often misunderstood by missionaries; in this instance they confused the idea of Ryangombe with local politics. The characteristic of Ryangombe as a ritual is sacred to all Africans. Max Gluckman refers to the ritual performance as being highly conventionalised and by which people believe that they are helped, by mystical means outside of sensory observations and control, to protect, purify or enrich the participants and their group (Gluckman, Max, [1966], p.224.)

In an honest pursuit of the question of African historical ritual, it is logical to start off by finding out what gave expression to the relationship, which is purported to exist between people and the surrounding world. Having done this, it will be fair to evaluate and discuss such claims without accepting or rejecting them out of hand. Leonard is quoted by David Roach ("Absolute truth claims break down; Imperil religious liberty", July 2003) as arguing that claims of truth are far from it. Decisions follow on the judgement of what is true and right, which shows that the basic doctrine of Christianity and its domination was seen in the eyes of those dominated as untrue. This is how the ultimate truth alluded to the African people and it remains debatable to decide on the truth of a claim, when it is found to be contrary to reason and to observable facts. For instance, psychological Christian conversion was found to be extremely exclusivist and it is argued by David Roach that exclusivism borders on an infringement of religious liberty (Roach David, July 2003).

What was clear, however, was that the culture that was adopted after conversion to Christianity was preventive, inadequate or insufficient for communication of the new type of individualism. The lifestyle advocated had no idea of the prerequisite of successful community restraints, and this was the inevitable consequence of the contradictions given the role of misunderstanding and the resentment over traditional beliefs and cultural practices. In fact, the debate over behaviour change must never be isolated from the ongoing deterioration of moral value. Even communities that had enjoyed decades of unity, social responsibility to one another and stability, still face the challenge of setting parameters in their daily operations in the community control of unacceptable behaviours and human relationships.

Bishop John Taylor's "Primal Vision" is relevant here. Taylor vividly describes the network of rituals that had given security and meaning to life in Africa. He explains the vertical relationships going back through father and grandfather to the ancestors so that people felt they were an integral part of the community (Taylor, J. V., [1963], chapter 8). Moreover, the ritual established a bond between those who performed the rites. In fact, local beliefs argue that the dislike of these rites by European administrators and missionaries was mostly to do with the way that they brought together different ethnic groups. For instance, in Africa Hutu, Tutsi and Twa during ritual celebrations there were one. Two of the things that impressed and attracted people were the ways in which rituals were conducted and the sacredness of the ceremony. During the occasion, all people became one, united without differences between Tutsi, Hutu or Twa, while the celebrant's focus was on the ritualistic ceremony. A similar example of such a ritual would be the Islamic ritual ceremony of Mecca, which unites Muslims all over the world. Returning to developments in Africa, local beliefs lamented the speed of change (Interview at Butare National University, August 1998).

Traditionally, when people decided what was good and what was wrong, they were guided by the approval or disapproval of their community rather than by personal appreciation. This tradition gave stability and security in an unsafe world, with local beliefs believing that, as anything new was seen to be dangerous, this perpetuated the Africans' reliance on Ryangombe consultation in decision making. Besides, Bishop Alexis of the Anglican Church at Gahini, Rwanda, observed that the work of a missionary or the work of any expatriate might miss the point if they do not try to gain some insight into people's ideas of what they want to change. (An interview with Bishop Alexis Birindababagabo in Kigali, August 1998).

The next chapter intends to briefly look at how the situation has led to the current crisis.

A number of commentators and theorists offer mixed interpretations of public reactions and have developed various theories of the source of why people disappeared and others were found killed. Unfortunately, many theories concerning the current crisis collapse into each other and I do not think this can be done; each refers to real and different aspects of the problems that Christianity in Africa will have to take into account. So far, available evidence reveals that in 2009 alone (according to media reports) there were 500 victims of ritual sacrifice in Uganda. However, different explanations gave various versions of theories from people interviewed by media reporters. For instance, one man, Richard Sonko from Mityana, claimed that human sacrifice was an act of conspiracy stemming from rivalry between traditional healers and African Christian pastors, who do this to discredit traditional healers.

It was further argued that as the rivalry is caused by pastors whose intention was to have a monopoly of healing powers, so Christian congregations in Africa grow in size. As a result, the smearing claims of human sacrifice were seen as the tactics of a campaign by pastors to discredit traditional healers' credentials and destroy them. It is argued that if one group of people in their mission can travel around the world to discredit other religions as false, that is why society needs religious liberty. Though this will not happen overnight, it will require a critical campaign to win the trust of the public if traditional beliefs and healing practices are to get a better deal from society and from the services that exist to support them. Bukedde added that the need for a campaign for freedom for traditional healers is that the voice of pastors is always heard in campaigning for burning all shrines in the country (Bukedde, Wednesday, 11th March 2009).

However, what needs to be added to this assertion is the variations around the beliefs concerning healing within the two groups. Some see the cause of the culture of human sacrifice as both reflecting and perpetuating a serious state of moral crisis in society and give the example of a parent, whose name is not mentioned for ethical reasons, who was caught selling one of his sons in Uganda for 3 million shillings. I will therefore argue that where traditional beliefs and community values are no longer regarded as adequate because of the loosening of community bonds, this was brought about by changes in society and wider prevailing socio-economic influences. This underpins what has been happening in community disorganisation for the last 100 years. In this respect, the social problems lie in social arrangements that are radically different from the former ways of thinking, acting and living. The needs of society are constantly under challenge to gain their own priorities. Similarly, there are forces within society that the church can continue to ignore and not ask what prevents people from responding freely to church teachings, which are capable of transforming individuals' lives and the society in which they live.

On the other hand, there are other parallel theories from a political point of view, which see the sacrifice of human lives as an evil act of political enemies whose intention is to spoil the government's public image and politically damage the leadership (Bukedde, Wednesday, 11th March 2009). On the other hand, the leader of traditional healers in Uganda, Mama Fina, in media reports, attributed the problem of human sacrifice to two things, fakery and foreign influences of witches who travel from different countries purposely to con their clients in the pretence of possessing special powers. Mama Fina added that even among traditionalist healers there are some fakes ones with hidden intentions characterised as devil worship. (Bukedde, Wednesday, 11th March 2009). On the other hand, Mama Fina's proposition of the outside influence of a combination of witchcraft and fake healers makes sense if it is perceived as related to other incidents, such as those reported in Tanzania, South Africa and Latin America of Voodoo religious practices or traditional healers.

A review of the local literature shows that something new seems to have emerged from the above theories, which is rivalry between the new Christianity in Africa and traditional healers. If this is true, it needs to be tackled by society as soon as possible. As such, it sets the context for a reasonable (although not exhaustive) effort to find out about the existing search for wealth, which seems to have triggered this resurgence of a demand for traditional religious ritual. If it is true, then the rivalry that is often associated with popular religious groups, which tend to evaluate other groups negatively, requires analysis of the subculture to be carried out to determine practical measures.

For the sake of clarity, two points need highlighting here. The first is how people develop an interest in becoming wealthier, which needs to be carefully considered to avoid hasty conclusions, as if every proposed theory above does hold water. The second is to be cautious and for Christianity in Africa to avoid preconceived ideas of what is good and not good for other religious groups, which should cease because it is not comparing like with like. The issue boils down to whether society wants to take a lead over religious (traditional) beliefs. For the church to assess if it is avoiding the issue or has competing motives is bound to be problematic.

Following the discovery of headless human remains at Kibaale, the Police are holding two traditional healers over the murder of a 16-year-old girl in a suspected ritual sacrifice. Her body was found with the breasts, private parts, fingers and hair cut off. The district officer in charge of criminal investigations, Michael Ogwal, identified the suspects, who were both residents of Nkooko village in Nkooko sub-county. Ogwal said the duo disappeared after the murder of the victim who was returning from school. He added that they hid in Kiboga district until the police got information about their whereabouts and arrested them. (Monitor, Sunday, 22nd March 2009).

What must be recognised is that these ritual sacrifices are condemned by traditional religious healers as well. The problem of the lack of freedom for an open debate over traditional theological issues surrounding these practices hampers any progress by isolating the wrong culprit and continues to give opportunities to fake healers to exploit vulnerable people by misusing and abusing traditional beliefs. It is even arguable that human sacrifice is a combination of greed and faking supernatural powers. While the traditional healers demanded clients offer ordinary gifts such as a white chicken or a goat for appeasing spirits, fake healers go a mile further to demand the most difficult gifts to create an impression and a situation that convinces their clients that they possess more special healing powers than others. The purpose here is to examine whether these devilish acts are a new phenomenon, or whether acts of the past might be about people's beliefs in the supernatural as a whole.

The question to ask is whether human sacrifice represents a resurgence of traditional healers, or whether fake healers might be related to the culture of greed for wealth, which has led them to impersonate traditional healers. In response, we need to look at what has been happening in other parts of Africa to examine whether human sacrifice is truly related to traditional beliefs and practices, or whether there is a new, developing hidden culture of which society needs to be aware. In the process of trying to identifying the source of the incidents of human sacrifice reported in the media, I will try to assess whether these acts are related to beliefs or culture that has not had the opportunity to advance, or be modified from the negative elements contained in traditional religious healing practices.

There is a danger in an approach that forced traditional beliefs into secretive practices and under which abolition or a preventive agenda steadily became the source of isolation of the same power blocks, whose support was necessary to move serious issues into the national debate, in order to weed out the bad traditional healing practitioners and to develop the good ones. It takes much more than legislation to change the cultural mindset of human beings. So far, what we have seen is evidence that the history of abolition has led to resilient cultures that are pushed underground when threatened by legislators and form a strong unifying cultural force for their believers. As argued elsewhere, there are absolutely no winners in this; there are just losers. This is why there is an ever greater need to identify and locate the root cause of human sacrifice to gain practical and theoretical knowledge in order to establish how society can get over the present state of confusion.

So far, the phenomenon of ritualistic sacrifice has scared society to the extent of describing the act in various ways: some see it as an act of superstition and others as Satanism or greed on the part of fake healers who claim extraordinary powers and offer success for wealth. All these descriptions could be true. For instance, Mary Najjingo, 16, was butchered in Nkooko sub-county in Kibaale district, Western Uganda. Esther Among, a Senior Two student in Soroti district, Eastern Uganda, was also murdered. Resty Bangi, 20, was picked up from Bweyogerere Pub and her butchered body was found in Bwaise. Gertrude Nattiba, 18, of Namakonkome Bbombo Road was kidnapped, raped and killed while going for night prayers at a nearby Christian church. (Chris Kiwawulo, Friday, 6th March, 2009, New Vision).

Another report covers the trial of a suspect from Kampala over the ritual murder of 12-year-old Joseph Kasirye. A witchdoctor, who says he was contracted by the suspect to sacrifice the boy, testified as a state witness. In the first part of his testimony, the witchdoctor narrated to the court how he befriended the suspect who revealed to him that he had spirits that used to help him to acquire wealth such as buildings and vehicles. "He told me that his spirits (misambwa) are in Kooki, at Kaziru landing site in

Masaka and in Bunyoro," the witness told the court. (New Vision Newspaper, Sunday, Sunday, 16th August, 2009).

A detective at Busia Police, John Leo Othieno, who went to Amboke, in Kenya to arrest a child trafficker, said he found children fetching water in big jerry cans. The trafficker, Ms Namutosi, confessed to kidnapping the children from Mbale town after "realising that she is barren" (Daily Monitor, Sunday, 16th August 2009).

The crucial issue is not whether we are talking about kidnapping or human sacrifice, but why this kind of activity has increased and how to convince local sources to exercise a degree of restraint, as often there is no evidence that all these acts of murder are necessarily related to traditional healers as the bodies are discovered with no marks. What remains conspicuous in many ways is that there are other scenarios in which women are raped and finally strangled, contrary to sacrificial ritual practices, which means there are a number of other factors that need to be considered and there is no concrete evidence that all these people were killed as an act of ritual sacrifice.

The analysis starts with the conversion of African Christians, because I want to develop the question of the history of Christian conversion to show how European culture had an impact on African societies. This draws heavily on the debate over conversion accompanied by behaviour change at the macro level in terms of the interrelations between an individual's actions and the structure of society. The conversion process can be considered in terms of the comparative transition between African and European concepts represented as the understanding in many ways of a European, rather than African ceremony, which marked the transitional process of baptism.

Of course, at this period there was no policy of not discriminating on the basis of race, colour, creed, national origin, gender, sexuality, age or disability. The intentions and methods of conversion represented the denial of all that had made sense, argued in a functional analysis from the local point of view to have been identified as a ritual constituting the authority of the powerful. In fact, while considering the rite of passage in the organisation of their daily lives, what was ignored was a social function that celebrated the changes and the actions achieved by individuals from childhood to adulthood.

Superficially, such a decision ignored the rite of passage and had great repercussions in the transitional period. Individuals used to be marked with a sense of expectation in respect of acting maturely and responsibly as an adult, to uphold social norms and customary laws and to act as a custodian of community values. This is why missionaries are criticised as not having cared, but if they had, they would soon have discovered the explicit or implicit influence of bias on the side of people's culture and beliefs. The conversion journey would have required first an examination of the nature and extent of the situation that motivated and contributed to people's behaviours.

The second question arising from the past is to take a critical look at the functional organisation that undermined African intelligence and led them to take different orientations. Most likely the source of the resurgence of ritualistic beliefs is the lack of mutual enrichment that systematised social arrangements and led to interaction. Instead, the two worlds created seem to work against each other in favour of the outsider.

This is most common in African experience where decision making is still prevalent from outside the continent to a greater extent than in the interests of local needs. However, the Catholic missionaries seemed to realise earlier than other missionary groups about the inculcation position and Pope Pius XII, continuing the line of his predecessors, supported the establishment of local administration in church affairs. In 1950, the hierarchy of Western Africa became independent, in 1951, Southern Africa and in 1953, British Eastern Africa. Finland, Burma and French Africa became independent dioceses in 1955. (Audience for the directors of mission activities in 1944 A.A.S., p. 208).

Ironically, decision making even then is defined in almost the same way under the same doctrines in line with a natural role that ought to be played. The African concept of God is portrayed as one who protects, which indicates that the conception of God is not subject to human limitations. The false use of distortion and demonisation proves that all institutions as a body are open to political biases if not manipulation, since they are made up of human beings who are prone to err. One undisputed fact is that the resurgence of traditional beliefs comes from people whose effectiveness looks as if it is a warning for the church in Africa to pay attention. Therefore, the next chapter attempts to analyse what happened, the changes in society and the broader social function. The one after that examines the shift of culture and behaviour in African society.

Chapter Four

4.1 The Paradigm Shift in People's Behaviour

An attempt is made here to draw attention to the influence of similar structures and processes. More generally, the central argument is that politicians and church leaders talk, people listen and people make decisions. That explains the impact and influence of people's experiences of public leaders. What people hear and see matters a lot because when they enter into forms of social relationships with other people, not only do they enter into an association that involves making decisions with others without referring to contemporary cultural influences, including business and either the moral basis for their collective lives or the ways in which this life form is definable and has significance, but they also enter into economic relationships with a clear knowledge of prevailing conditions in their economic environment.

The whole idea of how situations cue, or prompt behaviour to occur, is integral to methods used by society to address moral codes, which are an often overlooked component of influence theory in society. For the sake of clarity and as a matter of priority, I will give an example of how corruption initially starts from the top and goes to the bottom. If the prevailing conditions require bribing officers to obtain a trading licence, traders will be compelled to adjust to the new regime and pay the bribe, but the inventors of the bribe culture are not the ordinary citizens trying to obtain the licence, but those with authority to issue the licence. Influence theory, of course, has always regarded the environment as the prime determinant of behaviour. William Temple observed that it is in that interplay of mind and environment that value resides (Temple, William, Nature, Man and God, p.135).

So far, what seems to have developed recently in society is a mixture of hostility and negativity towards authority. In this view, communities are not strongly or effectively connected with pro-social and anti-criminal others and institutions. There is a willingness to excuse, overlook or justify some delinquent, anti-social or criminal behaviour in relation to the present crisis, where people seem to have lost human sanity influenced by greed. In essence, all sorts of corrupt culture explain what society has been creating for the last hundred years in the trend of wealth accumulation.

Most attention has been given to how individuals learn habits, which are internalised and effectively applied, whereby they use all sorts of means to become richer. This explains the role of external influences rather than people's beliefs in human sacrifice. We are in a situation where people are caught up in poverty and the present external climatic influences their conditions, so that often when individuals are faced with making decisions on big issues, it seems to be a serious dilemma for them. Also, bear in mind that these people tend to have little educational background and lack experience in professional business transactions.

It is therefore under these conditions when people relate their beliefs to the problems with which they are faced. It is the most urgent requirement to think how the church can engage meaningfully with people through communication when they are in precarious situations. There is also the issue of providing primary and secondary education for all. Of course, everyone desires to be educated and to be rich. However, it is arguable that these services should be introduced without politicising them, rather than using them as a political catchphrase to win voters, particularly for partisan gains. This should be also regarded as corruption in disguise, because the money used to provide these services is either from public taxation or donated grants from developed nations, purposely for universal education to eradicate poverty in developing nations. There is a much bigger social question than what appears on the surface to be a more complicated source of the human sacrifice problem, which is a systematic failure to confront the question of empty phrases.

It is argued that the current problem laid a foundation for subsequent social disintegration and immoral innovations, where almost everything in society has turned to fake means. There is nothing left that the corrupt fear. Today's corruption culture symbolises an anomaly, which is indicative of a larger undercurrent of moral decay in society. Something has to change! All these developments is society are argued as signs of a weak influence of the moral institutions whose effect has led to moral deterioration in society, manifested in wrong innovations evidenced in fake preachers, fake local industry manufactured materials, fake drugs and fake traditional healers, all impersonating the genuine article.

However, I wish to emphasise that the fake culture presents various problems that have affected every sphere of daily living, including the police, who are even impersonating other officials. For instance, in Uganda Fred Kiwanuka reported that a police corporal from Iganga district was arrested in Nakasongola district for impersonation and extortion of sh2.8m from a traditional healer. Corporal Hudson Bakidiseemu, who had been masquerading as a senior officer from the police standards unit, was arrested while allegedly extorting money from Sam Bampige. Also arrested was Bwiire Kironde from Iganga, who had been masquerading as Corporal Mbusa from the police standards unit. (Fred Kiwanuka reported, Report, New Vision, Uganda, Monday, 26th October, 2009).

In another incident the police recovered a fake document, which was purportedly signed by an assistant superintendent, Turyamureeba, which the suspects had been using. The police central regional spokesman, Lameck Kigozi, said the duo had earlier robbed a traditional healer, Bampige, of his motorbike and sh4m, after threatening to arrest him over flimsy charges. He said the same people went to the same traditional healer and demanded another sh2.8m after accusing him of defrauding a patient. However, this time Bampige had arranged with plain-clothes' policemen from Nakasongola police station to trap and arrest the duo as they were receiving the money. The two men appeared in court on charges of impersonation and extortion of money. (Fred Kiwanuka reported, Report, New Vision, Uganda, Monday, 26th October, 2009).

This alarming fake type of culture has arisen widely in various African countries and is used to rip off the public through people claiming to have powers, miracles or magic. In a way, indicative signs of broader social problems have been accumulated by the sense of success and symptoms of greedy behaviour, as a prime mover. Albert Mohler rightly argues that the biggest problem with the fake promises of wealth and prosperity is not that they promise too much, but that they promise far too little. The Gospel of Jesus Christ offers salvation from sin, not a platform for earthly prosperity. While we should seek to understand what drives so many into this movement, we must never for a moment fail to see its message for what it is – a false and failed gospel (www.twitter.com/Albertmohler).

It is this pathetic state of corruption that consequently reveals a deeply sick and weakened people who cannot endure or resist manipulation. Based on the above analytical use of brutal corrupt suppression, I am prompted to argue that these changes in society might be compelling grounds for highlighting challenges to human behaviour that seem to have uprooted the long-held traditional community values, which offered a range of variables for support, in particular in time of crisis. The consensus is that local communities have become less safe, facing major anti-social behaviour, violent robbery, mugging and vandalism. Certainly a plethora of scandals reveal gaps between goals and assumptions and serious cultural change.

It is arguable that after the abolition of traditional values this was a disaster waiting to happen: where society used to apply cultural and religious values to make decisions and guide daily activities, all these were no longer available. Likewise, critics often pay special attention to styles that depart from representational realism by adopting religious practices as an explicit or implicit standard situation. This indicates that the standard of integration of Christianity in society has fallen, due to the fact of having been despised. One feels that the suppression of traditional religious freedom suppresses the lifestyle of the independent mind, not only the religious, which exist as two-dimensional areas of contradiction.

We may then ask what correlation exists between historical actions in the process and the perception of missionary conversion. The reality is that this has contributed to the creation of a new modern ritual. How did this unwanted culture come about, what process can be considered for reversing it, and how did the result of the process naturalise this culture into an aesthetic ritual of sacrifice? One way of beginning to provide light is to consider how local people perceived the events on the basis of a fundamental sociological analysis of the role of corruption in society. Among its results are the long-term development of social and economic devices and the long-term deprivation of the last decade. In turn, it is liable to generate tendencies of cynicism and an authoritarian culture. But what appears to have happened is that when crisis strikes, many people find it difficult to cope and when they search for advice, they often fall into the wrong hands.

So far, evidence of what happens often obscures the facts from the public and misses much of the hidden interpretations of dealings in society, which are the source of the rise of the prevailing belief in human sacrifice. The history of conversion suggests that collective negotiation about traditional religious beliefs in society and a new approach to the issue of dealing with past misgivings are inevitable. The economic climate has swelled the numbers of those who, in traditional times, would have been looked after within communities and today are referred to as the "under-classes". This underclass constitutes the largest section of the population and contains the source of human activities in the present plight.

4.2 The Divisive Influence on Human Behaviour

The biblical word translated as "church" is *ecclesia*, which is the original Greek meaning "the people of God". The New Testament uses this word in two different ways. Sometimes it refers to people of God gathered together in congregations; that is our traditional idea of the local church. But at other times it means believers in general, wherever they might find themselves. God calls the Church to be transformers of society through their collective influence. Jesus prayed that His Church would be unified in order for the world to respond to Him. "May they be brought to complete unity to let the world know that you sent me and have loved them even as you have loved me." (John 17:23).

That there are causes and consequences of structural inequality may, then, be inept symbols of another issue. Equally important in a way is the question of how traditional beliefs, human conduct and behaviour have deteriorated or been corrupted while old beliefs are manipulated to con citizens.

Take the regime of Juvénal Habyarimana in Rwanda. The media strongly influences what people think about various issues such as political matters. In Jean-Pierre Chrétien's view, Habyarimana's regime became the favourite child of colonial and international cooperation and NGOs; the famous "pays des mille cooperates". (Chrétien, J. P., [1991], 42, pp. 127-129) (Chrétien, J. P., [1991]. "Presse libre" et Propagande Raciste au Rwanda: Kangura et "Les 10 Commandements du Hutu, Politique Africaine" 42, pp. 127-129).

Pabanel agrees that, in international opinion, the African government had successfully resolved the ethnic question and dedicated itself to development, thoroughly convinced that it would overcome it. (Pabanel, J.P., [1995], p.113). Furthermore, Rene Lemarchand added that France helped to give the Habyarimana regime a degree of credibility that proved totally illusory, and thus created false expectations about its commitment to democracy. (Lemarchand, Rene [1994]. Managing Transition Anarchies: Africa, Burundi, and South Africa in Comparative Perspective, The Journal of Modern African Studies, 32, 4, Cambridge: University Press, p. 603).

Above all, Habyarimana's regime was busy dominating the upper echelons of the army, security services, the civil service, the diplomatic missions and the university. (Interviews in Byumba, Gisenyi and Kigali July 1998). The commanders of the Presidential Guard were drawn exclusively from Habyarimana's relatives and village. Habyarimana came from the commune of Karago, as did his powerful wife, Agathe Habyarimana, and her influential brothers. (Interviews in Byumba, Gisenyi and Kigali July 1998).

Colette Braeckman argues that this made up a small group known as "Akazu" (a little household), many of whom were related to Habyarimana's wife. This explains the close connection between Habyarimana's government and the Akazu clique. They had access to the best land and houses, the most lucrative business opportunities and easy credit facilities. In spite of this and President Habyarimana's claims "to have instituted a programme to ease ethnic tensions and to create a balance between the two ethnic groups", most observers saw his government as perpetuating discrimination against the Tutsi. (Special Report, Rwanda: Accountability for War Crimes and Genocide, A Report on a United States Institute of Peace Conference, 2001, p. 3).

According to political sources, it was the family's children who obtained grants to study and train abroad and who were offered the best jobs in the country. In his report on Human Rights and Conflict Resolution in Africa, Nguema refers to the fact that institutional corruption, tribalism and nepotism were the consequences of poor leadership by heads of state. In sharp contrast, the Habyarimana household used absolute power to dispense state resources as if these were their personal property. (Nguema, I., The Challenges for Peace Making in Africa, Conflict Resolution, Addis Ababa, Ethiopia, London: International Alert Report, September 1994 p.7).

During interviews, residents of the Gitarama region said that they were accustomed to thinking that this regime belonged to them. Ethnic and regional segregation had been instilled in the Hutu from Gitarama, to the extent that they would say, "Any person who did not come from the north was Tutsi" (Interviews in Gitarama, July 1998).

Those from Gitarama came to believe their own propaganda, namely that the privileges they enjoyed were a birthright and that they would last forever. Throughout the

33 years of the regime, many communities psychologically tended to incite hatred and prepared by propaganda, which encouraged further hatred of the Tutsi. However, each regime advancing this ethnic ideology made claims of establishing a pure democracy of the majority, which had permanently overcome the minority of the feudal Tutsi. But the new democratic process excluded the Tutsi from national democracy, which referred to Africa as the land of the Hutu.

This new approach requires consideration: democracy under the Hutu was firmly associated with the ideology of ethnicity. Such a democratic approach carried with it considerable problems for the Tutsi in Gisenyi and Ruhengeri where Habyarimana and his clan mates were known as the "blessed region". (Interviewing survivors in Kigali, July 1997). Similarly, before the genocide in Rwanda, the Hutu were fed a constant diet of manipulative anti-Tutsi propaganda that made Hutus sympathise with the ambitions of their leader to be directly involved in the genocide.

Mob justice is another example of moral deterioration, which is a recipe for disaster, demanding that concerted effort be put on the rule of law to uproot such behaviour in society, arguing that it is likely to replicate itself in many different ways. If you are living in anarchy and a corrupt environment, the chances of making moral judgements are pretty close to zero, because your whole surroundings are corrupt and the population gets consumed with corrupt thinking and deeds. This reminds us Isaiah's cry of who will go for us (Is. 6:5-6), because we are all sinners.

Furthermore, it can be argued that corruption also plays a pivotal role in the making of "injustice", the redefinition of the responsible citizenry via the production of a public culture of the vilification of criminals and the construction of mob justice, which replaces the rule of law. This is related to the question of the climate in which the criminal justice system operates, which is crucial within a shifting cultural paradigm.

Richard Wortley observes how this may apply to immediate environmental stimuli: when Pavlov conditioned his dogs to salivate at the sound of a bell, he demonstrated not only that reflex behaviour could be learned, but that performance of such behaviour was situationally dependent. The surest way to prevent the dogs from salivating was to avoid ringing a bell (Wortley, Richard, [1996], p.96).

Pavlov's study is used as an example of an eliciting stimulus. Evidence of this are the many everyday influences where particular environmental conditions become associated with predictable physiological or behavioural actions; arguably it is all about choices (Ibid.). Richard Wortley argues that an environmental eliciting stimulus is established through classical conditioning as an active reflex or respondent behaviour. It is further argued that there is a cutting edge from corruption to mob culture, which is not going to be easy to say goodbye to, as it is a culture that many have been used to for a long time.

In a way, behaviour change teaches us how to have simplified lives: a healthy lifestyle, career and hard work avoid the influence of wealth accumulation with no regard for others, and a lack of focus in the process of decision making has led many to all sorts of misleading decisions.

It is arguable that for society to regain control over the situation that has poisoned people's minds, it will have to reclaim those moral values, which for generations glued communities together. The argument here is to put emphasis on the rule of law as a solution to the restorative proposition that, if society traces the backgrounds of each of the individuals caught up in these deplorable acts of human sacrifice, it will soon discover that some of suspects were ex-offenders.

Young people who were unresponsive to society's measures are likely to enter imprisonment at a young age and an earlier stage in their offending careers; others are victims of the last civil wars, or of HIV/Aids whose parents died when there were young and grew up in poverty; while others suffer the effects of parental marriage breakdown and grew up with a single parent.

Apart from the risk factors of social deprivation, there are other several variables not cited here, which are all indicative of a society full of wounded, damaged and traumatised people. The degree to which past beliefs are brought to bear on human knowledge has become a source of conditions for the resurgence of ritual in a society or culture. The lack of collective human interactions has created weak ties to conventional settings such as home and family, and school and work paint tough living influences, which have altered people's behaviour towards negativity, hostility, rejection of non-criminal others and not caring what others think.

There was also an effect from the politics from 1957 when Ghana became independent, followed by Nigeria in 1960, to the 1970s after African independence movements and counter culture and the politicisation of forms of marginal deviance, which involved some educated middle-class people, notably the drift to the Pan African movement. This Pan African movement, involving highly articulate, educated sections of the population, enormously contributed to the politics of this period.

However, we need to bear in mind that the independence struggle was also a struggle for human rights. As a matter of morality, any model that allows anyone to abolish or eliminate through force other people's values, beliefs and culture to evade responsibility for their rights, will not succeed in helping society to stop violence. In other words, the function of preventation in relation to the past has often been singled out as a negative factor surrounded the abolition of people's values. Greater meaning was added to the highly ambiguous precision of abolition and it is argued that a better approach could have been to assess the devilish element in the beliefs and practices of traditional mediums.

The fact is that the distortion is in the foreground and the abolition is in the background. Therefore, if there in fact was no hidden agenda concerning people's beliefs, the devilish element should have been taken as a priority to challenge traditional mediums into accepting responsibility for their own behaviour. In other words, the action to abolish or clear everything in the missionaries' way cannot be merely treated as misunderstanding or simply failure on the part of missionaries.

In my view, the decision to choose not to discover the importance of the traditional religious values and African culture demonstrates that effectively there was more than one agenda during this period. First, missionaries were conniving with colonialism and, secondly, the missionaries' mission was to change society to embrace the new thinking, belief and living in the European way. This is supposedly when society was losing everything that had meaning. This was seen as a mistake, for those using the technique did not consider the policy for long-term human relationships, since the central criticism was seen as the lack of assessing the devilish element in traditional beliefs. The importance of this assessment could have helped people in society, because the survey reveals a long-term systematic deterioration of human behaviour as sources of the present deplorable acts, because when people feel threatened they are most likely to return to their traditional rituals in search for help.

The long-term deterioration in human behaviour explains how the traditional beliefs and morphology of African ritual ceremonies are sacred. In a sense, traditional ritual ceremonies become sacred in so far as they are embodied in the social culture. That these rituals are still powerful reveals that there is something in them outside their normal status as something viable for people. In this circumstance, this is where the differences between fake and genuine traditional healers can be traced and phased out.

4.3 When the Past Becomes the Present

Let me reiterate that according to traditional religious practices, people who perform rituals are clearly marked and known within the community of traditionalists and become sacred by spirit possession or consecrated by being set apart for some function related to the sacred function. These persons and things devoted to worship and ritualistic use had to be ritually clean, not in the context that often degrades them to outsiders as merely set apart by tribal taboo. Sacrifices and exclusion of the customary laws of clearances must be practised to ensure sanctity in whoever approaches the shrine.

The trouble is that for so long traditional healers have been known to operate underground, which is seen as the reason why fake healers have used this to their advantage to abuse the practice. Therefore, as mentioned earlier, it is argued that in the present tough economic conditions, people will do anything to save themselves from repossession of their property, while others are simply searching for magic protection out of fear of living in poverty once again.

As a result of the devastating threat of losing a business, it is natural to feel scared and to search for help, but the most dangerous decision and action is sacrificing human life and it is against traditional religion. Indeed, these acts are symptoms of a disintegrating society, which must be discouraged and those proved guilty must put imprisoned to safeguard the public because they are dangerous and exploitive. On the other hand, the driving force of all this is individuals who either fear returning to poverty or are deceived.

An exclusively objective view is that the consultation of traditional healers tends to arise out of desperation and a number of factors such as lack of medical facilities, no money or the breakdown of relationships. Doubtless all crises can lead innocent victims to extreme decisions. For example, recent media reports in East Africa claim that patients in some hospitals go for days without seeing a doctor. They are just content to be in a hospital and are comforted by the thought that at some point a health professional will come their way and help them. Thus, the shift from reality to wishful thinking is arguable, as out of desperate conditions individuals may succumb to fake healers to help chase away demons or deter evil spirits, or seek blessings to protect them from any harm. Under these circumstances, it is incredible that fake healers demand human sacrifices just to exaggerate their demands and magnify the problem.

There are even some church leaders in Africa who would ask for money to offer prayers for wealth. The desire and belief in fake protection and blessings for wealth has very serious ramifications that have not spared even politicians. Evidence of this is that members of parliament have been warned against witchcraft and corrupt tendencies.

"You should not consult witchdoctors for success, but instead seek help from God," Fred Hartley said during a prayer meeting for parliamentarians. "I know witchcraft is a big problem in Uganda but as MPs, you should be exemplary," he said.

But if we trace the history of each of these so-called rich people engaged in these beliefs, we easily find that the majority of them are people who became rich from nowhere and from dubious means. This is part of a culture of "Okulira mu Kavuuyo", living by crafty means, in which some people say that those who hope to succeed through straight means have a problem in their mental faculties. On the other hand, psychological needs are fuelled by public commercialisation, when one is considering people's behaviour at the rational level, in terms of the interrelation between individuals' actions and the structures of society, or at a situational level, in terms of the understandings, intentions and methods use in the organisation of people's daily lives.

It is this state of affairs that compels church compassion for a decision to propose to stop lynching suspects of human sacrifice, having heard the evidence which at times is contrary to what the public expected. In the eyes of the public, these individuals should never cease to be seen as human beings who simply lost control of their decisions and, rather than killing them, they should be assisted through rehabilitation to retrieve the situation. This is an opportunity for Christians to show compassion and let faith shine in Christ.

Christians are expected to respond to the goodwill of our fellow humans, for those who know how corrupt society has destroyed every nerve of people in society and accept how difficult it can be to act in a straight manner. In this circumstance, the Christian role is to support all those who are in trouble to raise their faith in hope, because anyone who has ever been in trouble will then appreciate what it sounds like to hear the voice of comfort. All this is in the hope that something can be done by which those entangled in a crisis can realise their terrible mistakes. As a result, when they find their wholeness, they will be able to look towards themselves in love and to appreciate that taking someone's life will not get them anywhere.

There is also a need to help individuals realise that it is not necessarily true that acquiring wealth is an end in itself, because society has created this impression. Most of the so-called rich are people who have come from nowhere in terms of being wealthy, or with no educational background, but they have gambled their way through corruption to acquire what many lack and yet are regarded as worth everything in life. To some extent this is liberation from the ghetto, but what emerges from this modern lifestyle is a sense that if you have money you can buy anything; for instance, a nice house, a good car and beautiful women. All these things charm most people in any society, so they should not be outcasts, but rather they should be helped to realise the terrible things they are doing in their obsession for money and love for nice things, because love is what they lack and were deprived of from their childhood.

Such a restorative process has to be focused on the role of caring and guidance, because there are generations who from childhood have never tasted love, having lost their loved ones. Jesus Christ warns the church of false righteousness, which is found in those who trust in themselves as righteous or justified by their moral accomplishment, overlooking the fact that humans are healthy and fit to serve God when they are fed both psychically and spiritually. The failure of the church to recognise this is believed to be a social disaster in the making within the area of the normalisation of the long-term effects of tragic experiences of civil wars, and in the understanding of the impact on people's lives of the HIV/Aids' epidemic.

It is this state where, to an extent, to kill one or two people to save themselves from their misery, would mean little to someone. In this sense, it is through love they will find the wholeness they greatly desire. Until the past damage can be healed, they are not comfortable in their own skin. It is only when they can be themselves that they will no longer cause hurt to others, but find acceptance.

No matter how courteous, mild or apparently objective the missionaries seemed to be, they clearly underplayed the significance of culture and traditional beliefs. Yet the question of failure is not purely coincidental since it was the fault of both the church and society at large, which shows how constituencies to the present day have failed to admit the insincerity and highly immoral characteristics that established the church. This would have been both local and yet universal in character, signifying practices that were critical weaknesses on the part of missionaries' teaching values and meanings that varied from people's beliefs and traditions.

When a difference of values enters a cultural context and replaces what had existed, its value comes from within and not from outside. For instance, why did the church leadership find itself still implying that the African traditional religious concept of God was not truthful? The truthfulness value must have been characterised in the Western context of the missionary use of doctrine where there was an inherent conflict between materialism, spiritualism, body and soul in the concept of the church member's role, which in fact is so outdated and no longer heard of in most European churches any more.

This latter question will be explored in some detail to demonstrate what I mean about shallow teaching lacking the radical thinking that is needed to restore society's values. How can we demonstrate that a Christian lives justly, in imitation of God's justice? What are the practical ways to imitate God's passion for justice and righteousness? God's justice isn't merely punitive. As a practical outworking of loving God and others, true justice is restorative. True justice represents God's love to those around us, thereby honouring the image of God in people. It would be helpful to clarify the methodological apparatus that was used to override Christian messages with European culture in spite of the reality.

Having argued that, everyone needs the gift of freedom and boundaries in their own beliefs, culture and work to succeed, which was not the case in Africa. In contrast, in the story of Creation, God set up the ultimate work environment in the Garden of Eden (Gen 2:1-5). Using the argument of creation, similarly it was necessary for the missionary Christian doctrine to develop out of the African environmental culture, which had in the past restrained people from greed and indifference and would have prevented the continuance of a crisis that replicates the inconsistent and endemic system of corrupt facts and questions pertaining to the present issues in society. The continuing lack of commitment and venality of the majority Christian church in Africa bears out the shallowness and weakness in the church's teaching and the present Christian membership's truthfulness in living double lives.

In fact, based on the analysis and overall evaluation of the salient arguments, it is not surprising that the African church is reluctant and unwilling to listen to this argument, because this double living is a sign of weak Christian teaching and people's beliefs in Christianity exemplify a critical example for the church membership that frequently pays lip-service to the church, while surreptitiously denying it in their deeds.

Traditional healers were demanded for the soul's health; in the same way there are several people in society today who need the assurance of God's intervention in their daily lives. The God of the Christian church to some does not recognise human struggles, but rather is seen as over-representing the spiritual side of growth alone. The church has to strike a balance in its care where it is possible for people to obtain what they need for their daily lives.

All this brings me back to the question of how to make things working better in a society where the obsession for wealth has replaced social values as protection for individuals to fulfil their dreams; how to uproot a system that has corrupted people's minds to the point where there are simply caught up in the hysteria of wealth accumulation. It is argued that the best way forward is to build a non-corrupt environment that is stable and peaceful and may greatly help the public to realise their mistakes.

Unfortunately, the people who denounce ritualistic sacrifice are the same people who badly need to do something about this problem and offer a lasting common remedy, considering the unquestionable assumption that human sacrifice is caused by a deterioration of human responsibility to one another in society. The anxiety produced by this situation is enough to make people take wrong decisions where there are no advising agencies. There is a pressing need for general advice for those suffering from anxiety and stress who have no history of psychiatric problems.

As a matter of fact, each East African country urgently needs to create a Citizens Advisory Bureau to provide a professional and confidential advice service covering a range of issues in society and in particular to assist in building and maintaining links with national financial bodies to make the individual case where necessary with bankers on behalf of borrowers faced with financial crisis. This service would help people by introducing them to a communicative environment, which indicates that certain behaviours are appropriate or inappropriate. Ironically, if the church is judgemental when things go wrong, church members may turn to traditional healers for help. Perhaps some churches, especially those of an evangelical persuasion, need to learn from the traditional healer's approach to assisting those who are in trouble.

Traditional healers will not judge anyone; whether you're a thief or evil, they will only listen to your problem without questioning your integrity. Of course, this invites some sharp questions, to put it mildly. During a crisis people's reasoning is likely to be impaired and they may be suspected of making wrong decisions, leading to various problems. In some way society needs to help them to reduce difficult and traumatic experiences, either through loan difficulties or ill health issues.

In the current situation when borrowers first experience pressure from banks, they find it hard to handle the situation. At the other end of the spectrum, I must make it clear that the majority view is that the conditions of bank loan interest are just part of the source of the human crisis that ends up in beliefs in sacrifice. I do not mean to suggest that these were the only determinant as there were other enormous social and health problems.

It is for this reason that no one can make a simple judgement based on one particular incident. First, by looking at society much more closely it becomes evident that when people on the fringe lose control they may succumb to anyone who can offer an alternative. The prominence given to the role of being wealthy is an irrational choice and making situational demands to prevent the murder of these people is not the best solution. Instead, we are justified in asking society to consider a number of other issues, taking into account the external implications of the hidden long-term bias, which aims to draw out the influence of the conceptual distortion of traditional beliefs in both historical and contemporary times. But full religious integration must be part of the journey and the longer the distorted image of traditional beliefs remains, the harder it will be for the church to achieve a fuller Christian commitment in Africa.

All this has to do with a climate that cultivates a deep-rooted culture of corruption and inducement to bribery, which has an influence on people's behaviour. The argument of climatic influence dates back, if one is considering colonies, at least from independence. Since then, this complex corrupt culture of associations has been gradually built and has received empirical support from a number of incidents reported in various areas, correlated negatively with behaviour deterioration and unrelated to influential climatic variables.

I am mostly concerned here with the new overpowering wave of corrupt culture that needs to be considered seriously and how wrong it is to condemn victims of a corrupt climatic influence and weaker individuals crying for help.

4.4 Pertinent Questions

All human experiences are varied and complicated. But alienation and subjugation to imprisonment on account of your beliefs is inhuman. While it is not possible to describe the situation entirely accurately, it is nonetheless important to get a feel for what it is actually like on the ground and why traditional beliefs are still the issue for many who still feel the hurts of the past. The seed of today's grievances was sown in the nineteenth century and the whole history of conversion still has a strong effect on relationships. Yet after decades, in former colonies, the past is creeping into the present; for instance, many disputes over land are occurring between the ancestors of squatters and the families of former chiefs. Not surprisingly, society is still asking pertinent questions about demands for traditional rituals and culture, which had formerly united people together and created dual proprietorship of community-focused practices.

It will probably be useful to look at the facts of church missionary teaching, which seems to have maintained past policies and suppressed traditional practices, pushing through "divide and rule" policies and creating a new wave of divisions in society. The church has played these divisive policies for too long and the consequent disempowerment explains how some weaknesses in people's unity and cultural restraints were engineered by changes brought in deliberately from outside.

Overall, analysis of the key events in converting Africans to Christianity raises sufficient evidence to enable anyone to speculate that the deterioration of people's care for their neighbours and community values began at this period. Following on from this, when people turned in the opposite direction, we might say that if we need to ask questions such as, what does it means to be African in this situation? This might help to reach a fuller understanding of how the change to the worship of wealth occurred and turned away many young generations from relationships with one another other. This process partly shows how ritualistic murder developed out of a particular historical period and had a definite influence on people. Such a process is part of theological reflection in considering how imposed systems possess a history that irreversibly evolves and in which past events are never forgotten.

Three main areas are suggested:

1. Powers and pressures. What powers or influential factors were at work in the situation (e.g. colonialism, missionaries and Christian conversion) whose interests were powerful? What pressures were converts under?

2. Human consequences. What was the effect of the situation on the various people involved? Whose interests were likely to be overlooked?

3. Motives and values. What were the aims and different agendas being pursued by colonial and missionary groups involved in the changes (e.g. wanting to avoid change or risks)? What were the values and motives underpinning the aims and agendas (where Europeans instead could have had value and respect for traditional religious beliefs and their presence)?

All these points were necessary and were ignored by missionaries before they brought their own cultural experiences to shed light in the darkness, reaching a bifurcation when they abolished the existing system. What justifies criticisms of this change is that the ideas and theological themes that came from their minds were not relevant to the situation (bearing in mind that they were in different biblical times) and everything that has been heard recently about the exclusion of African ideas, prayers and expressions of faith. From the time of colonial rule, the disproportionate missionary influence was evident in the cultural shift in church teaching, which led to the disintegration of people's relationships in society.

Other developments that were taking place in the political arena suggest that after independence many African countries seem to run together; ideas sprang out of nowhere rather than developing integrative economic policies in the local developmental culture, which instead created various irregular changes and promoted some good and some bad philosophies.

To mention some of those characterised within as good, we could include Milton Obote's Common man's charter, Jomo Kinyatta Harrambe and later Fata Nyayo in Kenya and Uwujama in Tanzania. However, there were also empty phrases such as in Uganda on the long road to recovery since 1986, when the economy was dominated by three words: magendo (smuggling), kibanda (black market) and kusammula (speculation, hoarding). The reason they are described as "empty" is that they have no philosophical constructive meaning or long-term philosophical objective other than simply corruption. Other terms include Mafuta Mingi, which means excessive wealth; Okulembeka or Okulira Mukavuuyo, which literally means to profit out of chaos or in crisis, evidence of which is often seen when accidents occur and instead of people helping victims trapped in vehicles, they rob them of their belongings; Twarire from Western Uganda, which literally means that it was time for eating or being wealthier or an equivalent in Buganda, okuggwa mu bintu, which is falling into things.

In my opinion, when these views were introduced it marked a radical departure from the traditional setting and a greater cultural shift in society; from that period people increasingly lost the community spirit and moral or ethical values.

The nature of this social order is problematic because of the lack of respect of traditional wisdom: when all local values cease to be valued, what was once treasured in communities becomes watered down and degraded as valueless, living in the past and backward thinking. These divisive and immoral measures poisoned people's minds and will take a long time to eliminate from society. Both government and religious appointments need careful attention before anything can be done to reverse the breakdown of moral order that has been created. I question how quickly political leaders can forget what has happened, which simply highlights how bad leadership has an effect in determining thinking and behaviour.

In a corrupt system of social relations where members of society play roles occupying statuses that are functionally to do with wealth and success and the pressure of being richer, this has a considerably greater influence on people who get caught up in a crisis and indeed on the analysis of the external forces of people's beliefs. All acts, circumstances and consequences are related to the economic dimension, which has recently tremendously affected human behaviour, either by establishing or destabilising an economic order that is related to, and perhaps directly influenced by, the central value system of society.

Alternatively, we can cut into this aspect of political corruption by building up a perception of how politicians understand their role in the public arena and their intentions in political appointments. Against the background of the current crisis, it is further argued that religious and ethical values that had tried to modernise society and unite people are increasingly under threat due to too much emphasis on acquiring wealth. In this age of globalisation, this is a fact that we cannot ignore because it has such a powerful impact on aspirations for success.

The idea of success is particularly associated with postmodern critiques of globalisation, in which old identities have been replaced with new ones, especially in relation to consumption. In such circumstances, seekers of quick success become trans-located in traditional magicians, who promise to perform a magic astral ceremony of protection on their behalf. This ancient ritual will eliminate every negative power (harmful thoughts, negative vibrations, bad luck) in one's life and replace it with positive energy (solutions, luck and profit or anything one desires).

Many people who were fortunate enough to benefit from the magic ritual of astral protection saw their lives transformed. The fakers promise that very ancient beneficial forces will be at work, and the predictions made by the Ogams reveal many things to those who can understand them. Initiates of this ancient magic claim that it has already brought great happiness to many, who today are all perfectly content and sheltered from need.

Given the importance of people's sense of routine, the weakening of human resistance results in turn to benefits to the fakers. They often emphasise the urgency of performing the secret ritual as soon as possible, which remove forces that hinder one's success in finance and happiness. They promise amazing financial success ahead of one, followed by more months of pure happiness on a personal level.

This was not traditionally a common practice, although people in the past believed in hard work and educating children as a way of aiming at long-term success, but it has recently become normal for the corrupt and gamblers to become successful and rich, through ordinary domestic loans, mortgages and other means for obtaining credits. It is even doubtful whether such a thing as equality of bargaining power exists; in a sense an attempt to co-exist in every stratum is certainly a type of corruption.

I think that in reference to all these interests, there is a parallel between political leadership and hidden clauses in loans, which have driven many people into all sorts of corruption. There is an evil influence, regardless of the way it is done or at which level. Everywhere you go in African society and whatever you do, there is some form of corruption.

The classical theory of corruption undoubtedly plays an important role in economic and social development and it is tempting to consider, to an extent, whether some critics of corruption scrutinise the scandalous appointments of close relatives to government jobs in many African countries. It is incredible how political leaders never learn from the mistakes of others. For instance, corruption started from the period of Mubutu in former (Zaire) DR Congo, but there is exactly the same concern today, what has now become the “Kazu-(household) syndrome”.

Although it is difficult, and perhaps inappropriate, to keep moral indignation out of the discussion, I find it disheartening to take this route of exposing the source of corruption and how it has become institutionalised as part of the culture of leadership. Monitor argues that leadership is instrumental in institutionalised corruption by accepting bribes in open daylight (in reference to the money rewarded for agreeing with wrongful decisions), while politicians cleanse and defend unscrupulous deals, such as scandals, to justify flaunting of procurement laws and accept illegal shoddy purchases, disrespecting civil liberties and perpetuating acts that are tantamount to state-inspired terrorism. (Kiboko squad, Black Mamba etc.) (Daily Monitor, April 27th 2009).

This means that the leadership position is so often contradictory in its policies that it is like constructing a highway and not expecting the public to use it. As much as the leadership may pretend to fight corruption, it is likely to fail because it is a bad example from top to bottom. Therefore, the question of transparency in leadership plays an important role. Transparency should not be misused to suggest one household’s control of the leadership, but rather leadership must be transparently a broadly formed government that represents national interests from all communities equally.

The key concepts that emerge from the above analysis suggest that some important policy engineering is required in conflict-prone countries where there are cultural differences. It is arguable that the separation into superior and inferior religious beliefs was a product of conquest, which leads to the conclusion that the past has now been excavated from its ignorance and error. It is for this reason that it proved to be a hard task after independence for leaders that inherited systems that were not founded on democracies to establish democratic rule rather than an authoritarian regime.

Rather than testing the traditional religious winds to see which way they are blowing, or investigating the definition of traditional marriage, Christians must turn to God's word for his view. Once follow-up data on the outcomes is available, evidence is analysed to identify factors correlated to the outcome of cultural and social policies, which are all part of a systematic process to reduce people to horizontal inequalities. Policies towards investment, employment, education and other social services should aim at reducing imbalances and inequalities. These are factors during the process of change that created enormous conflicts, not only in politics, but in every sphere of life, and are strongly associated with the divisiveness that characterises the current crisis.

Chapter Five

5.1 The Question of Abolishing African Traditional Beliefs

The main aim of this chapter will be to trace the consequences of church teachings, which represent a more fundamental problem than the issue of the alleged ritualistic sacrifices of traditional healers that highlighted the dangers of demonising traditional beliefs. That it is a serious challenge shows the danger of missionaries abolishing traditional beliefs and the local culture. All of a sudden, we hear of all manner of suspects masquerading as genuine traditional healers. The disturbances of ritualistic murder are argued as a warning to the church to realise how past events pushed traditional beliefs to operate under cover, which was unhealthy, and that suppression of people's traditions and cultural values leads to a very damaging position for society.

This is examined to understand how historical events are associated with the current deterioration in human behaviour and debates regarding the strategic function of forms of society, which are needed to establish cultural values. The church needs to realise the importance of integrating a variety of traditional values into church teaching, which has a healing purpose that presents the most important shifts in terms of the restoration of social values and social conduct. In a sense, unity is more important than ever for people today: in the past it was seen as of absolute importance, but that situation has greatly deteriorated today.

Considering further the issue of God's revelation, it can be argued that knowledge of God can be revealed even in the most backward or darkest place, even where there is no physical development. Furthermore, it is also arguable that

God's revelation cannot be restricted by space, time, environment or circumstances. I can only say that those are human-made assumptions, cloaked beneath assumptions used to reveal something God wanted certain people to know, but that requires the elimination of inconsistencies and contradictions for the general knowledge of God.

It is apparent to me that God views the place where you receive these truths as a high position: whether in a city, in a high temple or in a bush under a tree; it is the same way. But no doubt others will persist in viewing such places as despised. My suspicion is that as humans we are only capable of such rigour in narrow domains and for limited periods of time, which is why the church has to evaluate Christian teaching in an attempt to isolate how it drove colonial values to unleash ill-proven intentions on society and how Christianity was manipulated in conversion activities to dominate weaker societies.

Scholars attempt to isolate such domains for Christian church teaching to capitalise on high Christian principles through bursts of rigorously logical thought. It is argued that Christian faith in the love of God carries with it, necessarily, a hope for the future, which is both as a mission and for the human community. The basis for this hope lies firmly in God's own procreative, transformative, resurrecting power and action. It is arguable that missionaries were called to act as co-creators in the process. In the light of the steps gone through above, it is essential to take any useful way forward is essential to take, whether looking at the situation or taking into account new attitudes, bearing in mind the realities of the situation.

In Innsbrück, Franz Weber noted that his European colleagues take up contextual theologies from Africa, Asia and Latin America with eagerness, but the paradigm shift in practice did not change their Western outlook and superiority complex. European theologians treated African people as if they were exotic fruits that supplemented their traditional European dishes. (Weber, Franz Mission. Gegenstand der Praktischen Theologie? Frankfurt am Main, 1999, 228).

Therefore, the emphasis in this chapter is to highlight the relationship between personality and the Christianity established during the missionary conversion. The historical question of abolishing traditional beliefs was not only a problem for Africa, but included several other areas where Europeans had conquered indigenous people; for instance, in Australia among Aborigines, the inhabitants of several West Indies islands and Native Americans. However, Francis Wijsen observed the cause of this as Western "knowledge export", one-way traffic, a manifestation of a Western superiority complex in which we presuppose that our rationality is the best, that our methods are the most appropriate. Are we prepared to learn from "the others", or do we want them to adjust to our criteria? (Wijsen, F., and J. van Slageren, Missiologie-beoefening in Nederland en België, in: Wereld en Zending 27 [1998/4], 25-34)

When trying to understand the ideas behind the alteration of the societal structures that were found in Africa, it is clear that other African customs and traditions - that can in no way be interpreted as heathen in nature - should be allowed to continue among African converts. The way Africans praised and the revelation concept could have been adapted as means of transmitting the Christian messages. As to exactly what customs should or should not be allowed to continue, the legitimate Christians would have made decisions within contextual amendments. In the absence of European culture, the responsibility for making such decisions should have rested with the head of the African Church. In short, customs and traditions that were not contradictory to Christianity should have been allowed, while those that were clearly contradictory should have been tolerated, laying the foundation for the church and advancing the Christian doctrine under any circumstances.

Therefore, the advance of missionary messages can be considered as causing contradictions in how people see things, especially when they have been indoctrinated to believe that the accumulation of wealth and success is satisfying in itself. To begin with, there were surely bound to be contradictions, since it has been revealed by the passing of time that, although Christian conversion was concerned with spiritual matters and changing minds, this type of teaching played a large part in deterring African social conduct. Such attitudes were adopted on the basis of outsiders' interests, but ignoring the fact that human assumptions are carried over to new situations. Indeed, it is more important to follow a rigorously logical analysis and claim that it should have been gradual practice to help people fully understand the meaning of the Christian message in a practical way and how it can be conceived in social reality.

In addition, this makes it possible for those involved to design messages that are context specific, which eventually helps them to modify behaviour and encourage the development of desirable community habits. In theory, it is a profound mission of the Anglican Church's commitment to contribute to social development and play a positive role in spiritual renewal. The fact is that weak involvement leads to weak theology and strong involvement, on the other hand, leads to a truly incarnation-authentic understanding and practice of the mission.

This also raises the argument that is was a blunder of the missionary church to abolish local values during conversion, because they would have helped in the process of moulding people's behaviour change and expectations and meeting social demands that could have continued to hold true among converts. What is criticised as a mistake for missionary was abolishing and discouraging the local acknowledgement of traditional beliefs and culture to enter the church, despite it being recognisable that Christ was already present in non-Christian cultures.

U. Hannerz argues that after modernisation and globalisation most societies in the world are not multicultural in the sense of a patchwork quilt or mosaic of separate pieces with hard, well-defined edges, but consist of a cultural mix or cocktail, for which Hannerz uses creole languages as a root metaphor. (Cf. U. Hannerz, Cultural Complexity. Studies in the Social Organisation of Meaning, New York 1992).

Language is important not only in itself, but also because it shapes cultural perceptions and attitudes. In its metaphor and metonymy, it serves to represent the expression of several trains of thought in a singular representation as the principal axes of language, but the choice of one word over suitable alternatives, at any given point, is regarded as a spill forward of the linguistic chain and consequently likened to the paradigmatic and syntagmatic as well.

This level of similarity is evidenced today not only in cities like Amsterdam, Paris or London, but also Jakarta or Nairobi, which create youth cultures that are a mix of Hindu, Sikh and Muslim traditions, combined with secular-political and ethnic ideals, bound together particularly by reggae or rap music. Whereas some scholars speak of cultural homogenisation, for example Ritzer's "McDonaldisation thesis", others foresee cultural differentiation and fragmentation, as is the case in Huntington's "Clash of civilisations" (Cf. G. Ritzer, The McDonaldisation Thesis. Exploration and Extension, London 1997; S. Huntington, the Clash of Civilisations and the Remaking of the World Order, New York 1996; B. Barber, Jihad vs. McWorld, New York 1995).

Some scholars even question whether cultures even existed, as is the case in Hobsbawm and Ranger's "Invention of Tradition". Wijsen notes that the export firm that the church used to be had become a multi-national import firm. (Wijsen, Francis, Intercultural Theology and the Mission of the Church at the University of Nijmegen on 7th March 2001).

Wijsen and van Slageren argue that there are two types of religion in the world today: religions of the imagination (which men and demons have made up) and the religion of revelation (Oswald J. Smith, The Roman Catholic Bible Has the Answer; Cf. Grand Rapids, MI: Faith, Prayer and Tract League, [1953], p. 6; Wijsen, F., and J. van Slageren, Missiologie-beoefening in Nederland en België, in: Wereld en Zending 27 [1998/4], 25-34).

This brings me back full circle to the point that the African departure from their own revelation of God occurred when it was undervalued by missionaries in a context that characterised traditional religion as devilish, which was self-defeating. God is telling the church that the means it is choosing will defeat the end. Waiting on God is neither dishonourable nor unfaithful. The danger of undervaluing traditional religion is that from that moment any value and beliefs were made inferior, it spelled the destruction of the entity of people's thinking and beliefs in society.

In contrast, I wish to say that the lack of use of people's experience does not only mislead people, but leads to a closed system and to the misapprehension of the depth of mystery that characterises everything that is. I will perhaps stretch the word insight to connote a deepening apprehension, which in this case was distorted to undervalue the African concept of God's revelation. The conception of difference could extend to almost any length and yet the fact remains that people's concept of God for who He is was a vital basis for the contextual understanding of their theological knowledge. It is also arguable as conveying the message that to choose to seek the mind of Christ (1 Corinthians 2:16) was to be faithful to Christ depicted in an African environment.

In this view, African contextual theology purposely communicates the Saviour's love and the mode of choice is then transformed into a theory of love. The significance of contextual theology is that it represents within the cultural world the most certain image and clearest embodiment of Christ as the source of God's love of all beings, who convey their meaning through each other and have their being determined by their mutual relations.

It is further argued as incumbent on Christianity in Africa as a requirement subsequently to reverse all the distortions of people's culture and beliefs. Burden argues, "Theology is about the nature and will of God for humanity; the Bible encourages us to look at our present experiences in the light of the nature of God and his will for community". (Shriver, W. D., Woodstock Report, March 1996, No. 45).

The object of these quotations is simply to reinforce the obvious, but well hidden fact, that the reaction is not to dispute the claims they make, but to observe that they seem simply to justify the missionaries' abolishing of traditional religious beliefs. However, strangely after centuries these beliefs still thrive as much as ever in those countries. Therefore, the quick response to the question of abolishing traditional beliefs is a strong no. It was totally wrong, a miscalculation and a misconception of missionaries to abolish traditional beliefs and classify them as evil and satanic. It is argued that these policies led to the traditional beliefs being unable to participate in their full capacity, from the early conversion to the present Christian world view of an African conception of truth. The evidence of traditional beliefs' survival to the present day proves that it was a mistake to abolish them and if traditional believers had been fused together in Christianity, traditional beliefs would not still pose a problem to the church.

In other words, African beliefs should actually be firmly entrenched in African Christianity's liturgical worship. The integration of people's beliefs is a fundamental right for developmental action and is necessary for the structural dualism, which relates to traditional beliefs within society. In fact, what are the reasons for having foreign religious pluralism rather than having religious structural pluralism? In plain language, this would mean that to develop a healthy society must have its own beliefs and keep its own cultural entities with a distinctive cultural heritage and sustainability. This is the inescapable bind for all past suspiciousness and stereotyping.

It is arguable that people are practically forced into the resurgence of traditional acts as a reflection of their past source of protection. The spiritual forces that are trusted in society inform the mistakes of the past and serve implicitly to show structures through a pattern of the implicit source of the crisis in traditional beliefs. John Urry quotes Bauman who outlined the conception of power as not necessarily exercised through real co-presence, as one agent gets another to do what they would otherwise not have done through interpersonal threat, force or persuasion. (John Urry 2001:60).

Nonetheless, to understand the source of the problem we need to examine how the problem of power was constructed in the Christian philosophies of conversion, which interpreted the Bible in the church doctrine of the "Truth". Speculation on the part of missionaries about traditional beliefs can be argued as developing the interests of European dominance, power and control of less developed societies. Studies over several decades have found that the use of threat, force or persuasion gives them the power to abolish traditional beliefs, ritualistic practices and African culture, which during this period can be termed racism overshadowed by a simplistic view of racial or cultural incompatibility, as was often featured in the decisions made in conversion.

A central feature of the past Christian conversion in Africa served to reproduce the dominant structure through a pattern of implicit discrimination, so the decision to abolish traditional beliefs can be described as prejudiced or biased, where prejudice is an unfavourable opinion or feelings formed before and or without knowledge, thought or reason, often unconsciously and on the grounds of race or colour.

Ideally, one asks what does this past has to do with the present crisis and does this past exactly inform what was happening during this period? Yet even here biases, assumptions and the attendant rationalisation were used to institute these assumptions and contradictions inevitably crop up. In a way, they do not show a purposeful or long term goal-seeking social improvement of human behaviour, but rather the imposition of new ideas contrary to current behaviour, which required premises, semi-conscious or unconscious assumptions or behavioural codes.

However, justified criticism of the new codes of rules is their neglect to realise that these premises or codes of rules were not corresponded to as sensitive goals or clear-cut rules. In that particular environment there needed to be a process of integrating new ideas, which would be relied on by society far more than imposition of new rules or a new order. The reply is that, if the church is my primary concern, it has to change the attitudes of people in society today, but first has to engage with the past to know the source of the crisis.

These developments raise far-reaching implications of ignoring Christian conversion's use of baptism as a transitional or liminal phrase from traditional beliefs. It is argued as the mechanism according to which society would have owned the transition to full development of Christian conversion without demonising or abolishing the traditional beliefs, but when conversion did not then reflect the reality of person being initiated. The person baptised occupied a "betwixt and between" position; having lost his or her former status in society, he or she had not yet fully acquired a new one.

This is why the church today needs to re-examine the core contradictory message of Christian conversion, which accorded agents of change with the ability to control society rather than deliver the "Truth". In this instance, it is argued that the message of "Truth" had the implication of according power to make things happen in the colonial interest and to prevent local ideas and beliefs from developing.

This approach seems to have betrayed a pattern to which the Christian revelation is seen to be strikingly relevant, and thus the door was open to constructive theological reflection, inhibited by an over-emphasis on the sweeping change and the dangerous influence of distortion that had existed at the expense of new ideas, philosophy and new religious beliefs. This, in the long term, would create dependence to stop the traditional beliefs from advancing from their status, instead ushering in European religious dominance.

From the philosophical point of view, thus far, the explanations for both the church use of distortion and colonial rule's use of forms of power show how the process inflated and intensified social divisions. Developmental disparity and institutionalised social inequality, including the suppression of religious beliefs and practices was intrinsically fostered for decades, Speaking from a local point of view, the purpose of change was not only religious, but was rather conceived as a colonial enterprise, where the emphasis of Christian teaching was the preservation of a valued European cultural way of life and legitimised their (rule) on the weaker societies, although it can be shown that Christian missions varied in different colonies with different strategies.

In fact, the changes undoubtedly degraded African ideas. Upholding African traditions became intolerable and were eventually pushed underground, which has turned out to be a source of resurgence and a hiding place for fake traditional healers. The population is caught up in a broken and dysfunctional system and arguably this exploitation culture is traceable in people's cultural lag. It has developed out of changes towards cultural corruption in a society where law and order no longer count, which has been weakened and marked by deterioration in the moral values of human behaviour.

In fact, to assess how it is possible to make things better by succinctly examining the situational prevention of human sacrifice, situational techniques need to be differentiated from other crime prevention approaches, which aim to improve social behaviours. (Cf. Clarke 1992, 1995). This is arguable as a failure to recognise people's culture and beliefs, which prevented them from recognising their potential or changing in their own way. That is a rational perspective on the impact of the phenomenon, although some of the most profound and noticeable changes in the conduct of social change pivoted around issues creating the crisis of a loss of human value, leading them to degrade each other in the name of wealth accumulation, as reported in the media. Of course, not all people are the same, but those who do this are quite open, without shame or consequences.

On the other hand, let us not kid ourselves that there was a time when society's morals were perfect and that society has suddenly arrived at this situation, because in fact it was a gradual shift. I will be quick to add that neither has Christianity's religious influence fully erased the past. It is symptomatic of the fact that society has no respect for the value and sanctity of human life above all else, because that is the foundation for morality. Indeed, the purpose of this assessment is to trace the reasons for the rise of these beliefs as a recent phenomenon, which will be traceable in both social changes and economic influence.

Trying to make sense of the changes and to find the framework through which religious institutions in society can integrate traditional beliefs does not mean necessarily a conversion to traditional beliefs, to which I believe many Christians are already converts. However, the cardinal principle for the process of religious integration of traditional beliefs is rather to create harmonious relationships or multi-cultural religious beliefs, and to allow freedom for each group by promoting the best attitude to adopt when listening to each other's story.

The notion of missionaries that traditional beliefs will easily disappear or go away was also a wrong one, because all the evidence, as we see today, is that rather than disappearing they keep rising in different forms. It is the aim of this chapter to revisit the past through memories of missionary conversion in order to assess the past, make sense of it, but also to recreate in the present what can only become a fiction of it. This should not be used as revenge driven by subjective anger of the victims, since by definition subjective anger pays no respect to standards of evidence, proof and proportionality and therefore tends to breed further injustices in another spiral of violence and revenge. Justice, on the other hand, seeks to replace subjective anger with the desire to restore social equilibrium, so that society may function healthily and for the good of all.

The problem with mob justice and lynching is that it is very degrading and dehumanising and leads to a wild society without a system. What is morally objectionable in the use of lynching is that once human life is treated as an object lesson rather than as a person, it must be so far internalised in society that the naturalness of human life is not thought to be a right. Such treatment is simply a devaluation of human life, which is contrary to civilisation and utterly repugnant to human reason in modern society. And once one human life is treated like that, we all know that our lives have been reduced to that much.

However, this should not in any way give an impression that the defence is to suggest that offenders to go free. Both in the past and in contemporary society it should remain practice to safeguard both the general public and suspects in ritual murder. It is therefore argued that all suspects must have a free and impartial trial without any prejudice or any outside interference or influence. By law the suspect is not guilty until proved guilty. It is argued that people's ethical rights under this treatment are marginalised by an overriding focus on the idea of punishment. The prerequisite for society is to enforce the rule of law as a necessary human right.

On the other hand, in the present human sacrifice crisis, where a suspect is proved guilty, two points should be considered: firstly, representing the ultimate human rights' position of an individual with reason for life imprisonment and, secondly, to apply a degree of restraint in the acceptance that those proved guilty should not be terminated, but punished. To kill punishes the family rather than the guilty person. Families suffer emotionally and financially and community relationships many be strained forever. The idea of prison or detention centres is that once the offender is convicted the approach has to be holistic, taking a collective view and seriously considered by society. This is an alternative theoretical approach, which sees society as a kind of system composed of inter-related parts known as structural functionalism and is largely aimed at society adopting a more humane approach to improve its inability to deal with social change and social conflict.

This does not sanction the state taking away the life of those found guilty through an excessive punishment. Four key aspects of the rule of law should be used to foster acceptable links for punishment. From the social religious aspect, punishment of those found guilty has to be used as a means of rehabilitation. What I mean by this is that restorative justice requires much more than punishment alone. It is a process that requires offenders to go beyond the pain and humiliation of the sentence to a fuller acknowledgement of what the human consequences of their actions have been, why they are wrong and what they must do about it. The prison punishment method also plays a double purpose: its vital element in dealing with criminals is the protection of the public, as well as helping criminals through widely used rehabilitation services; for instance, prison chaplaincy, education, medicine and probation.

In the final analysis, the past distortion and claim of truth argues that whatever is done, and however it is applied to the abolition of beliefs, was a matter of dialogue, which the church needs to listen to and revisit in order to repair the damage in this area. Neither does it imply that there is nothing useful in the belief; for instance, a faith based on divine revelation.

The church trying by all means to continue condemnation of the traditional healing practices is no reason to doubt the church's sincerely and truthfulness. The fact that most church members still trust traditional healers argues that that should be an eye opener for African church leaders to wake up to the reality and to assist individuals or groups who are still searching for spiritual help. However, church teaching still insists on missionary claims and distortions and it will not solve the spiritual hunger of church members by simply dismissing African traditional healing and practices and expecting people to turn away from the loving Creator, whose loving and healing message is received. If the church is able to establish rapport and end marginalisation, this could bring about Christian reform and allows Africans to appreciate their own church and tradition. The unity and peace to our divided world would yet be beautiful.

Of course, the advocacy of African traditional values, beliefs and equal rights for their heritage would allow traditional healers to supplement modern medicine, which is a way to recognise the fact that traditional healing practices still have a vital role in society. One of the areas, if not the most dominant, in which bias has been clearly perpetuated is the denial of developing ideas of traditional healing, in African societies and on the continent as a whole.

There is a clear indication of a conspicuous trend in the development process, where the emphasis on colonial and missionary ideas was perceived as one-sided and tended to focus on the privilege of developing their own ideas. Instead of concentrating on developing people's ideas, they are rather used for medical experimental trials as guinea pigs and this exercise is somehow indirectly still carried out. For instance, in Rwanda there was a report of research carried out on blood specimens collected from over 1,800 volunteers from Rwanda, Zambia, Ivory Coast, Kenya,

Nigeria, South Africa and Ugand.a (The New Times, Rwanda, 12th September 2009).

This is why it is necessary for the Christian ministry to profoundly scrutinise the theoretical claims of traditional healing and to express through teaching and church example glimpses of the kingdom of hope, symbolising creation renewed and where imperfect is made perfect.

When you consider the history and the development of modern medicine, it shows that medical development has come a long way to where it is today. For instance, the significant improvement in medical plastic surgery took place between the nineteenth and twentieth centuries largely due to improvements in technology. Podnett-Hood determatome, named after the plastic surgeon and engineer who developed it in 1938, was designed to remove sheets of skin suitable for large skin grafts. Another example is the development of titanium plates, strips and screws in 1980. Titanium is light, malleable, strong and biologically inert. It is used to cover small defects in the skull; strips of standard lengths and breadths are used instead of plates. (Cf. Dermatome English, made by Down Brothers Ltd, Steel 1980).

Modern medical and surgical instruments were introduced after the First and Second World Wars to operate on victims during and after the wars. More recently the service was professionalised and centralised and has even become commercially focused. In addition, the invention of the latest technologies, such as the Internet and new media, has acted as reflector to amplify knowledge and has contributed greatly to the advancement of medical breakthroughs.

Nevertheless, Africa has to bear in mind that the developments that took place during the colonial period did not favour or allow colonies to develop their own knowledge. The central colonial period's use of power was partly through policy making from both a legal and commercial point of view and a prestigious role was awarded to medical practitioners. In essence, legalisation of their knowledge and medical practices meant that anything not done by colonisers, even after independence, was not to be trusted as safe for use.

The medical control and abolition of traditional medicine and beliefs was a combination of both capitalism and monopoly theories. Functionalism understands a legitimatisation role for monopoly (Persons 1951). Yet African traditional healers' practice of medicine is an important part of traditional religion. Mediums and medicine men/women are reputed to have professional knowledge of illness (pathology), surgery and pharmacology (roots, barks, leaves and herbs). Some of them are also reputed to diagnose and treat mental and psychological problems. The role of a traditional healer is broader in some respects than that of a contemporary medical doctor. The healer advises in all aspects of life, including physical, psychological, spiritual, moral and legal matters. He also understands the significance of ancestral spirits and the reality of witches. This is why both the church and civic leadership must realise that the most urgent question is whether they have really engaged traditional believers and mediums, or assessed the paradoxical nature of what is called healing.

It is my view that the traditional healer's view hasn't been heard. What is often heard from the public is a repeat of the past distorted claims of missionary teachings. The symbiosis of modern and traditional contributions would assist those who search for traditional interventions through discourse. To be fair to traditional healers, the debate must be brought into the open to engage professionals in what is being done in secrecy and find a long-term solution. Father Richard Nyombi observed that the decline of African traditional religion (ATR) was as a result of the arrival of Islam and Christianity in Africa, and that the presence of Christianity and Islam were a greater hindrance, since "its propagation was carried out by living it other than by preaching it".

Christianity arrived in Egypt and the Mediterranean coast (Roman "Africa") in Roman times and penetrated to Nubia (where it died out in the sixteenth century) and Ethiopia, but it did not spread further south until the era of Portuguese expansion in the late fifteenth century. In the sixteenth and seventeenth centuries it penetrated into the Congo kingdom and took root in the Portuguese colony of Angola, but at the end of the eighteenth century Christianity was restricted to a few coastal areas. A new era began with the settlements of Black Christians from Nova Scotia in Sierra Leone in 1787 and the missionary advance inland from Cape Town began with the arrival there of J. T. van der Kemp in 1799. New missionary societies (the LMS, the CMS, the Holy Ghost Fathers, the White Fathers etc.) began work in many parts of Africa, though, apart from the extreme south and the Horn, the interior was hardly touched before the last quarter of the nineteenth century. The missions founded in 1875 on Lake Malawi and in 1877 in Uganda mark a new beginning.

Over the next 30 years, with the political "Scramble for Africa", missions were established almost everywhere and churches grew. In general, missionary activity benefited from the conditions of colonial rule, but some missionaries voiced criticism of abuses and in the later colonial period relations were often strained. e.g. in Zimbabwe, Mozambique and South Africa. Since political independence, they have varied.

(http://www.interfaithdialog.org/reading-room/the-problem-mission-and-or-dialogue.html/1/10/09).

The Christian expansion in Africa was followed by a preoccupation with its practice of abolishing ATR. It was from this period that ATR dogmas and doctrines increasingly had a very small role to play in the life of their followers. (Father Richard Nyombi in African Traditional Religion). However, considering the current point of view on human sacrifice, as far as traditional beliefs and cultural views are concerned, condemnation or continuing to campaign for keeping the practice underground are not the best measures to help society and are not even a solution to the problems abolition has caused for people. Instead, the church should wake up and realise the danger of keeping the practices underground as the source of all sorts of dubious groups who abuse traditional ritualistic practices, rather than helping people who are simply trapped in spiritual moral dilemmas. (Father Richard Nyombi in African Traditional Religion).

This has led to confusion over ritualistic sacrifice and has raised the debate to the need to find a solution to the wider problem. In the analysis of forcible intervention in society, traditional beliefs are a central issue that requires an urgent response. It is a situation that calls for the church to act in the way Christ himself treated outcasts and sinners, to reach out to traditional believers because it is in the name of Christ that the church operates. The church will have to stop its prejudicial teachings so that their effects on traditional believers can be overcome.

Informed politicians and social scientists know that cultural bias and prejudice towards African beliefs was unmitigated colonialist fiction; therefore church leaders must study traditional religion to help traditionalists fully turn to Christ. The church's relationship with traditional believers should be empowering, not judgemental. Africa did not need to be "saved" from its own tradition and culture. To call traditional beliefs demonic worship was a

European cultural value judgement on something they did not understand and moreover never bothered to understand.

Let me further explain what may be advantageous to know about the psychological characteristics of magic and witchcraft. In Human Mythology and Magic, Eric Maple asserts that "magic as a force can probably best be defined as the interpretation of one mind upon another, with suggestion as its primary mechanism; psychic power is nothing more or less than a peculiarly effective type of thinking." (Maple, Eric, p.3019).

Magicians have the ability to capture people's energy and magnetism, by clairvoyant flashes based on someone's photograph or name. They can provide a clear description of someone (whom they have never met), tell you about their profession, their problems, what they have already experienced and what will happen to them in the future. It is believed that mediums possess an internal power, which enables them not only to heal the sick, but also to identify witches in the community.

It is necessary to identify the role played by mediums, magicians and sorcerers in society to understand that there is quite a clear distinction between magic and witchcraft; in fact, they are two different elements. Magic is related to spirits and performs two roles: sympathetic and protective. Sorcerers use witchcraft to cause harm and its use is negative, while magic is the traditional medium in sacred ritual, which is protective and is performed to prevent spirits from causing harm, or to undo harm caused by spirits to the individual or to the family. Magic is a highly conversational performance by which people believe that they help, by mystical means outside of sensory observations and control, to protect, purify or enrich the participants and their group.

In recent reports, both are classified as "witchcraft", which is wrong because magic and witchcraft have separate roles. Magic rituals give expression to the relationships that are supposed to exist between humans and the surpassing world and is therefore positive. (Gulckman, M., [1965], p.224). Witchcraft ritual is negative but confused, because it generally involves religious elements dealing with spirits and the afterlife. However, witchcraft in the media is generally characterised as magic according to the police.

Unfortunately, the church's attitude, especially in African missionary-founded churches, shows that it is still dwelling on the past shallow teaching of negativity, which will make it impossible for people to be able even to contemplate positive steps to discard evil practices out of traditional healing. Harmonising positive practices prevents risks and if the church ignores this, it would be negligent and prevent people being saved from a lack of knowledge about their own culture and beliefs and the falsity of human sacrifice. It is impossible to grasp fully the source of the resurgence of ritualistic sacrifices without understanding their religious dimensions.

Chapter Six

6.1 The Question of Exclusion under the Conversion "Truth" Doctrine

The previous chapter tried to explain how missionaries excluded people's traditions and beliefs in the process of conversion, yet argued that in every human society beliefs are vital in human development. In order to survive, people in any society must live by their beliefs and develop their ideas about how to relate to each other. The failure to recognise the fact that traditional religion was an integral part of African society was a mistake on the part of missionaries. This approach is argued as stemming from the effects of domination, either by the church itself or in alliance with colonialism, using biblical scriptures as a major part of achieving a paradigm shift in society.

In fact, the advent of the Christian mission in Africa was preceded by teaching that harboured an attitude of mistrust of anything that was not known to them. This informs us why they chose to demonise traditional beliefs, but their mistake lay in not considering the long-term impact on society. The missionary assumption was that after abolishing the traditional beliefs they would cease to exist. In this form of conversion, as we shall see, the truth claim was a dominant factor (John 14:6).

However, it is important to emphasise at this point that normally conversion is subject to two possibilities: truthfulness and based on someone's faith. It may be contended that many disagree with this, because the prerequisite of conversion was measured by coming forward for baptism, which was diplomatically or courteously claimed as a sign of faith in order to attain some material gains. It can be reasonably argued that this process was too delicate in terms of effects when one considers the aspect of abandoning one's faith on the other hand. The question of genuine conversion can be analysed by looking into the benefits and status before and after conversion.

The idea of conversion methodology was partly motivated either by some material benefits or by the aspiration to status, glory and power for some. In this view, the colonial authority and the missionary church system as a whole soon monopolised everything that it was possible to monopolise. Through the support they got from converts, they gained control of all political and religious institutions, with powers to determine what people must believe, or do and what they should not. Looking back in history, the method of conversion contained incentives to attract needy people to convert. The emphasis in conversion was put on charitable work. To improve the social welfare of converts, they were rewarded with benefits such as handouts of clothing, salt, soft pins and other imported objects. It is argued that in a way, conversion through charitable inducement is a forcible conversion. Conversion should only happen through spiritual persuasion and not through the gifting of material possessions.

This kind of charitable service is not entirely bad, but it should not have been mixed with religious conversion to attract ordinary Africans, who frequently visited missions and were eventually, without much difficulty or imagination, recognised by the way they were persuaded to convert to Christianity. The process of conversion only turns problematic when it abolishes traditional practices and demands that converts abandon the past. Some converts sensed that this endangered and undermined their traditional beliefs, identity and culture that had existed for centuries. Nationalists defined identity as African, regardless of origin; African leaders defined it as black African.

A political impasse transcends personalities. Every census is a fundamentally political document. The state thus distinguished non-indigenous races from indigenous tribes. All races were governed under a single law; civil law. There was never a single customary law for all tribes as natives; a single racialised group. Each tribe was ruled under a separate set of laws, called customary laws. Racial discrimination distinguished between master races (Europeans) and subject races (Asians, Arabs, coloured and so on).

Without beating around the bush, this traumatic experience explains how people accepting baptism could have misled missionaries that those coming forward had truthfully converted to the Christian faith. In the first instance, most of the missionaries who spread the gospel had a conscious or unconscious colonial orientation to lifestyle and religion. This was coupled with the fact that missionaries worked hand in hand with colonial administrators, so the ethnocentric superiority of the faith was transmitted to African society. In effect, accepting the Christian faith implied accepting and abandoning one's culture and living in a European culture, without reasoning unconsciously how to live in real life in society.

To that extent, the Christian converts therefore had no reason to question the faith they had received. In the course of the process of conversion, it might be disputed by the church, but it would not be wrong to suggest that it was a period of African submission to colonial rule, indirectly through religious persuasion but not conviction. This raises the question of the truthfulness of Christian conversion. It might have been conversion for many in the early stages because it was the status quo that was supported and looked natural to everyone. However, the assumptions of the disappearance of traditional beliefs seem to have been discounted by the present resurgence of traditional religion.

The church today can only condemn, which is a sign of loss of the power of effective guidance in matters of traditional religious beliefs. In my opinion, this condemnation is not a solution in itself, but is just seeking public acknowledgement of the church being sympathetic. However, the profound danger of the resurgence of traditional religion still poses a challenge to the church and a threat to human lives.

The early concept of the church's teaching was based on claims of Christianity as the only religion that holds the "the truth and the only way". (John 14:6). Where it is still believed that there is no other way to access God's salvation, the church needs to think twice. The church needs to engage with society and learn to listen to their traditional beliefs rather than condemn. The abolition and condensation of African traditional religion is worth discussing, the reason for its failure perhaps being related to the fear of punishment in the fires of hell for amplifying points in the conversion message.

The theory is often criticised by society as being totally wrong and still the fault does not lie with traditional believers. However, if the church had analysed this, it would have realised that the doctrine of hell fire was flying in the face of common sense, rather than being a historical instrument of change. The implication of change is that the new problems of the new order that converts encountered, prevented and denied the possibility of traditional beliefs and cultural development.

The logic of this is to argue that the key element of this was the negation of the old order and the fundamentally and widely advocated colonial agenda in the nineteenth and twentieth centuries for changing the world. Societal breakdown and cultural disintegration marching in step with the progress of industrial societies was seen as a problem that created the inability of control arrangements to cope. For nothing was more traumatising than the breakdown of community values that is traceable to the wicked philosophy of "truth claims" distorting the African concept of God and yet, in Genesis, the Bible says that God let us make mankind in our image, after our likeness. (Genesis 1: 26).

This statement of creation makes it clear that the image was in no one's image but a heavenly image. This is why it is necessary to bear in mind that the background of missionary conversion teaching was the source of a social breaking point, which has created a greed for wealth and accumulation to an extent that society cannot control. Subsequent changes were all more or less constructive versions of the missionary "philosophy of change" spectrum and missionary rigour pioneered evangelism through early Christianity in Africa. This is seen by local people as a severe restraint to the development of local cultures where local values were mortgaged to the culture of individualism and wealth, in which what matters is wealth and whom it hurts does not count any more.

The culture of this corrupt system left victims defenceless and courts reluctant to convict. It is further argued that so many people have become over-confident and the obsession with wealth has turned their motives to generate more wealth, which has created conditions in which the richer they become, the more they lose the sense of community values and Christian virtue.

It is argued that it was a mistake to dismantle what made an African what he or she was, because any neutral analysis of African traditional religion shows that behaviours and virtues were connected with the communal aspect of life. In view of all the changes, African history at this period was being erased, a process by which they were merely turned in observers, while the younger ones in particular became curious and excited about changes in the process. It is these changes that presented the rationale for implementing new forms of state capitalism, with the superior technological knowledge supplied by European civilisation. This negated social behaviours such as respect for parents and elders, appropriately raising children, providing hospitality and being honest, trustworthy and courageous. In traditional beliefs, morality is associated with obedience or disobedience to God regarding the way a person or a community lives. For the Kikuyu, according to Mbiti, God, acting through the lesser deities, is believed to speak to and be capable of guiding the virtuous person as one's "conscience". (Mbiti, J.S., 1975).

According to African religion, a person is expected to have a good or bad conscience depending on whether he or she does the bidding of God or bad spirits. The point of concern here is how conversion to Christianity worked hand in hand with colonialism to distort the traditional beliefs of converts and lead them to despise their African heritage endowed in traditions. The teaching organised the learning situation, in the former without consultation with society and, in the latter, total rejection.

In the early stages of authoritarian conversion, this conversion based on outside culture is similar to the New Testament, but not the Old Testament, although as the eventual outcome is that the process becomes a replacement of the old culture, the learning context itself is implicit in the theory. All of this explains the deep impact of conversion on converts in terms of the transmission and interpretation of Christianity, which in the process of conversion remained between understood or misunderstood when the emphasis was to reject converts' own heritage.

The preference was for the distinctive characteristics of the new identity and embracing European cultures and beliefs, yet degrading or distortion did not only endanger local culture and beliefs but African memory as well. Just for the sake of clarity, during the period when wider colonisation was taking place, the theories of post-modernism were in sense so ambiguous, because they do not refer either to a period of modernising alone, but of changing physically and spiritually with a commitment to acclaimed truth, the reason for this truth (John 14:6). In this regard, the change argues that the truth is rooted in the nature of industrialised society, which seems to target and be focused on control and advancing industrialised knowledge, formulated and legalised in a new powerful philosophy. This was viable through the influence of Christian teaching, ideologies and doctrines in order to put pressure on the colonised, which was especially a task that defied the collective efforts of missionaries during the colonial period.

From the above assertion it does seem necessary to discuss the following questions:

1. The implications of the "Truth claims" (John 14:6) raise questions about the influence of imported culture. The claim was applied as an instrument of change that enforced on society an inherent materialism, whose philosophy and irrelevant theology served as a precursor for social disintegration in Africa. If a credible explanation was to be established of the precise cluelessness of the concept of distorting and destabilising traditional structures, culture and people's beliefs are located here. This "Truth claim" is argued as having developed either to abolish traditional religion through legislation, or to apply persuasive ideas of dominance explicitly as a mode of control in converts' minds.

2. Narrating what has changed today provides an understanding of the exact intentions of the "Truth claims", in effect pivoting this discussion around the dominating and controlling modes. It is important to know that the conversion did much to refute the early traditions, both

religious and social, which were opposed, distorted, demonised and persecuted for decades.

The atmosphere of world movements during this period of the history of post-structuralism or post-modernism rejected premises of the nature of local beliefs in "colonies". On the other hand, it was an analytical device that makes it appear as if colonial administrators and missionaries had put their heads together before embarking for Africa. If looked at this way, this disguised domination was carefully planned and introduced by both colonialist policies and through persuasive teaching mechanisms operated by missionary agents of change in everyday life. This is sometimes described as the mechanical approach, which is a social theory claiming the reality of the "Truth claim" instrumental apparatus, for the social change phenomenon is argued as mediating access to what was claimed as "Truth" in a religious setting. In the religious sense, Christian conversion was turned into ideological and theoretical control of the mind. But the similarity of the "Truth claim" to reality does not just happen; it involves a doctrinal code.

Understanding what was happening means understanding something of the ordering code. More specifically, when colonialism is deeply examined its mission and impact confirm that it was not just accidental or as innocent as it may sound, because perceptions depend on coding, which suggests that during colonialism the influence of conquest was high on the agenda and many European countries demonstrated their powers by their dominance of weaker societies. In this case, Africa was approached by colonialism in various ways of dominance. Hinga notes that the image of Christ that prevailed was the postulation of Christ as the conqueror, a warrior King "in whose name and banner (the cross) new territories, both physical and spiritual, would be fought for, annexed and subjugated". (Hinga, Teresa, (1994). p. 263). It is this past observation of influences that underlines the need to dispel the misconceptions that were created in conversion.

The principal issue is: What is truth? It is a problem of being clear about what you are saying when you say that a particular claim is true. The most important theories of truth are the correspondence theory, the semantic theory, the deflationary theory, the coherence theory and the pragmatic theory. (Cf. Bradley, R., and Swartz, N. [1979], Donald, D., 1984 and Strawson, P. F. Vol. 6, [1949]).

Importantly, though, I want to give a sense of the complexity involved in trying to understand both the conceptual purpose of "Truth claims" and also how 'Truth claims" (John 14:6) appear to be apparently contradictory to each other and never seem to agree, even among different groups of Christians. What is more, the capitalist colonial ideological analysis of difference illustrates the histories of the key practices of Christianity as social theories were embedded in it. The influence of Christian conversion can partly be considered at this period as packaged with colonialism, in that the religious influence had a tangential significance as its technique impinged on beliefs and supported colonialism.

This is why we must mark these two terms used as ideas and techniques. The Christian change of African society in principle set apart the past, which at the time was too far removed from people's own experiences. The early concept of evangelism was a change to save pagan worshippers and to free them from worshipping the powers of darkness (Satan) into the true worship of a true God. This argument will be explained further under contextual theology in Chapter Eight.

The main objective of theories of the Christian use of hellfire can be argued as an agenda construct derived from nineteenth-century (Victorian) values, as we shall discuss later. However, we should note that the use of the "power of darkness" was not without purpose. The possible explanation had deep roots in ethnocentric theories that represented black generic inferiority. Popular culture was interwoven with Christianity, laying the theoretical ground work for distorting anything black in missionary teaching. In contrast, a number of Darwinists were describing Africans as people who were simply closer to the monkey than to the human; it is thus relatively understandable that the abuse of Africans, (slavery, colonisation, genocide etc.) would be more or less acceptable. The idea of "survival of the fittest" was even applied to women. If we accept the beliefs of the period, only the European male had managed to become most fully evolved. So his desire to conquer all "lesser evolved" beings was regarded as completely natural (http://www.mamaafrica.com/article/articleone.php/16/9/2009).

Though all the changes were criticised, the objective was to establish a new order. Very soon it appeared as if the old order had disappeared, which was not true, as we shall see in the development process. The missionary teaching with threats of hellfire and punishment was normalised and was something to be found in the social, political and cultural theories of control and economic climatic influences supporting control of Africans through ideological and religious influences, political and colonial rule. All these were radically different from the African context, where the New Testament interpretation of individualism and the industrial culture of competiveness were embedded in the teaching of Christianity in Africa, where the salvation doctrine was the only "way and the truth". (John 14:6).

For other societies, cooperation (communitarianism) seemed much more "natural" than competitiveness; caring for each other in society more "natural" than ignoring or even exploiting each other; ensuring that everybody in the community had sufficient resources to live on and no one had more than their individual needs and community goals were to obtain more resources for the community to depend on. It is conceded as foolish to begin talking about God and salvation before the way was paved for such notions and without considering ethnographical issues and cultural anthropological dilemmas about where the recipient of the message was fundamentally situated, taking into account problems, questions and all sorts of issues surrounding converts.

The next section considers the operation of social ordering and traces the history of the concept of social control, in order to identify its beginnings and highlight how absurdly African traditional religious beliefs were excluded, by placing emphasis on selected biblical scriptures to condemn them as evil and devilish acts. In setting out an approach that is more transformative in its outlook, seeking to compare truth (John 14:6) claims shows the problem of how differences in claims are divergent and cut through all denominations, rather than attempting to be only claimed as a Christian monopoly. For instance, it is argued that in the contemporary context the church teaching on the truth concept needs to redress the past biased emphasis on the monopoly on "Truth".

Firstly, when seeking to expose the "Truth claims" there is no unilateral agreement among Christians about the salvation doctrine and different denominations in the church had different emphases in theological teachings. Secondly, there are differences even among other world religions such as Judaism about "Truth claims", especially in Orthodox Judaism where truth is the revealed word of God, as found in the Old Testament and, to a lesser extent, in the words of the sages of the Talmud. (Cf. Tarski, Alfred, Research 4 [1944].

For Hasidic Jews (an Orthodox sect), truth is also found in the pronouncements of their rebbe, or spiritual leader, who is believed to possess divine inspiration. Kotzk, a Polish Hasidic sect, was known for its obsession with truth. In Conservative Judaism, truth is not defined as literally as it is among the Orthodox. While Conservative Judaism acknowledges the truth of the Old Testament generally, it does not accord that status to every single statement or word contained therein, as do the Orthodox. (Cf. Tarski, A., 1994). Moreover, unlike Orthodox Judaism, Conservative Judaism believes that the nature of truth can vary from generation to generation, depending on circumstances.

In respect of halakhah, or Jewish law, (which loosely speaking can be described as the will of God as expressed in day-to-day activity), Conservative Judaism believes that it can be modified or adapted depending on the needs of the people. In Orthodox Judaism, by contrast, the halakhah is fixed (by the sages of the Talmud and later authorities). The present-day task, therefore, is to interpret the halakhah, but not to change it. Reformed Judaism takes a much more liberal approach to truth. It does not hold that truth is found in the Old Testament, but rather that there are kernels of truth to be found in practically every religious tradition. There is neither deliberate disobedience nor a rift in the Body of Christ. There is, however, a disagreement about how concepts and interpretations within scripture are to be regarded.

Most avid readers of scripture defer to the opinions and perspectives held by the early church fathers who, in considerable wisdom and after much deliberation, determined that certain scriptural writings should be considered as divinely inspired. But we forget that there were disagreements about their decisions to either include or exclude various writings. Not only were there significant disagreements about the concepts presented that resulted in decisions that were far less than unanimous, there were also highly political and deeply social influences that resulted in successful alliances resulting in majority choices. The deeming of divine inspiration of one piece of scripture versus another was a very messy affair. Today, we forget that such processes are full of inconsistencies. We just accept and see scripture as definitely holy and divinely inspired, almost as if the decisions that were made came in unanimity with the glowing presence of the Holy Spirit shining all around. Not so.

For eighteen centuries, many texts were lost or were deliberately suppressed because these texts and the perspectives they propagated were deemed contrary to the direction and viewpoints that those in positions of power desired to allow. But the Truth cannot be suppressed forever. Eventually, it makes its way out from under the piles of darkness and breaks free. Think of the many men and women who have been innocently incarcerated after prosecution, defence, judge and jury have all given their best efforts, under oath, to assure the correct decision in determination of their guilt or innocence. Yet people have been innocently incarcerated because the jury made victims of people who had committed no crime, despite every intent and effort to free the person if wrongly accused. Moreover, the attitude towards the Old Testament is, at best, to document parts of it that may have been inspired, but with no particular monopoly on truth, or in any way legally binding. (Bradley, R., and Swartz, N. 1979, Donald, D., 1984 and Strawson, P. F. Vol. 6, 1949).

Buddhism differentiates between two levels of truth in Buddhist discourse; a “relative” or commonsense truth (Tibetan: kun-rdzob bden-pa; Sanskrit: samvrtisatya), and an “ultimate” or absolute spiritual truth. (Tibetan: don-dam bden-pa; Sanskrit: paramarthasatya). Stated differently, the Two Truths’ Doctrine holds that truth exists in conventional and ultimate forms and that both forms are co-existent. Other schools, such as Dzogehen, hold that the Two Truths' Doctrine is ultimately resolved into a non-duality as a lived experience and that they are not different. The doctrine is an especially important element of Buddhism and was first expressed in completely modern form by Nagarjuna, who based it on the Kaccayanagotta Sutta. (http://www.iawwai.com/EternalLife.htm/4/2009).

In Hinduism in the Upanishads of ancient India, truth is Sat (pronounced Sah't), the one reality and existence, which is directly experienced when the vision is cleared of dross. This is poignantly described by Ramana Maharshi: "There is no greater mystery than that we keep seeking reality though, in fact, we are reality." (http://www.iawwai.com/EternalLife.htm/4/2009).

Father Richard Nyombis's similar remark that "For the African, religion is literally life and life is religion", fits the Hindu approach to the mystery of the revelation of God. Humankind can be likened to a blind person who touched an elephant's trunk and described it as the branch of a tree and another one who touched the back of an elephant and described it as a rock, which is truly how we are in many ways. Jews used the Old Testament and Europeans cleverly used both Old and New Testaments to claim a monopoly (Father Richard Nyombi in African Traditional Religion ARR).

These claims agree with Sharrock, Read and Kuhn's observation that the influence of the colonial scientific and philosophical revolution, under which such claims were constructed, was characterised by Victorian values, even in Africa from where Christian teachings emanated. On the other hand, it was also influenced by a mixture of the European Enlightenment's mission and power to colonise, to rule and to change heathens who lived in the dark continent of Africa. I will therefore briefly assess the concept of the Enlightenment. (Sharrock, W, Read, R., Kuhn, Philosopher of Scientific Revolution).

I will also be quick to argue that the truth (John 14:6) claim was developed in one way, which was of benefit to European culture and influence over all that had existed in African society, which implanted far-reaching changes, included the acquisition of power and deepened the ability to impose a revelation that undermined any other sources of revelation. This is an argument based on the fact that the lack of meaningful consultation with society's institutions represented a deliberate exclusion of any other ideas. It is further observable that the Enlightenment regulated society and intervention in contemporary society was viewed as effectively harmful to other beliefs and cultures. F. James Davis added that it was based on the mythology that God had created blacks to be slaves and that one drop of "Negro blood" made one Negro; persons of mixed descent were believed to be against nature and fated to physical extinction. (Davis James [1992], pp.41-2).

6.2 The Critique of Missionary Teaching

Revisionism of traditional rituals is emerging out of the community and the practice of ritual sacrifice; how it is related to missionaries' teaching and the church after independence is being criticised. The outcome of the analysis of oral history source materials is as follows: cultural differences and representation that addresses the questions outlined above suggests why the church has to realise the need for change. In the process, there needs to be dissemination of research findings, such as articles in journals, a publicly accessible digital press archive, ongoing, community-based knowledge transfer workshops, exhibitions and conferences. The research needs to be used for public education in the interests of understanding stereotyping and how racialisation works, understanding cultural diversity, anti-racism and social cohesion.

I intend to provide a detailed analysis of cultural theories that are argued as transgressing local values in Christian conversion, the representation of local views in the existing literature on race and research from press and magazine coverage of some areas where ritualistic murder sacrifice was reported, locating and scanning source materials, selecting material for detailed analysis and beginning content analysis.

There is a need for missionaries to stoop beneath and humble themselves to reach the local people by being trained in the life history of the people. Reading written materials, analysis of written life stories from the area and careful listening to selections from the existing oral history of elderly people offers a catalogue of information.

I will endeavour to give a brief description of Christianity's advent in African society. According to Oliver and Fage's account of the pioneering missionary work and the exploration of the interior of the East African mainland, there were two German members of the Church Missionary Society, Krapf and Rebmann, who in 1947-9 were the first Europeans to see the snow-capped peaks of Kilimanjaro and Mt. Kenya. (Oliver R. and Fage J. D., [1962], p.142).

As pointed out earlier, the first missionaries who came around the fifteenth to eighteenth centuries during the slave trade were Portuguese and Spanish, who worked in Angola or Mozambique, but whose impact was not significant. In 1622, the Holy See had organised in Rome the Sacred Congregation of Propaganda, but because of Spanish and Portuguese interests this did not take place until France officially sent missionaries from Europe who started out from Algeria. Also, towards the end of the eighteenth century, a group of pietistic Lutherans called Moravian

Brethren and Calvinists developed a concern for conversion of the non-Christian (heathen) peoples of the world. (Oliver R. and Fage J. D., [1962], p.138).

The first missionary group from England was sent by the Baptists in 1792, followed by Congregations' group from the London Missionary Society sent to the Pacific and South Africa. In 1799. Anglicans of evangelical persuasion founded the Church Missionary Society, which concentrated its mission on West and East Africa. (Oliver R. and Fage J. D., [1962], p.138). They were later followed by Methodists whose mission work was in West Africa, South Africa and some parts of East Africa (Ibid.).

In 1848 France sent the Congregation of the Holy Ghost, whose members began with West Africa, into Gabon, in the lower Congo and East Africa. Later, in 1868, Cardinal Lavigerie's the Sisters of Our Lady of Africa, known as the White Fathers, came from their original base in Algeria and the mission covered various countries in East, West, North and South Africa.

Today, all these missionary groups have a greater or lesser impact on the areas' methodological problems. This is not an ethnomethodological critique of a historical account of the missionaries' approach to Christian conversion in Africa, but rather a theoretical criticism in the sense of trying to highlight the problem of the approach to conversion. Therefore, its chief contribution emerges from empirical research. The analysis of conversion within the ethnomethodological tradition offers various insights to compare what went on during Christian conversion in various colonial countries and since then. The twists and turns of the wider implications of change in society have moral repercussions that beg for redress.

On the other hand, the critical analysis that follows does not in any way suggest that the missionary work was all negative and not vital for society. Of course, it was and is still important. The only criticism is that it needed to undertake a detailed, empirical study of people's beliefs and to learn about their cultures rather than taking them for granted. Through knowing the social order, one comes to realise that it is nothing more than a fragile set of "commonsense" assumptions about the world. The question of the current crisis in human sacrifice can be traced to multi-agency changes in African society. What arises next is to ask why, if the missionary work was necessary and good for society, do we have to revisit the communication activities of missionaries during the early days to assess various dimensions of society and whether the abolition of traditional religious beliefs had anything to do with current issue of human sacrifice?

The crucial question of the missionary approach of conversion to Christianity, whether it fits relevant sociological categories, might have been generated by the teaching that advocated abolishing the local beliefs that were found, to fit the European culture, lifestyle, value system and life world. Of course, in this period, African societies were constructed through a struggle between two competing beliefs.

The violation of rights that occurred from this period proceeded under numerous strategies employed by both colonialism and missionaries to set one group against the other, following the divide and rule theory. For example, "one ethnic group" versus "another ethnic group" approaches; "conflict" of "one tribal group" versus another "tribal group"; "consensus" approaches and "materialistic" versus "spiritual" approaches. In fact, we cannot hope to do justice to these here.

I only offer insights to get at least some appreciation for the complexities and contradictions of the so-called early dialectic of enlightenment, as well as suggesting some similarities between approaches that have increasingly come to characterise bad and good missionaries. The good missionaries encouraged converts to comply with Christian values of behaviour, in the sense of wanting to take Christian action to safeguard human value and guide people to salvation.

I will therefore endeavour to assess the bad missionary teaching, which is often referred to as indoctrination. My correspondents sought to extend the concepts it harboured of the triumphalism of political dehumanisation within the doctrine of means–ends capitalism, and a colonialist rationality over an emancipatory rationality. It is quite clear that excessive force was used under this category of Christian conversion to forbid the traditional beliefs and practices and distort their messages. This is why there is a need today for the church to trace the source of the resurgence of ritualistic human sacrifices, rather than trapping converts and pushing their emotions into a box of non-existence and yet leaving their souls boiling with questions. It is also argued that the resurgence comes from where that boiling soul was kept strictly and firmly locked.

It is accepted that there were many different "life views" of those who tried to understand those cultural and traditional beliefs, which were consistent with Christianity and a diversity of cultures who avoided the use of oppressive practices, instead trusting in the Lord to mould converts appropriately and that their performance was an essential role in safeguarding African souls.

Due to this unique calling, society should praise and respect any person involved in selfless humanitarian work, irrespective of his or her religious beliefs. (See Dhiru Shah, Mother Teresa's Hidden Mission in India: Conversion to Christianity). But as soon as that work is done with an ulterior motive, it no longer remains a saintly deed. Those missionaries who were described as bad are those who had a political perspective, reflected in two aspects, spiritual and colonial, in the way they regarded themselves as "agents of change". Society became overloaded with rapid changes. Neither colonial administrations nor religious institutions were conscious of the local experience, which they ignored or neglected, while they also ignored the claims of some other divine source of revelation in social amenities and the development of infrastructure. All of this highlights the missionaries' disregard or lack of knowledge of African people's knowledge of God.

The ideological influence that seemed to have been attached to the situation explains how the traditional physical, institutional and structural systems that had sustained people's relationships became static and in the process destabilised the community. It is arguable that for an efficient and effective approach, the Christian church must consider the fact that up to the present day many Christians and non-Christians still traditionally believe in the existence of sorcery and spirits and have recourse to witchdoctors or ancestors' spirits, and that this belief remains a central influence in society whether the African church wants to believe it or not. Furthermore, there is still great trust in society of medicine-men and their practices.

The argument here is that the reason for this is that it was irrational to impose ideas and beliefs without considering how important those beliefs and culture were to the people. Mawinza, in religious research at Nairobi, wrote, "The fact that everything was ruthlessly condemned as paganism and superstition inflicted a deep wound in the heart of many African people." (Mawinza, J. [1970], p.43).

As mentioned elsewhere, considering the instrument of change, the advent of Christianity's impact on society channelled social decisions and crucial policies to govern a way of broadening western cultural influence and employing dominating agendas that came from western culture.

6.3 Unrealistic Missionary Moves and Actions

Missionaries seized their opening and got away with convincing converts that Christianity cannot be restricted by cultural parameters simply because the African approach to all important aspects of life was different from the European one. Probably the missionaries' confusion was relating African traditional beliefs to European paganism's use of sorcery with evil intent. For instance, one of the largest groups was that of Alphonse Louis Constant, which existed from 1810 to 1875. In Britain, there was a pagan movement in 1888 under the Order of the Golden Dawn. What a perfect example of how a tiny Christian mission turned things around and took over the situation from millions of Africans, who were afraid to defend their beliefs because no one could reason with a white man. The word "change" was effectively put into action and some young Africans at that time saw a bright future ahead, or certainly a golden moment for opportunities to increase.

Of course, because humans are always discontented and desirous of a better life, young Africans became easy targets for the sale for new ideas. So much so, in fact, that one of the quickest ways for the idea of change to be executed effectively was through them. Obviously, some changes are positive and some are negative, but too much change, or change for the wrong reasons, can leave people scrambling for the higher ground of stability. Where Africans were forced by circumstances to ride those rolling seas of change, after abolishing the traditional beliefs, some individuals felt forced into what is described as a paradigm shift that sent traditional believers underground to cling to and maintain their emotional and spiritual equilibrium. (Cf. Psalm 61:2).

In fact, in 1974 at the All-African Conference of Churches, delegates called for a moratorium on foreign missionaries. That was the start of the realisation that the idea of Christ's incarnation was being used through tinted lenses in which God could not be known, loved and honoured by all cultures.

Irrespective of their rich traditions, the existing concept of God that had developed was all but ignored. The root of the problem was the cultural arrogance of a small minority of that period, because of which everything valuable for Africa was thrown away through the most persuasive message of conversion that Christ incarnate was to make all things new, for him to be known to all nations and all races. However, whichever theory was advanced in "Truth claims", there are a number of additional issues that need to be addressed. Can claims about the future be true now? Can the predicate be completely defined in other cultures, without alteration of meaning, from the contextual point of view in which it occurs today?

Then there is a choice of rational theological pattern, which draws on psychological fears for many in the process that were persuasive of punishment in hell, which was only to be overcome by conversion to the Christian faith and being saved in Christ. The argument seems to support the idea that there are several brands of Christian teaching today that seem to be inconsistent in the "Truth claim". For example, Nikolai Ge's *What Is Truth?* depicts the New Testament's account of the question as posed by Pilate to Jesus' assertions of truth based on history, revelation and testimony set forward in the Bible, which are central to Christian beliefs.

Some denominations have asserted additional authorities as sources of doctrinal truth; for instance, in Roman Catholicism the Pope is asserted to be infallible on matters of church doctrine. (Cf. Richard F. Costigan, The Consensus of the Church and Papal Infallibility: a Study in the Background of Vatican I [2005]). The criticism was that missionaries were ramping together practitioners of ritual magic, which is probably the practice of fake healers today. This ritual magic is often conceived as belonging to a vast underground movement with its roots in antiquity. In fact, the European neo-pagan movement consists of large groups who share the common beliefs and are violently anti-Christian, but others claim to be Gnostic Christians.

Chapter Seven

The Question of Identity

7.1 Past Grievances

In the first instance, it is argued that there was an attempt to erase African identity in the process of converting to Christianity by emphasising change in the interest of promoting European culture, philosophies and changing people's way of life and thinking to the expense of African values and beliefs. Of course, if someone aims at disarming you, they will first take away the tools you may use to manufacture weapons to fight the opponent. In the first place, African identity was replaced with a new form of Christian identity, which was the reverse of people's beliefs. Missionaries still either defend or downplay the importance of correcting distortions and command the church to act as if they were religious "sect", an exclusive association of religious virtues that overlooked the misinterpretation and distortion of African history and culture. In contrast, a universalistic "church" established for the salvation of the world must take into account the past to find the remedy to the history of how and where African identity can be found and a commitment to doing so.

It was profoundly argued in the first place that the Christian identity needed to be assimilated to the African concept of God and beliefs, cultures and customs rather than abolishing what they did not understand. That doesn't mean that you abolish everything you don't understand, but the right approach was to enquire about its validity as the fulfilment of God's mission for receiving people in their own environment. What all this means is that it begs the church leadership to create a universal church for all humanity, which must be committed to seek to know what

God has done in the past and is capable of today and what the Old Testament Bible says about God, because the New Testament has long talked about Christ who is not fully incarnated in African society. More importantly, under this subheading, the aim is to show that grievances require a unique response from society to reconsider a combination of approaches with two principal variables; to consider the danger interpreted in the light of a constant pressure to rubbish traditional beliefs and thinking to fix European culture as the church's identity.

The greater crisis in Africa was that converts had to ask just who they were. This is why interference with people's traditions and identity is criticised, the reason why for decades loud protests against interference have been repeatedly heard. In this case, it is even right to argue that ever since conversion to Christianity in Africa, the whole exercise has been seen by many Africans as an attempt to erase African identity. The criticism is that the Christian mission seems to have marked the start of a long strategic process to distort African traditional religious identity in various ways. Christianity was ushering in a new culture and religious beliefs with new values and practices, interpreted as masking dangerous values. Furthermore, the criticism of those masked values was that concepts and policies did not allow people's tradition and culture to develop.

This was a characteristic experience of a subjugating and dehumanising process that had a profound impact on local people's conceptualisation of the world in relation to themselves, which led to self-rejection and hatred of their own heritage and identity. The identity issue highlights that Christian conversion was of course partly representational of another culture. This demonstrates how this caused a great psychological effect on converts, because it would be ridiculous to assume that there was nothing useful in people's previous beliefs and culture. The use of the language of demonisation as both the instrument of change and a structuralist order, degraded and put African religious beliefs, culture and identity in an inferior position. The new identity received after conversion led to an identity crisis that in a way was a self-rejection, because the process included a rejection of both culture and tradition (natural heritage) in favour of the Western (European) lifestyle characteristics.

However, a distinction needs to be drawn between social morality and individual ideals. Ethically, the church's teaching strictly speaking is concerned with the claims and counter-claims arising out of adding cultural ethics teachings by missionaries outside the culture they belonged to which had provided for their cohesiveness. The Africans were free to remain as before in the personal ideals according to which they lived, as long as they did not conflict with any rules governing social behaviour; African ideals were essentially important because they were what society desired.

The trouble with the approach to Christian conversion was that the basic ethical issues were not at stake in the conventions which had held society together. Those ethical matters, whether primitive or not, were still regulated by customary law and without them the future stability hung in the balance. It can then be argued that any reform had to include the reassessment of traditional beliefs and healing practices.

This is why the questions of right and wrong, good and evil, were in the end found by society in some cases to be a justification for a gradual functional role of a fundamental organisation of traditional beliefs and culture in Christianity in Africa and other religious faiths. How to settle these issues, except by reform, is the aim of this discussion. What went wrong in the process of change through development is perceived as offering better living standards or, on the other hand, colonial cruelty and ruthless measures. The church needs to repair its degraded and distorted use of history and culture, to restore public confidence and values.

Nevertheless, it was occasionally assisted by greedy African chiefs through the slave trade, whereby an African lost everything that had identified him or her as an African. Those who were sold in slavery lost their culture, religious beliefs, language and their African names and acquired a new identity. But slavery and colonisation (inter alia) were used to distort the encounter between people of different ethnic groups and marked a permanent legacy where black people have, for centuries, been identified by the colour of their skin rather than their Christian identity.

In Africa, converts to Christianity were baptised and given names whose identity ever since has become a subject of debate within and outside the continent. In a sense, converts had misconceived interpretations that the missionary identity meant abandoning your tribal and local values. Christian converts assumed this to mean a new relationship of brothers or sisters in Christ. In fact, the words, "brother" and "sister" define far more for Africans than they do to European Christians. This superficial uniformity between the converts and dominant groups concealed differences in opinions, cultural sentiments and beliefs, but not in the real sense of a Christian European or American, who will always identify themselves first as British or American and then as Christian.

However, there is mounting body of evidence indicating that the history of any religious belief is a history of institutional resistance. Therefore, Christian identity at this stage was still at the level where it demanded an assimilation process. In this sense, the identity of conversion can be argued to be redundant, since whether accepted or not, the identity was fundamentally a shamelessly flawed process, representing the advantages of social assimilation rather than a misplaced emphasis on abolishing beliefs and practices.

Of course, there are various theories attributed to human sacrifices. One suggests that the ritualistic murder is not related to traditional healers, but to magicians who travel to different countries in search of clients in order to make money, such as those from West Africa, Tanzania and Congo. Therefore, in consideration of this, the Christian identity demanded a striking shift in both traditional and cultural contexts, which forced traditional beliefs to operate in secret. That is why it is argued that the prevailing state of ritualistic murder could be both magicians and fake practices in the disguise of traditional healers.

In the Bible, God's designs are always qualified as efficacious and can never be frustrated by humans. It can be argued that had God intended all humankind to be saved by the death of Christ, then all would be saved. This is because there are no conditions to be met in order to be saved (salvation is by grace not by works, even acts of faith), and both repentance and faith are secured for those for whom Christ died. (Romans 5:10; Corinthians 5:21).

Doctrinal differences in a way seem to have led to confusion when missionaries added conditions such as abandoning local cultural observances, forbidding converts from their responsibilities in society and insisting on monogamous marriage. Paradoxically, the insistence on cultural and social structural change is linked to later crises when converts began to disobey established structures, traditional concepts of hierarchy, authority and societal obligations. Identification with and the suspension of belief in traditional concepts is seen as having been directly responsible for the contradictions and ethical constraints on people's behaviours and characters. Yet it could be argued that when converts attempted to resolve these contradictions, the Bible did not condemn established authority. Peter 2:1-18 says honour every authority and structure of leadership; therefore, for instance, in Uganda the case of young converts misguided by the idea of a perfect world (utopia) by missionaries were led to martyrdom after shifting their allegiance from the King of Buganda.

The acceptance of Christ led many other converts to disobedience of the traditional institutional authority, which was unnecessary and unwarranted. In fact, this was the inception of a far-reaching undermining of all traditional institutions and culture and since then traditional institutions have never regained their authority. This is why the Christian approach is criticised. The conversion effect certainly explains how the missionary agenda was to replace the traditional power structure, authority, beliefs, practices, medicine, philosophy, culture, music and all forms of African ideas, which are all grievances aired in public or privately today.

While European countries are conserving their historical sites, Africans are busy demolishing their own historical monuments. The notion of Africa as the Dark Continent is a parochial European idea, which gained currency, because Africa was the last of the continents to be opened to the gaze of the outside world. Because it was the last to experience the full impact of European people, ideas and techniques, it marked a feature of world history from the sixteenth until the early twentieth century. (Roland Oliver and J.D. Fage, [1962], p. 13).

Africans often argue that the question was not whether their ideas were true, backward or not modern, but that their African identity above all had its development restricted, prevented from recognition and that the freedom of traditional beliefs and practice had been in jeopardy for quite a long time. In missionary schools Africans began to be taught colonial history and how to live a European lifestyle; European dances and songs, as well as games such as cricket, chess, draughts and also gambling, which eventually was a method used to usher in a culture of corruption to society. Therefore, it is argued that what is happening today is a long process of ignoring local values, which consistently and continuously poses a danger to society. For a long time the question of the culture and beliefs that were denied existence and practice in numerous ways has not been addressed.

This calls for the African churches to consider the best way for Christianity in African society to resolve these grievances. To do so is to emulate, for instance, the Latin American practice of the Voodoo religion, which is said to have been introduced to the western coasts by slaves from Africa. To understand the nature of the survival of African religiosity in Latin America and the Caribbean, one has to examine some of the African-influenced religions and religious expressions that exist within the region. According to Leonard Barrett in The Diaspora Caribbean Experience, this includes what have often been referred to as retentions or samples of African Traditional Religion. There is Shango, a feature of the Orisha faith in Trinidad and Tobago, Santeria in Spanish-speaking Cuba and Vaudou in the French and Créole speaking republic of Haiti. (Barrett, Leonard E., The Sun and the Drum: African Roots in Jamaican Folk Tradition, London: Heinemann, 1976).

The Voodoo practice of worship is believed to have started in Haiti in 1724 as a snake cult that worshipped many spirits pertaining to daily life experiences. The practices were intermingled with many Catholic rituals and saints. It was first brought to the Louisiana area in 1804 by Cuban plantation owners who were displaced by revolution and brought their slaves with them. The Latin American

Voodoo religion has countless deities, demonic possessions and animal sacrifices (human sacrifices in the Petro or black magic form of Voodoo), but Voodoo practitioners cannot understand why their religion is so misunderstood. Also, Ras Tafarianism is a religious phenomenon that emerged initially in the 1930s as a Jamaican cult in response to the need for people within the Diaspora to maintain an attachment to the ancestral homeland of Mother Africa.
(http://wwww.erukies.com/site/articles/views/5).

Everywhere during colonial rule, traditional religious beliefs faced restrictions or punishments, persecution or imprisonment and interpretations that negated their existence. Such values subsequently developed a culture of resistance and a greater commitment to the beliefs and practices, as strategic means of survival. In fact, the history of suppression was one of escalation, representing most clearly church teaching's attack on traditional beliefs, which proves that among the positive strategies for traditional healers, was a conspiracy to resilience in the wake of the mighty Western Christian influence on society.

The hidden strategies of traditional practitioners are said to include acting as an underground movement in practice, when to avoid visibility, church members belong to two camps: on Sundays they belong to the officially recognised religious institutions, but on weekdays they consult traditional healers, which in my opinion shows why it was a mistake to forbid the practice.

Human beliefs and culture are preserved by natural instinct and deserved to be respected as a human mechanism for development, since human survival depends on the beliefs offered by society. Basically, this is a strategy of engagement. It is not a strategy of isolation in the hope to aspire people to work together; in these circumstances traditional beliefs should have been carefully considered and what is good may be maintained as long as people want it themselves. Also, the main role of Christianity in Africa is not as a strategy for the evangelisation process, but as a significant contributor to the total process of salvation of a believer or humankind without bias to tradition, which may sound like a statement of traditional religious preferences.

Both missionary and colonial events involved a great expansion and dispersal in which indigenous ways of doing things were absorbed in domination, control and economic interests. In particular, a real understanding of the potential of the colonial and missionary vision of Africa came with the Second World War. According to Oliver and Fage, after the Second World War there was a greatly increased demand for the strategic raw materials Africa could supply, as well as shortages of foodstuffs and of many raw materials. The colonies suddenly became of immense economic value. Therefore, economic reasons partly paved the way for spiritual needs that were a combination of politics and a social economic continuity strategy. Even later, after independence, church leaders and politicians continued to condemn traditional beliefs as devilish.

The issue of identity appears throughout and is often summed up by African people as a period of dispersal of African ideas and the fundamental concepts of beliefs and morals that had glued communities together for centuries and acted as major moral restraints. It is argued here that it was totally wrong to have undermined the system, all in the name of civilisation and progress. It was a violation of human rights.

It is helpful to distinguish between three methods of conversion that created contradictions in African society. Firstly, the trouble was that missionaries often saw themselves as agents of change, for there was no other way of establishing their consolidating and perpetuating, mythopoeic mentality about people's beliefs and their cultural values. Secondly, Louise Pirouet rightly reminds us that we must not assume that these new missions were only concerned to send people from their countries to evangelise other parts of the world to Christianity. The missionary approach deviated people from internalised cultural norms, values and religious beliefs, so that societal values become less effective in guiding people's actions and as inhibiting rules. Instead, the new rules in society became the new order, which constituted part of a move to destabilise the previous social order and to suggest that the new order determined the practical Christian influence that penetrated the depths of society, spearheaded by Christian conversion.

Finally, Kinyatta argued that if Africans were left in peace with their own culture and social values, Europeans would have to offer them benefits of white civilisation in real earnest to develop a way of life that was really superior to the one they had lived, rather than robbing them of the material foundations of their culture and reducing them to a state of false impressions that were incompatible with human happiness. (Cf. Kinyatta, Jomo, [1938], p.138).

Effectively, the influence of Christian conversion and the changes it brought about weakened the deterrent societal cultural effect. The church must take this into account in today's ministry, because specific thought would have informed missionaries that in this society different working rules were likely to be enforced. The new rules were not enforceable and are seen as the source of deterioration in human behaviour.

But that was in earlier, better days. As the pattern of violence against traditional beliefs and practice developed in later years, it is argued that things in society may have stayed the same, but many other things changed greatly, either for better or for worse, leading some people to lose self-control and make irrational decisions. The plight of traditional beliefs and cultural values in these circumstances was that they were under long-term suppression and persecution, which was a familiar practice in various African countries during colonial rule and missionary days. No traditional medium even dared to speak out against the persecution for fear of facing greater hostility, suffering and even the personal danger of being imprisoned.

As more traditional mediums and believers were suppressed, internal resistance for survival began. One area where such trends have been particularly evident is in the resurgence of traditional beliefs, since there is very little evidence to show that attempting to prevent a person's beliefs is effective and, in fact, it can actually be harmful. Christianity during the colonial administrative changes acted as an ideological façade whereby society at large could not tell the difference between politics and Christianity.

This moralising of the Christianity mandate was in many respects misleading at best. Under these tactics the consequences were that missionaries undermined African culture and the traditional structures that had glued together people's relationships in society and their synthetic understanding of how to live and relate to their society. The moralising of Christianity overlooked the existing nature of the African way of life, which meant that missionaries were presenting misinformation on cultural reality. Since then this has caused divisions that have sprung from contradictions between people's culture and traditional practices and the Christian set of rules, which became problematic in the process of foreign advancing interests in gaining more power and conversion.

In fact, it is appropriate to question how the prevention and elimination of traditional rituals would have been achieved without engaging with traditional believers.

However, in defence of the contradictions among various groups of missionaries' approaches to conversion, Louise Pirouet observed that the nations of Western Europe were no longer Christian nations, (though people often spoke as though they were). (Cf. Pirouet, Louise, [1989], p.4).

This is critically characterised as the pessimistic outlook of a cynical colonial state in the sense that it had abolished, prevented and eliminated people's traditional beliefs, which aggressively targets the family unit and traditional institutions for destruction. The primordial driving force of conversion and cultural change seemed to have been a belief in the value of local lifestyles and the transcendent dignity of the human person.

Abolishing the source of virtue for African people and their traditional values, including their treasured history, had the purpose of denying evidence to the next generation. But traditional medium men and women did not become enemies of the church. If traditional religion had cut off people's access to the church and to God and if it had denied its believers, the free exercise of Christian worship and witness, then it would have been evil and should have been fought.

However much the church is inclined to sympathise with traditional beliefs, it can be argued that it is anti-Christian to hate, abolish and repress anyone, despite differences of opinions and beliefs. A regime that harasses and imprisons people because of their traditional beliefs is equally guilty, whether it did so in the name of Christianity or to eliminate evil or devilish worship. No wonder the young generation today in a quest for ritualistic protection are often heard questioning why Christian morality did not adhere to ethical principles and was more committed to the revolution than to the gospel teaching of love.

Respondents claimed that the reason why they chose to erode society with inadequate teachings was at the best confusing and one-sided. Whether it was out of Christian morality or for inter-disciplinary reasons, the repression of people practising their beliefs in their own right cannot be supported. There was a great tendency on the part of colonial administrators, including some missionaries, to be so enamoured of African beliefs and practice that they neglected to consider whether traditional beliefs were moving people further away from God or not.

The appropriateness of missionary approaches depended on each missionary group and the most important theories that contributed to conversion thinking in the nineteenth and early twentieth century. To do this, missionaries needed ethnomethodology – the study of the methods employed by people as they go about their daily lives – to recognise that people differ according to their environment, beliefs, lifestyle and the kinds of social arrangements they form in order to be sensitive to their different needs. They would maintain the "Christian Truth" as rational, but customs are also rational and culture and societal traditions can also be rational. Furthermore, the word "truth" can be distinguished from the Platonic dialogues.

However, the doctrine of creation and redemption, law and grace, challenges the use of technical philosophical concepts. In many respects, the irrational ignoring of the African truth of their concept of God, sin and redemption, struggle and disenchantment, which was set from prehistoric times, long ago against a background of seething violence and widespread corruption, whether knowingly or unknowingly, was argued by my respondents as preparing the soft ground for corruption in society.

Therefore, the doctrine of general redemption argues that death of Christ was designed to cover or include all mankind, whether or not they believe. The difference is that the use of Greek philosophies is rather to be seen in the nature and the method of the salvation proclaimed, in the concept of sin, of redemption and the specific norms of morality and not in the usage of the word "truth". Earlier, these terms were used interchangeably with metaphors by those who believe that redemption applies and those who do not believe that it provides the benefits of common grace and the removal of any excuse for being lost.

This brings us to the most difficult subject of justifying Christianity as the only truth, which was under the increasing influence of philosophers like Socrates, who were forces of reasoning decades before colonialism in Africa. Of course, some of the agents of change had been intoxicated by scholarship intermingled with European cultural philosophies and theological reasoning, to the extent that even the African concept of God was given negative explanations, ranging from attributing the African concept of God's divinity to devilish, evil spirits or demonic worship.

This, in fact, was contradictory and did not make sense, because at this period there were those who believed in universalism, which was a valid argument that the African concept of God was not either devilish or demonic. If missionaries were consistent in their teaching, it may be that the African concept and God's revelation would both have been convincing as devilish. Fieldhouse added that during this period, when most political philosophers began to defend the principles of universalism and equality, the same individuals were still defending the legitimacy of colonialism and of imperialism. (Fieldhouse, D. K., [1961], X1V, 2, p. 80).

Yet the relationship between God and truth in the Hebrew and Greek scriptures is quite different on a number of points from Greek philosophy, mainly because the concept of God is also quite different in Hebrew. Differences between Christianity and the African concept of God also lie in philosophical usage, not in theological content, which argues that there are important distinguishing differences. The Hebrew asserts that God tells the truth: he tells what is true, his assertions are the truth. The Old Testament is different in the sense that the meaning of the divine revelation of God, in the Hebrew plain usage of truth (Genesis 42:16; Deut. 13:14; 17:4; Prov; 12:19), concerns legal satisfying evidence. The New Testament "truth" gives more added meanings to the word "truth". (Galatians 2:5, 14; Eph.4:21).

The first theological attempt at a systematic exposition of the concept of truth was by made Augustine, whose aim was to refute scepticism. Thus, it is argued that the biblical truth was a figurative description: when Christ says "I am the way, the Truth, and the Life", the word "truth" is just as figurative as the word "life". It means that as Christ is the cause of life, so He is the cause of truth. (John 1:14, 14:6, 9). Therefore, the use of the truth could be defined as a theory of prejudice and was used to disadvantage Africans solely on the ground of their location, colour, culture and traditional beliefs. Such a definition was clearly prejudicial in that it restricted and denied other sources of revelation or any other concepts of God, though such a figurative description raises the question of doubt that anything other than the European values and revelation experience could have been accepted at this period of colonial rule.

We must distinguish between the three aspects that are inextricably and prominently related and were mutually reinforced:

1. Use of words such as the "Truth" by a group of missionaries who seem to have been motivated by a religious bias against African traditional beliefs.

2. Their approach distorted everything that was of value in society and did not reflect an honest spirit of inquiry, perhaps because their mission was intended to abolish anything that had previously existed, to arouse

appreciation of people's experiences, beliefs and culture. This distortion succeeded in generating a poisonous atmosphere, which was exploited to satisfy the needs and aspirations of colonisers and missionary religious establishments.

3. The doctrine or theory of prejudice, bias or psychological attitudes in conversion. With the demonising tendencies, there were hardly any incidents that were not attributed to traditional beliefs.

There is no doubt that slight differences existed not only in fashion or detailed rites and practices, but in the proper terms to describe people's beliefs as devilish, which portrays arrogance and a demeaning of the African ability to differentiate between truth and falsity. The evidence of this is a lack of appreciation of other humans' experience and knowledge, or to examine whether there was anything in common between African claims in their revelation of God and other religions, such as Judaism and Islam.

This was clearly deemed as contradicting the authenticity of African beliefs and exposing them intentionally to an over-emphasis on the devil, aimed at turning Africans against their own beliefs and cultures, which had protected them for generations. This was like turning away from your parents because they were out of date, black and degraded. This did not show of appreciation of the historical facts, open-mindedness or even logic. As such, for the missionaries the ends justified the means; distortion, abolition, lack of honesty, half-truths and at times sheer ignorance of whatever existed in the long run was bound to have an effect on society, though it is arguable that the missionaries could have appreciated the free use of human knowledge, belief, culture and experience. This shows that it was not a coincidence that the messages and motives of conversion were often connected with the missionary and colonial project to convert. Yet, looking at the biblical interpretation of the truth, it is clear that the use of what we mean by biblical truth can be used figuratively, by metonymy, in which the effect is substituted for the cause.

The purpose of an initial definition, whether it was sufficient or not, was to distinguish what is different from the familiar and, in a sense, was used as a means to condemn the unknown. This is why it is argued that behind all the condemnation of anything unknown was either misunderstanding, or purely the prejudice of missionaries and that there was a need for appropriate instruments to neutralise these past distortions and the church to explain and restore the integrity of Christ's body the church.

This is what Lisa Miller describes as the transformation of the belief system in ways that resemble Hinduism. Hinduism is radically polytheistic and syncretistic. According to Hindu belief, the many gods and goddesses of their veneration all represent one fundamental divine reality. If we can see beyond what is a "continuous lie", it does not mean that it is the truth. The pendulum is shifting away from the idea of a singular and exclusive truth, which is antithetical to classical Hinduism. Miller suggests that contemporary Americans, including many who consider themselves Christians, are abandoning the exclusive truth claims that were carefully orchestrated in the form of theological European cultural relativism.

More tellingly, it was identified that white evangelicals shared this belief. Miller cites Stephen Prothero, a leading researcher on American religion, who defined this "divine-deli-cafeteria religion" as "very much in the spirit of Hinduism. If going to yoga works, great - and if going to Catholic mass works, great. And if going to Catholic mass plus the yoga plus the Buddhist retreat works, that's great, too." As Lisa Miller correctly recites, Jesus did say, "I am the way, the truth, and the life."

(http://www.twitter.com/AlbertMohler).

On the other hand, from analysis of the knowledge of truth, it is also arguable that the Bible's use of truth was written in colloquial language and the senses in which it uses the term truth are not so different from colloquial usage anywhere. If the implication of the use of the words "Truth claim" is looked at from the positive and negative angles, it could represent the ideas of where the positive use of "Truth claim" (John 1:14, 14:6, 9) is shown to rest on a series of knowledge logics.

Those missionaries who argued this way could have been purely aimed at conversion and saving African souls. The African thinking that religious beliefs underlined moral injunctions suggests that the conversion approach stemmed from a much more sinister colonial idealism, in the shape of cultural relativism; the view that supported this conclusion of truth is only one kind of truth and it is not to be especially privileged. (John 1:14, 14:6, 9).

On the other hand, the criticism of the biblical misuse of context in Ephesians 4:20-24 speaks for a conception of truth that has no intellectual basis and did not take it seriously as a moral and spiritual effect on people. In other words, totalistic relativism is an epistemological theory denying an objective, universally valid human knowledge and affirming that meaning and truth vary from person to person, culture to culture, and time to time. The common conception of truth is as a fact, or what is real and morally or spiritually significant.

However, aside from the general legitimacy of relativism, critics say that it undermines morality, possibly resulting in strain, anomie and complete social Darwinism. If not from God, then where from? The Darwinists believe it is from evolution, while others disagree. Relativism denies that harming others is wrong in any absolute sense. (Metron's 1938; Rorty, R. Consequences of Pragmatism).

The majority of relativists, of course, consider it immoral to harm others, but relativist theory allows for the opposite belief. In short, if an individual can believe it wrong to harm others, he can also believe it right, no matter what the circumstances.

The problem of negation also arises. The reply of the critical analyst to this objection is to claim that, while we ordinarily suppose that factual judgements are basic, we are actually mistaken. Then, there would be no objective standards of right and wrong. If everyone with differing opinions is right, then no one is wrong. Thus instead of saying "all beliefs (ideas, truths etc.) are equally valid", one might just as well say "all beliefs are equally worthless".

Such a comparison is intended to provide ways of seeing realistically how the early missionaries used techniques that exemplify the argument that if relativism presupposes that "all beliefs are equally valid", this nullifies Christianity as being just one of many valid beliefs. Most monotheistic religions, Christianity or Islam for example, do presuppose that they are, individually, the only valid belief system. However, this creates a direct self-contradiction: relativism presupposes that any belief, including one such as Christianity, is valid. (Cf. Lewis, C.S. in mere Christianity, 1952).

On the other hand, Christianity believes that only Christianity (and therefore not relativism) is valid. Relativism states that Christianity is one of many true beliefs, while Christianity states it is the only true belief, which only results in contradicting relativism's presupposition that Christianity is one of many truths. In simple terms: If A, then B. If B, then not A. (In this case, A is relativism, while B is a belief system such as Christianity or Islam.) An argument made by several scholars states that some forms of relativism make it impossible to believe one is in error. (Cf. Feyerabend, P. Against Method, p. 296; Baghramian, M., Relativism, [2004], p.85).

In some cases, the question does not relate to how informed people were before the missionaries' arrival in Africa, but rather highlights the fact that the conversion approach diminished the African way of doing things in order to relate it to the Biblical scriptures in an unquestioned, uncritical reading and comprehension of people's way of thinking. This is where lies a crucial danger; to question if there is no truth beyond an individual's belief that something is true and then an individual cannot hold their own beliefs to be false or mistaken. (Cf. Feyerabend, P. Against Method, p. 296; Baghramian, M., Relativism, [2004], p.85).

A related criticism is that relativising truth to individuals destroys the distinction between truth and belief and a methodological approach to problems is inherent in using the biblical interpretations of missionaries. (Cf. Feyerabend, P. Against Method, p. 296; Baghramian, M., Relativism, [2004], p.85).

The overplaying of Christianity and underplaying of the role of traditional beliefs is forced to change, because the question of whether the words of scripture should have been taken the way they came to Africa, and people forced to receive them, overlooked the fact that it was forcing people to knowledge and experience that the scriptures should have been allowed to speak in contextual situations. Therefore, this is arguing for Christian teaching centred in church leadership and firmly grounding biblical interpretation in the wider context of a moral restorative doctrine.

In other words, this signifies a new attentiveness to - and sympathy with - people in their current situation. It is now admissible that to some Christians such a question was not relevant or important, because scripture should not be reduced to a situational level, but on the other hand it can be questioned why and for what purpose they were written. I am afraid that this is the line on Christianity in Africa that is taken by some churches where it is on the upsurge day in, day out. This consists of describing and analysing the major forces driving where people are finding themselves.

Another argument is to advance the view of people's social and economic struggles to survive, which have effects on people's attitudes and behaviour in society. One of the most important debates on behaviour change in African societies is that between theorists of structure i.e. those who feel that social life is determined by "structural" forces outside of the individual, and theorists of agency; namely, those who argue that the individual is an active and creative agent who constructs his or her social world.

However, African tradition is entirely different from these beliefs and has never been against any religion in Africa, but has been a victim of mistaken identity on the part of missionaries and persecuted by the church out of misconceptions.

In fact, there is a great need for the church to end these superficial claims of one biblical verse often being misused in claims of salvation ownership or monopoly in Christ that will save them. Moreover, much more needs to be done to implant Christianity, although the church in general has to stop acting as if to become a Christian is only to look for high status and wealth. It also has to end the misuse of faith in Christ alone as exploitation of others and seek a deeper relationship.

If the church considers seriously what seems to discount its effectiveness in modern society, it is the church's deterioration in its commitment to just leadership and love for Christ's church. Yet according to traditional religious beliefs, personal responsibility and accountability lie in the ancestors' ritualistic life and the public impression of the church identifies too much with the secular world. Traditional beliefs start with life here and concede that life hereafter is a life in God, of everyone and of all those who together and now participate in this life. Christianity's promises of heaven defer to the traditional religious views of personality as a cross-situational enduring predisposition.

In today's world, these are similar claims in Christian Science that Truth is God. In thirteenth-century Europe, the Roman Catholic Church denounced what it described as theories of "double truth" i.e. theories to the effect that although a truth may be established by reason, its contrary ought to be believed as true as a matter of faith. The doctrine of "double truth" was revived by the scholastics under the rubric "two truths". The current doctrine of the Roman Catholic Church rejects the doctrine of "double truth" or "two truths" and holds that there is only one truth and that Catholics should accept as true such scientific doctrines as the age of the Earth and the evolution of species. In a sense, attributed to the Evangelical movement, a misemphasis on salvation is basically laid on the "grace" of God: as long as you believe in Jesus Christ as your personal saviour, then your sins are washed by the blood of Jesus.

In charismatic Christianity in Africa, the emphasis of teaching for salvation is put on receiving the power of the Holy Spirit. In the Anglican traditional church teaching for salvation, the emphasis is put on the Word of God and a daily relationship with Christ renewed through the general confession of sins to God and through the ritualistic reunion in the Holy Eucharist, plus several other minor doctrines. The only link between all these Christian denominations is based on Jesus Christ as the only way and truth and the monopoly of salvation, which is a significant sign of how an emphasis on the "Truth" had an agenda in the functional role of Truth claims. This allowed the powerful to rule weaker societies and disallowed the weaker the ability to develop, or enrich, the revelation concept and expand the imagination of their own path to salvation. It was an approach that was more "abolishing than transformation" in its outlook, seeking to abolish the old beliefs of converts, rather than attempting to reform or mould them. This is why the increased prominence of cultures was degradation, as is the case in Hobsbawm and Ranger's "Invention of Tradition". (Hobsbawm, E. and T. Ranger [1983]).

But Africans were instead grouped in a form of a plurality that underplayed their religious values and overlapped cultural orientations, in such a way that each person was always involved in a multiplicity of such orientations at the same time, while none of these orientations coincided with only one society or one territory. Hobsbawm shows that the classic understanding of culture as discrete bounded units, which are closed into themselves and which produce a total field of life, still has a wide circulation outside anthropology, notably in the philosophy of culture and theology. (Cf. T. Ranger and O. Vaughan, [1993], pp. 62-111).

In contrast, the Christian church must reconstruct its own African image to protect its future. From a contradictory point of view, professions can be seen as interest groups protecting their own privileges, rather than as groups operating a service to others' ethics. A source on this approach is the Roman Catholic church, which commands worship of the Virgin Mary. (p.130). It is asserted that "many things are asked from God, and are not granted; they are asked from Mary, and are obtained, for She is even Queen of Hell and Sovereign Mistress of the Devils." (pp. 127, 141, 143).

"Mary is called the gate of heaven because no one can enter that blessed kingdom without passing through her."

(p. 160). "The way of salvation is open to none otherwise than through Mary, and since our salvation is in the hands of Mary, he who is protected by Mary will be saved, he who is not will be lost." (pp. 169-17). "All power is given to thee in Heaven and on earth, so that at the command of Mary all obey - even God and thus God has placed the whole Church under the dominion of Mary." (pp. 180-181). "Mary is also the Advocate of the whole human race for she can do what she wills with God." (p.193). (Martyn, Lloyd Jones [1968], p.6).

Brian Schwertley's article states that the Roman Catholic church teaches that Mary was born without original sin; this doctrine is referred to as the Immaculate Conception. It also teaches that Mary never committed actual sin and is the Mother of God. The Roman Catholic doctrine has it critics too, however. Martyn Lloyd Jones argues that it teaches that the pope is infallible when he speaks on matters of doctrine. The pope, according to Roman Catholic teaching, is the Vicar of Christ, Christ's personal representative on earth. The Roman Catholic Church claims to have the power of conferring indulgences. It does exactly the opposite of what the Bible teaches in the Roman Catholic doctrine of justification. (Martyn, Lloyd Jones, [1968], p.6; Cf. Pope Pius IX on Dec. 8; 1854 Schwertley Brian, p.1).

Lloyd Jones argued that Roman Catholic priests, theologians and scholars insist that saints, Mary, statues and relics are not worshipped; they substitute words such as honour, veneration and adoration for the word worship. Yet as he has pointed out, this clever semantic sleight of hand completely breaks down in everyday church practice. (Martyn Lloyd Jones, [1968], p.6).

However, whichever is the case, the long-growing turbulence between Christian faith and cultural issues requires the prevention of situational conflict and involves the effort to reducing theological differences associated with the "Truth claim", which was linked to conversion. The eternal reward of the afterlife (salvation) was judged to outweigh any other perceived rewards in any other religious life. Yet, from my findings, in traditional belief to belong to society is to be "in transit", neither here nor there, without position or place. Therefore, the rite of passage symbolises a specific type of community emerging, which had no internal authority structure; its membership is in constant "transit" and submissive to the general authority of societal and ritual leaders.

Strictly speaking, Christian conversion was culturally shifting people away from where they were and distorting their entire concept of the world and the life they had lived for no reason. It is argued by Loraine Boettner that the plain fact is that the church cannot hold its people when they become spiritually enlightened and discover that the church's distinctive doctrines are merely man-made inventions. (Boettner, L., [1962], pp.78-79).

It was a misguided strategy, not only because of the uncertainty about what the long-term dangers might pose, but also because of the certainty of the damage that these proposed doctrines would impose. In addition, the issue of conversion was very damaging to people's beliefs and cultural values and to those who were converted. Unfortunately, some church members are now polarised between the old beliefs and Christian beliefs' demand to attend worship and make a financial contribution to the church's upkeep. Nevertheless, the latter is far from being a panacea when church members' faith is on trial and this suggests that the present church leadership needs to work out an alternative way, considering the demonising of traditional rituals, which are now used as deplorable acts of human sacrifice.

Prominence was given to the damnation of those who believed in and worshipped images or traditional religion. However, Martyn Lloyd claims, "Go to St. Peter's in Rome and you will notice that there is a sort of monument to the apostle Peter and if you look at one of the toes you will find that it is smooth and worn away." Why? He says it was because so many poor victims of Roman Catholic teaching have been there kissing the toe! (Martyn, Lloyd Jones, Roman Catholicism, London: Evangelical Press, p.6).

He further argues that Christians in Rome bow with reverence and worship images, statues and relics. They claim to have relics of certain saints, a bit of bone, something they used and it is put in a special place and they worship it and bow down before it. This is nothing but sheer idolatry explained as rational choice. The restriction of such purposive action in African Christianity is justified to maintain the crucial role of Christianity as the only way the truth for salvation (Ibid.).

Most modern theologians now acknowledge to a greater extent that the refusal of Christians in Africa to embrace their own heritage was relatively shaped by the "Truth claim" of missionary teaching. The first question mark was the erosion of the image of European society and its disciplined bureaucracy. The reason why they did not recognise that behaviour and conduct is variable and is shaped by environmental influences was that the process of transformation did not realise that the cultural environment determines that a particular behaviour is either acceptable or unacceptable conduct. This is often a breeding ground for antisocial behaviour that has led people into demoralisation and into petty crimes such as mugging, street robbery and corruption, which all leads to social dislocation and disruption, outweighing the importance of human lives.

In this view, to attempt to play devil's advocate for many may sound like suggesting shaking hands with the devil. However, I will be quick to argue that it is overdue for Christianity in Africa to re-examine realistically the possible ways open for a new point of view of the situation surrounding the crisis in local beliefs and find a new practical framework. The more I think about missionary work, the more I agree with the view that questions whether the church in Africa still needs a gospel filtered through a Eurocentric prism in order for us to accept it.

Surely we have learnt something since 1877 when the first missionaries arrived. There is a myth of obligation raised by missionaries that people voluntarily accepted and understood, but the question of cultural factors, which were radically different to the European ones, was not seriously considered; therefore, the criticism is that missionaries' expectations were far removed from people's environment.

The African church needs to do something about the question of integrating theological thinking which places people's beliefs more firmly within Christianity, in order to recapture the previous traditional structures, which contained community values and promoted social behaviour and individual obligations.

There is increasingly a need, considering the continuous crisis after crisis, to stress that the naive assumption that individuals are capable of self-regulating their practices needs to be altered and regulated by the state. It is this theory which is, in a very real sense, far more convincing and persuasive than an attempt to dispense with the idea of self-regulating, which comes up against the inherent social reality of individual social attitudes to restore the old values to their former place and restrain individuals from acting contrary to the community's expectations.

The question of wealth accumulation reverberates right through the church and the system of social governance. So what went wrong if all the above assumptions of self-regulating safeguards were in place? The prevalent level of corrupt culture is argued as stemming from past religious problematic issues surrounding conversion and condemning traditional values and beliefs. In some colonies, even Christian moral values may well have been used as presentational, rather than being operational working restraints or inhibitors.

In this circumstance where the infringement of African assumptions of independence of mind and self-regulating responsibility can be located, community values ought to go hand in hand with the rule of law or the state, which make rules of sufficient elasticity for individuals to assimilate or to handle departures from unidealistic beliefs, such as believing in fake healers or too much emphasis being placed on wealthy accumulation or materialism. For example, the aim of reaching out to those who were for so long classified as devil worshippers, is to protect society, which cannot be protected from the rise of recurring incidents that deny people's beliefs and begs for the Christian church to take seriously the question of denying the development of people's ideas and beliefs, lagging behind their culture.

This denial of or blindness to society's cultural richness and the failure of converts to develop their own culture and religious philosophical values, so often appears in life interpretation as causing irritation and yet human beings are active decision makers who undertake cost–benefit analyses of situations.

Most recently, educated Africans came to realise that the rejection of their culture was not only a rejection of African values, but of the concept of their own revelation of God. I will give an example of clergy working in a pluralist society where there are civil liberty campaigners for minority rights and defence of diversity in beliefs. The church should champion the rights and protection of human values and the interests of those with different beliefs to ensure that policy and legislation reflect their needs. However, national policies and laws are still biased and delivered like in the past; therefore the church's contribution is vital to achieve positive change and the tolerance of traditional religious practices.

Like in any other free society parish, there are likely to be Jehovah's Witnesses, members of the church of the Latter Day Saints or Mormons, Muslims, Seventh Day Adventists, Methodists, Catholics and several other religious groups. Therefore, Christian clergy have a duty to learn about each other's beliefs, which is the practice in Western society, so that they can equip faithful parishioners with knowledge of what to say when confronted with various teachings. What happens in Africa is self-evident in that all the mischief is caused by seeking to address the past bias and distortion of people's beliefs.

As a matter of fact, all places have their own culture and beliefs and it is these two elements that uniquely separate humanity from the rest of the animal kingdom. Historically, the beliefs and hopes of all societies help to guide people and offer them aspirations and dreams. The way people interpret their world and the way they live are very important for the Christian church in Africa, because denying people a sense of who they are causes damage to their self-identity. The issue of creating contradictions in society and a lack of social support in the system are general concerns for society that must be addressed. In fact, every society has a system that runs it, whether it is backward or insufficient, but it is a system that has served to inform people what was right and what was not acceptable, in order to build constancy and stability in society.

Therefore, the question of African Christian identity is arguably not formed from within and was not truly Christian, but almost reproduced European culture, which led to deterioration in human conduct and fast and furious disabling of community restraints. The instrument of change is interpreted as a framework for understanding how changes were built into the state of affairs in society. This is the reason for my interpretation that abolishing African traditional beliefs was wrong and from the Christian point of view did not stem from a radical zeal of evangelism, but on the contrary the dominant messages targeted what was good and bad for Africans. The neglect of cross-cultural understanding is equally indispensable if one seeks to communicate to people from other cultures in terms of their own thinking, values and traditions.

This is why criticism of this approach is likely to become such a long-term problem in society. The process of change failed to rise to the occasion, but rather was a moment for a sober distortion of people's values. There is much evidence that the present crisis at any rate has to do with the historical changes that abolished what was precious for society, but should have been integrated, to become a key part of the explanation of Christianity. The criticism is that the lack of consciousness of how cultural variables had generally been of significant value to both conversion and communication.

In order to grasp the meaning of people from other cultures, it is now realised how crucial it is to seek sympathetic identification with them in terms of their own presuppositions and their historical roots. In this view, the church must start from the point of listening to various voices expressing concerns, fears, cultural issues bothering local communities, parents' fears of children disappearing and the discovery of bodies with part of their organs removed.

The assertion from these findings is that the people of God will find life entirely and exclusively through listening to God's Word and obeying it. Once again, I wish to emphasise that what is important is that the message is relevant in church teaching. In most cases, the lack of relevance is a serious problem and one of the causes of the schism that still reappears from the past church's distortion of culture and beliefs. We need to be aware that Christianity was introduced into Africa during the colonial era and seemingly prospered largely because it was supported by the ruling governments.

In conclusion, this does not in any way seek to undermine the great contribution to development of missionary work and the significant improvements that were made in education, modern medicine, industry and developing infrastructure in the colonies, which many people are appreciative of, so much accustomed to and cannot possibly live without today. Not only did it seem foreign in itself, but it was also a shared responsibility for the injustice carried out by the colonialists. Therefore, the above findings paint a negative picture of hurried changes that were made either knowingly or unknowingly and that denied local people their own cultures and traditional beliefs and the self-expression of their practices alongside Christianity.

Chapter Eight

8.1 The Question of Traditional Healing and Identity

In the last chapter I discussed the crucial problem of the abolition of traditional beliefs and healing practices, which still appears to be posing a problem in society. In order to consider this problem further and to begin a discussion of the relationship between traditional beliefs and Christianity, I will raise different voices from other areas to show the apparent state of people's dilemma. In the first instance, the God of the church in the eyes of church members in Africa was said to be uncertain, unreliable and slow to respond at their immediate needs. Therefore, the traditional ritualistic quest for church members' consultations is seen as a result of church members being in the middle of a spiritual crisis without knowing who to turn to, when they turn to traditional beliefs in search of help where the church could not provide a protective remedy.

This chapter will attempt to address only one particular view of traditional religion, which suggests that the neglect of local beliefs and culture begs the church to find a realistic discourse capable of engaging church members with their history. As an example, the Aladura movement in Nigeria and Ghana happened at a time when Christians were confronted with a spiritual need and a challenge to the Christian church in Africa (Turner, Harold, W., [1969]. The Place of Independence Religious Movements in the Modernisation of Africa: Journal of Religion in Africa, 2, p.43-63).

Interestingly, before converts to the Aladura movement were accepted as full members, they were prepared in the new Christian life, whose instructions took a totally different approach from that of missionaries. Aladura preparation aimed at making disciples who would soon take up the change of evangelism. H.W. Turner observed that the Aladura movement taught the problems of suffering in the world and spiritual powers through fasting and the use of prayers and psalms. The simple analysis of this type of preparation would be classified as receiving the six positive commands and six prohibitions. The six positive commands were to pray, fast, give alms, love, preach and read the Bible. (Turner, H. W., [1967], p. 69).

The instructions given aimed at promoting evangelical leadership. That is why the six positive commands points at the main duties of members, which were required to be fulfilled in the church of the Lord. The most urgent one was preaching and praying for the sick. The six main prohibitions were concerned with magic and idolatry, sex, foods, alcohol, tobacco and litigation (ibid.). After the instructions, which in most cases were carried out in not less than six months, the candidates were brought to a minister for baptism. For those who were baptised as infants, rebaptism was done "due to their own desire rather than official pressure". (ibid, p.196).

It is further observed by Turner that the baptism services are usually conducted on the river and there is another service at the church for receiving the baptised as full members in the church.

Membership in the Aladura movement is treated as of greater significance than in the missionary churches. All Aladura members are encouraged from the day of being received into the movement to participate in witnessing and interceding. Turner pointed out that the Aladura book of rituals gives converts - and especially those who are initiated into the order of cross bearers - a position that is higher than that of a communicant member in missionary churches. The position of an Aladura convert cross bearer is equivalent to a church minister, anointed to preach, to heal the sick, to raise the dead and to work miracles, looked on to take the responsibility of a church minister where there is none. (ibid, p. 10).

The most noticeable growth in the Aladura church movement took place between 1934 and 1937, expanding beyond national borders to other neighbouring countries. The influence of the movement soon covered the three English-speaking West African countries, namely Sierra-Leone, Liberia and Ghana. In 1961, one of the apostles of this movement, Adejobi, while studying at the Glasgow Bible Institute in Scotland, gathered together West African and other African students in London and established the first branch of the church of the Lord (Aladura) outside the continent of Africa. (ibid, p. 7).

The unique characteristic of this church was its adoption of the African cultural and traditional religious context. This was the best way and the same Christ should have been proclaimed through African cultural packaging as a response to the question of African needs, which European missionaries did not consider as important and yet constituted a fulfilment of the perceived needs of Africans, rather than imposition of European culture.

All this seems to suggest that the situation was begging for Church missionaries to find a realistic discourse capable of engaging Church members with their history. The Aladura movement allowed drumming and dancing, which in missionary churches were forbidden as the dance of the devil. It helped those who desired to worship God in their own culture, the way they felt and understood, as something acceptable and holy before God. It was essential to use the experience of people to address their fears and to provide a better understanding of the current debates in society, as well as to communicate in a medium that avoids the issue of culture being neglected. The appreciation of this was mentioned by E. G. Parrinder, saying, "At last God is enabling Africans to worship Him in their own church and their own way." (Parrinder, E. G., [1987], p. 93).

This was vital because almost all Africans in worship express love and sorrow in their actions. The direction of expression is said to show triumph over enemies or difficulties. (ibid, 1953, Religion in an African City, London). In most cases, dancing was always purposely done to please God, like in the Old Testament King David did in Psalms.

Though Aladura uses prayers and psalms for protection from enemies and healing, it is not clear how it began. J.D.Y. Peel states: "So far the analysis of Aladura doctrine may seem somewhat intellectualist, especially in view of the scenes of mass emotions at the great revivals or even today in many Aladura churches. It is well to emphasise the ratiocinating side of the religion, but it should be realised that these doctrinal formulations may be merely experience of religion." (Peel, J. D. Y.P, [1968], p.135).

He further pointed out that it was both the Cherubim and Seruphim and the Christ Apostolic Church that first claimed this power of healing by using prayers, psalms, blessed water and handkerchiefs. However, the use of prayers and psalms seems to stem originally from Yoruba traditionalist healers. This expression of what religion was about was certainly in line with traditional Yoruba religious views, according to which a whole range of people had "power" of one kind or another, obas ba balowos, witches, men with power juju.

Peel also says that the use of psalms was an influence of Islamic belief in the Yoruba people: "Alfa from Ilorin, explaining the effectiveness of a certain Muslim ritual, involving sacrifice and the drinking of water in which powerful texts had been washed, with prayer, described to me how it had power tabi agbara." (Peel, [1968], p.136).

However, the use of Muslim ritual, involving sacrifice and drinking of water mixed with the texts of the Quran, had been in common practice in East Africa for a long time and it was generally believed by old people to be true. For example, the use of a rubric from psalm 7 as magic to save worshippers from their enemies was a new experience to outsiders.

So, the relationship with God was the key focus. God related to his people on a personal and intimate level. And obedience was the key to a healthy relationship with God. Decisions were not made based on reason and analysis, but by obedience. "The fear of the LORD is the beginning of wisdom." (Ps. 111:10).

This is why many of the miracles performed in the Bible went against natural reason, i.e. feeding five thousand, crossing the Red Sea, retrieving a coin from a fish's mouth, walking around Jericho to win a battle, etc. God constantly wanted to check the leader's obedience, not his knowledge. Knowledge and reason came into the early Church with the Greek scholars in subsequent centuries. This is when the church began to affirm oratory skills among Church leaders. Gradually, over many centuries the focus on knowledge and reason has become more accepted in the Church.

Loss of intimacy with God has been the fallout as a result of the influence of the Greek spirit. The primary focus has been teaching and discipleship instead of the development of a personal and intimate relationship with God. This has resulted in a form of religion, but one without power. In the early church, the rabbi was there primarily for quality control, not as the primary teacher and speaker. He did not even address the people from an elevated platform. The whole congregation was in a more circular format, each sharing what they believed God was saying. The focus was on the power of God working through each individual, not one individual. (1 Cor. 14:26).

It looks as if that was due to the fact that the Aladura movement broke away from missionary churches, simply to respond to the epidemic disease that was killing people as the influence of a desire for these experiences among the converts. However, in other parts of Africa the beliefs of the Aladura movement did not enter the church as they seem to have in West African independent churches. This shows what mistakes were committed by historical mission churches in the past and provides valuable insights into the type of reactions that could be expected to particular policies or circumstances.

In these instances, as African churchmen began to see it, European missionary Christianity had some serious shortcomings in terms of missionary conversion and the reaction in society encapsulated many of the issues related to a culture of resistance among converts. While Christianity itself was deeply important, it was felt that the way in which it had been presented had failed to challenge the African personality. In some cases, this was the basic cause of the growth of independent churches. The fact that many other members of the Pentecostal (independent) churches in Africa today had attended mission schools and even catechism classes without ever seeking full membership of the missionary churches, also points to an indirect reaction of not being happy with the church's teaching.

The real attraction of independent churches for young members derived from their original, creative attempts to relate the good news of the gospel in a meaningful and symbolically intelligible way to the innermost needs of an African. I have argued that, anthropologically, the church did not go deep enough. However, the independent churches are in the process of reaching a high percentage of young people and have already been very successful.

Another area of importance is that of ritual theory, which has many functions, both at the level of the individual and of groups or society, through which they can channel and express emotions, guide and reinforce forms of behaviour, support or subvert the status quo, bring about change or restore harmony and balance.

St Thomas Aquinas and his disciples maintained a delicate view of reason and faith. Reason is seen here as a viable avenue of Christian knowledge and revelation of the truth. In spite of the misemphasis on the scriptural revelation of culture, there is a certain basic structure to African society given in creation, and it is defined and supported by customary rules.

The ability to create friendships was also important in conditions of ethnic division and alienation, where there is a great need for an intimate circle of friends and where individuals can receive recognition and feel at home. This is a necessary component of relationships in independent churches. Individuals are encouraged to regard one another as "brothers and sisters in the Lord", which breeds a sense of solidarity and gives rise to a new type of extended family.

At this juncture, it is fair to draw a comparison between the independent churches (Pentecostal) and missionary Anglican churches. This is not to imply that everything in the independent churches was rosy. There is also a negative side, which continues to be noticed to the present day. Rivalry was the order of the day for some pioneering groups and there were leadership struggles from the very day they began. Individual leaders' struggles for status and control of the finances occasionally caused disputes in some independent churches; in most cases they promoted the birth of numerous other independent churches.

Though after independence some churches ventured to adopt some of what had been rejected throughout the colonial period, somehow society reflected a conscious effort, which unfortunately did not go much further. According to informed respondents, in many instances the church's attitude appeared to show little concern for the people's real world during missionary days.

In short, the case against missionary forms of reductionism disintegrated African communities rather than uniting them. Once, community values and moral restraints were dispersed by the new system as irrelevant, moral restraints became difficult in a process by which ethical judgement was reduced to individual decisions and depended on missionary approval or disapproval. For instance, it is argued that missionaries did not do enough to explain how to live as Christians; instead, their emphasis was placed on public confession for "those who are on fire", forgetting that the wider section of the population was not on fire. (Cfr. Osborn, H. H., [1995]. Revival – A precious heritage, London: SPCK, p. 99).

This abolition of societal values is interpreted as a failure on the part of missionaries to distance themselves from the reality of people and the church's weakness, which often has left church members silently angry about the lack of guidance in Christian daily life. In fact, this is simply common sense: how can you stop people living by their culture and social order and then expect them to change without knowing why they should change? On the other hand, this was not the case, because there is evidence of missionaries engaging in the colonial advancement of their policies, either in school curricula or directly and indirectly in church teachings. However, in places the history of the missionaries shows that the strategy was based mainly on evangelising and on enthusiastic conversion to the state of being "born again", so as to save perishing souls.

8.2 Contradictions Within Missionary Teaching

Returning to the daunting question of contradictory missionary messages in conversion reveals how, in the beginning, the mission seemed to have had clear intentions to convert Africans to the Christian faith, recruit catechists and train them as agents for change and to teach the way of living as a Christian. This is where the main criticism of contradiction lies, in the questions surrounding the conversion messages and the lack of relevance of the theological contextual point of view. Of course, no issue alarmed converts more than knowing that they had lived for centuries in belief of God and in worship of God. That is why the question of contradictions arises. Why did they not encourage catechists and African priests to interpret the gospel in an African concept of God for the integration of the Christian faith into the societal understanding of God?

On the other hand, the question of value vanishes when insufficient attention is paid to the particular distinctive characteristics that stimulate an appreciative response from people in society, which it had not yet at the time. In this respect, the conversion attempt is criticised for not maintaining the use of local methods of communication, which is a question that cannot be answered now.

Furthermore, why did the approach used in the conversion to Christianity not consider people's background or their experience? These questions of people's culture, experience and knowledge were vital and should not have been summarily dismissed in the light of any preconceived theory. In fact, the conversion to Christianity involved a high degree of strain, both for the converts and the communities to which they belonged. If they were members of a community, they were liable to be treated as traitors, whose alien manners must, once and for all, be rejected. While the change of hearts and minds was essential, it was perhaps a mistake for what Father Hillman referred to as "Black Europeans", a new anthropological category devised by Julius Nyerere (Hillman, E., [1975]. Polygamy Reconsidered, African Plural Marriage and the Christian Anglican Churches, New York: Orbis Books, p. 14).

South Africa has been witnessing the resurgence of polygamistic marriages. Jacob Zuma is arguably the most famous African polygamist. (New Times, Rwanda, Sunday 8th November 2009). Apart from being the leader of Africa's biggest economy, Zuma is also the only known world leader married to three women. He has paid lobola (bride price) for many more and has been photographed dancing at traditional marriage ceremonies.

Recently, another South African made headlines by marrying four women on the same day. The catch was that the women said "we do" instead of the expected "I do". (Ssenyonga, Allan, Brian, article, "Are Africans repackaging Polygamy?" November 2009).

A few years before, a businessman in Western Uganda married two sisters on the same day and he made it to the front page of a newspaper. The ICC-wanted Sudan leader has also been quoted to have advised men to marry more than one wife in order to increase the population of Sudan. We should also not lose sight of the recently pro-polygamy legislations that were debated in Uganda and Kenya. (ibid).

This fits well with the observation made by a respondent who argued that things such marriage and religious belief are distinctly cultural and traditional, passed on deliberately through communication and imitation, generation after generation. I will return to the issue of polygamy later to contrast missionary teaching with what happens today in Christian countries about marriage. According to observers, missionaries seem to have suffered from ethnocentrism (the belief in the superiority of one's own cultural group or society) and a corresponding dislike or misunderstanding of other such groups. ((Hillman, E., [1975]. Polygamy Reconsidered, African Plural Marriage and the Christian Anglican Churches, New York: Orbis Books, p. 14).

Furthermore, it is argued that the criticism during the period of revivalist conversion was not about conversion as such and how converts must behave, but rather the basis on which the newly acquired faith was to be practised in society. The criticism is about the powerful pressure that converts experienced in this period, either to remain traditional or to become modern. Festo Kivengeri once said that changes would change you even if you did not want to change. (Kivengeri, Festo, in his speech at Bishop Tucker Theological, Mukono, 1975).

For instance, a combination of economic interests and power to control and prevent local ideas and beliefs from developing meant that the system changed significantly under colonialism in the nineteenth century. The imperative of Christian mission raised the question of how universal truth claims are applied to the particulars of a given culture and locality is one of the most popular ways to depict the changes to place during this period. For example, Chinua Achebe's *Things Fall Apart* outlines the changes in the Igbo experience when they became overwhelmingly Christian under colonisation. (Literature and Theology Advance Access originally published online on 4th February 2007, Literature and Theology 2007, 21[1]:49-65; doi:10.1093/litthe/frl06).

The dilemma for many after years of colonial rule was that society looked for kinds of spiritual guidance that would appreciate the tradition and their culture to reconcile them with the past. In the process of struggling to search for spiritual help, they turned to missionaries, but often found that these missionaries were also part of the fellow colonial system, preaching submission and obedience to those in authority. (Interviewing elderly church members at Kigali, August 1998). In their view, this meant submitting to the colonials' authority.

If society decides to follow the emphasis of openness, it may end up with a combination of an ideal approach from people's knowledge and the sort of practice in public debate that is desirable for society. In this view, it is essential to use the experience of various traditional healers, including various religious communities and any other faiths, to examine the way forward in an attempt to address people's fears and to provide a better understanding of the current debates in African communities that have proliferated within a culture of neglect.

Many of those engaged in these rituals will give the excuse that it is their right to perform ritual acts as a traditional belief, which indeed must be respected as people's freedom of belief and freedom of expression. Following this argument, it is these reasons that have prompted this book to try to assess whether these are truly African traditional beliefs and whether human sacrifice originally comes from traditional beliefs. What is accepted in today's society might reflect popular sentiments and may deserve proper modification of an old custom based on reason to promote good health for all and unity among ritual celebrants.

There is, therefore, a role for traditional healers to play in such a situation that implicates them. If society still invests trust and faith in traditional medicine, the mediums have to persuade fake healers that it is wrong and deceptive to sacrifice a fellow human being. Then the importance of the ritualistic celebrations will return to their rightful use and the practice of faking will fade away and the demand for human sacrifice fades also. This is argued as a matter of educating society to distinguish between what is genuine and fake. It is easy to dwell on the former when at times it is incredibly difficult to discern how individuals can be convinced that these horrible acts, in certain circumstances, are able to make any comprehensible change in one's economic life. In actual fact, the point of transparency in society is very crucial and a major concern, which needs collective effort from African society to seriously redress it.

I will even go further to exemplify the significance of the colonial and missionaries' suppression of culture when everything that had existed in society as being of value was abolished. African society adopted a culture of secrecy and this secrecy embedded another culture of corrupted minds. When society becomes accustomed to a culture of secrecy, this leads down a slippery pass to wrong innovations. Indeed, it is these wrong innovations that are the very corrupt culture, which becomes itself coercive and is a value in itself. What is observed in society is well exemplified by innovations of ritualistic witchcraft and human sacrifices and what is required is that religious leaders, genuine traditional healers and law enforcers work jointly to support a policy of transparency in traditional healing.

The indirect recent reaction in independent churches encapsulates many of the issues of complex cultures of resistance among converts. The fact that many members of the Pentecostal (independent) churches in Africa today had attended mission schools and even catechism classes, without ever seeking full membership of the Christian church in Africa, also points to an indirect reaction of not being happy with the Christianity in Africa's teaching.

The real attraction of independent Christianity in Africa for young members derives from its original, creative attempts to relate the good news of the gospel in a meaningful and symbolically intelligible way to the innermost needs of an African. I have argued that, anthropologically, Christianity in Africa did not go deep enough during this period, or in fact today. However, the independent churches are in the process of reaching a high percentage of young people and have already been very successful.

Another area of importance is ritual theory, which has many functions, both at the level of the individual and of groups in society, through which they can channel and express emotions, guide and reinforce forms of behaviour, support or subvert the status quo, bring about change or restore harmony and balance. Christianity in churches is not primarily designed to provide service and spiritual guidance alone, but to go further to provide the scope for forming friendships and a ground on which to unite.

Missionaries had always seen themselves as agents of change. Another point to consider is that missionaries were few and did not have enough time and resources to examine several traditional cultures, even if they wanted to. In some places they were simply overwhelmed by claims of differences of cultural beliefs.

John Mbiti underscores the important belief and sense of community among traditional Africans. In traditional Africa, the individual does not and cannot exist alone except corporately. He owes existence to other people, including those of past generations and his contemporaries. Whatever happens to the individual is believed to happen to the whole group and whatever happens to the whole group happens to the individual. "The individual can only say: 'I am because we are, and since we are, therefore I am. This is a cardinal point in the understanding of the African view of man." (J.S. Mbiti, [1990], 106).

For instance, if we look closely at the history of the revivalist mission in Africa and other areas, it shows that the revivalist heritage strategy was based mainly on evangelising and on enthusiastic conversion to the state of being "born again", so as to save perishing souls. However, another major historical argument as that during colonial rule and the missionary impact on society, these beliefs were pushed underground to operate quietly as if they did not exist.

It was a widely criticised approach and missionary conversion methods are regarded as the embodiment of impersonal, rule-bound authority, which enforced Christianity and constraints on another society through the tight cultural requirements of Christian living. This situation is suggestive that people had no choice or freedom about whether they were baptised or not. Baptism was conceived in consumerist terms: if people needed the goods or services offered, they have to accept a seller's terms, no matter how onerous these may be.

It is a situation of inequality of bargaining power, in particular between the Christian mission in Africa and clients of its service. It may seem that the idea of freedom of choice remains a big question and now seems a very out-of-date principle, which needs to find a fitting substitute. The net effect of analysis of the notion of absolute "Truth claims" (John 1:14, 14:6, 9) was misleading and it was a falsehood to use Christ as "the only way and the truth" and to impose Christian religious authority at the expense of local beliefs and values to strengthen their power, portraying concepts of Christian belief as the only way and the truth for salvation.

If all that I have said about the disclosure of God in terms of the African experience had closely accorded with Christian conversion, it seems to have been both confusing and contradictory at best. In the African concept of revelation, God is perceived as being interested in men and women as themselves, as products of their culture. George Mulrain in African Religion in the Diaspora Caribbean Experience offers the best explanation, saying that they seek to respond in worship and service to God. As pointed out earlier by Christopher I. Ejizu in African Traditional Religions and the Promotion of Community – Living in Africa, the concept of God between Africans and Caribbeans is synonymous and concerns the Creator (Olodumare among the Yoruba or Chukwu among the Igbo); God created everything that exists and set everything in its place.

Traditional Africans basically view the universe as comprising of two realms: the visible and the invisible. They grasp the cosmos as a three-tiered structure, consisting of the heaven above, the physical world and the world beneath. Each of these is inhabited by different categories of beings. The Creator and a host of spirit beings, including arch divinities, inhabit the heaven above; other divinities, ancestors and myriads of unnamed spirits dwell in the world beneath, while human beings occupy the physical earth. Human beings may be less powerful, but their world is the centre and the focus of attention. It belongs to human beings as sensible beings to maintain the delicate balance in the universe. This is what assures the happiness and prosperity of individuals, but tragically young people in Africa did not understand that the free-market capitalist system was what makes profits and prosperity possible and its influence on community values.

Around this period, Paul Tillich rightly said, "The universe is God's sanctuary. Every work day is a day of the Lord, every supper a Lord's Supper, every work fulfilment of a divine task, every joy in God. In all preliminary concerns, ultimate concern is present, consecrating them."

(Tillich, Paul, [1959], Theology of Culture, New York, O.U.P., p.41).

Christopher I. Ejizu, describing the concept of the African perception of the universe, goes a little further to show that it is one that contains both visible and invisible worlds. The cosmos is spirit filled, with a supreme spiritual being, a number of lesser spirits, human beings and nature. The cynics refer to this cosmology as tainted with animism, by which they mean the attribution of lifelike qualities to lifeless objects. Behind the idea of animistic beliefs, though, is an acknowledgement that truth is not confined to that which is empirically testable. There are spiritual truths. (Christopher I. Ejizu, African Traditional Religions and the Promotion of Community – Living in Africa).

George Mulrain argues that although they are not visible, there are spirits pervading the universe. It is equally the case that animists try to understand the reality of God and the invisible world with the help of physical, visible objects. (George Mulrain, Article, in "African Religion in The Diaspora Caribbean Experience").

Focusing on visible objects can be of assistance in the process of meditating on that which though unseen is real and people's beliefs as part of the conversion process. It also appears that the missionaries had not envisaged that the truth claims of Christianity would in the long run become the source conflict in religious interests, a situation that was waiting to happen in Africa. Yet from the traditional religious point of view, the best worldwide broad evidence of similarities is in ritual celebrations, which interestingly have some points of agreement about what gives protection in the same practices. Dr Kwenda says that the wide variety of African indigenous beliefs and practices makes generalisations difficult, but some commonalities may nonetheless be noted. In general,

Zairians believe themselves to be subject to a number of unseen agents and forces.
(http://afgen.com/religion.html/09/09).

A far more through and persuasive attempt to dispense with traditional beliefs and ideas as an African way of life demands to be revisited by African churches to assess what society has to say about different groups scattered all over the world that still hold to ritual celebrations. The reason for this revisiting and reassessment is to witness for them how traditional religious ritual celebrations have held to history and become interlinked in many ways. For example, Voodoo officially is a culture and religion of the approximately 7 million people of Haiti and the Haitian Diaspora. (http://wwww.erukies.com/site/articles/views/5). It has its primary roots among the Fon-Ewe peoples of West Africa, in the country now known as Benin, formerly the Kingdom of Dahomey.

Available evidence also shows that Voodoo has strong elements from the Ibo and Kongo peoples of Central Africa and the Yoruba of Nigeria, though many different peoples or "nations" of Africa have representation in the liturgy of the Sevis Gineh, as do the Taino Indians, the original peoples of the island we now know as Hispaniola. Haitian Voodoo exists in Haiti, the Dominican Republic and parts of Cuba, the United States, France, Montreal and other places to which Haitian immigrants have dispersed over the years. Other New World traditions to which it is closely related or bears resemblance include Jeje Vodun in Brazil, La Regla Arara in Cuba and the Black Spiritualist Christianity of New Orleans. Haitian Voodoo also bears superficial resemblances in many ways with the Nigerian Yoruba-derived traditions of the Orisha service, represented by La Regla de Ocha or Lukumi, aka "Santeria", in Cuba, the United States and Puerto Rico as well as Candomble in Brazil. (http://wwww.erukies.com/site/articles/views/5).

Therefore, like other places where the church integrated traditional teaching rather than using draconian regulations to prevent its existence, the situation could have been different in Africa, because culture develops as a patterned set of understandings, which helps people to cope with and adjust to the pressures and tensions which contort them. The culture of the people – the values, norms, beliefs, perspectives and community rules – informed their conduct and, of course, was not monolithic, universal or unchanging.

As in the above countries, there are millions of believers in traditional religion, which is the reason it is arguable that if during conversion there had been an attempt to understand these beliefs and their cultural role in society, the entire situation could have been different. There are differences of outlook within every society, according to such individual variables as personality, generation or cultural trajectory and structural variations according to how society values things and life itself.

The organisational styles and cultures of society vary between different people, places and periods. This is because informal rules are not clear-cut and articulate, but embedded in specific practices according to particular concrete situations and the interactional processes of daily occurrences, where successive generations were socialised into them. Tragically, when the pattern changes were engulfing them they turned passive, but as manipulated learners. It is further argued that by being aggressive, missionaries pressed their claims while African were silent on their culture and traditional values, norms, perspectives and development. The characteristics that differentiated missionary conversion were sharply different from the communal culture of the traditional era.

If missionaries' own culture was not promoting European superiority, it was shown by their knowledge of science, demonstrated through a disrespect of local culture and values. (Cf. Osborn, H. H., [1995]. Revival – A precious heritage, p.96). This is one way of seeing such abstractions, but it is argued that it would have been easier to refer to God through traditional concepts, in a formal way known by locals. Kinyatta added that "they would have left to let the African choose what parts of European culture could be beneficially transplanted, and how they could be adapted." (Kinyatta, Jomo, [1938], p.318).

8.3 The Loss of Traditional Religious Influences in the West

According to historical evidence, ghosts from the nineteenth century still haunted Europeans based on theories formulated in the past. In summary, generally religious influence was argued by men like Charles Darwin, Muller, Marx and Durkheim. Freud's *Interpretation of Dreams* is seen as the key work, as a personal relinquishing of legitimation for economic and political aspiration to opt out of the state of the poor and oppressed, offering compensation for deprivation in fantasies of an afterlife. All three – Durkheim, Marx and Freud – ignored the supernatural in religion as a myth to disarm a rigorous logic, capable of scoffing at its embroilment in contradiction. Their views about evolution and religion still undergird much of what is taught in the physical and social sciences and in the comparative study of religion.

In the field of religion, it all began with the publication of Charles Darwin's (1809-82) *The Origin of Species* in 1859 and continued with the tireless efforts of Friedrich Max Muller (1823-1900), epitomised in his massive compendium *Sacred Books of the East*. In Darwinism, scientific theory joined hands with a dominant philosophy of history and embraced evolution as the guiding principle of method; a principle adopted and applied with assiduity and vigour in the field of religion. That God may be considered dead, man come of age and religion abolished is evolutionary theory in practise. (cf. Eric J. Sharpe, [1975], pp. 25-6, 35-46).

In the fields of sociology and psychology as related to religion, Karl Marx (1818-83), Emile Durkheim (1858-1917) and Sigmund Freud (1856-1939) propounded functional theories of religion, which, they asserted, is functional to social cohesion and solidarity. Marx, as early as 1843-4, when he was about 25-years-old, addressed himself to the subject of religion in some brilliant epigrams, such as "Religion is indeed the self-consciousness and self-esteem of man who has either not yet won through to himself or has already lost himself again", or "It is the fantastic realisation of the human essence since the human essence has not acquired any true reality". Therefore, the resurgence of traditional healing cults is clear evidence that this threat is real and needs to be addressed by society before it gets out of hand.

Let me give two examples. Firstly, Uganda's Argentinean coach, Pedro Pablo Pasculli, was sure that Uganda lost to Africa because of witchcraft. "I am still shocked by this witchcraft that I witnessed for the first time in my football career. I have played in South America and witnessed many things in football, but this was too much for me," said Pasculli. "This witchcraft issue disorganised my whole team because they were so taken up and failed to concentrate."

Most people think that witchcraft only exists in Africa, but clearly the Argentinean coach must have proved otherwise. According to BBC News, Zimbabwe lifted the ban on the practice of witchcraft, repealing colonial-era legislation that made it a crime to accuse someone of being a witch or wizard.

Secondly, a police officer based at the Kenyan port city of Mombasa at the height of the Kenyan post-election violence, stated that it is amazing how witchcraft can turn out to work "for good". He asserted, "Whether ghosts exist or not, our work has been made easy. I wish there were ghosts all over the country." In what turned out to be a somewhat comical sideshow amid the mayhem of post-election violence, Mombasa residents started returning goods they had looted from shops for fear of being bewitched. Most of the "looters" were returning the goods at night to hide their embarrassment. Television footage then showed fearful, if not shameful; looters and their accomplices returning beds, sofa sets, planks of timber and other items, after rumours that victims had deployed witch doctors to punish the thieves started circulating.

Police officials confirmed the report, saying witchcraft had facilitated their business of tracking down crooks. But welcoming the move, police did not arrest anyone who had willingly returned the stolen goods, but gave an ultimatum to all others to follow suit. (News, article from uganet website, 2009).

Of course, the above two examples speak volumes, especially in an area like Mombasa where there are stories of Swahili (Magini) beautiful female spirits who fall in love with men in drinking places, but when entering the bedroom they vanish. How true that is I can't tell, but I will add an observation of the source of the resurgence of traditional beliefs, which is added to psychological magic by traditional healers. In fact, before modern medicine, African healers were not necessarily traditional healers. The traditional healer is a derogatory term as used in modern society, but healers were elderly people who used local herbs for medicine to take or to rub on wounds or fractured limbs. Then, in trying to express the effectiveness of the medicine, they often added some form of magic, which in a sense was just reconditioning clients or patients to strictly observe the procedures of the prescription; if they did not use this form of superstition, the prescriptions of the medication would not be strictly adhered to.

Though there are many traditional African beliefs, they have always shared common features. They never sanctioned sorcery or the misuse of any powers of nature. They have always emphasised healing, the driving out of evil spirits and the reconciliation of people within communities. This is the religion that has always been part and parcel of African culture. There was never any dualistic tension between faith and politics in Africa. Such co-existence had also been possible, mainly because of deeper cultural values, such as the sense of community, the clan; the traditional leadership and the mechanism in social relations were natural cultural restraints. For instance, if a patient went for medication to an elderly traditional healer, after diagnosis the healer gave them medicine to use at home with instructions that sounded like a mystical, magical part of the medicine.

It is necessary as well to try to see what is behind the magic characteristic of traditional healing which, for instance, requires a patient to sit at the entrance of their house and rub in the medicine at 6 pm and 6 am every day until they are completely healed. The magic is an imaginative reconstructed idea to suit the occasion, which is only known by the healer. However, the use of this added meaning is open to abuse by fake healers as inherently they can claim anything psychologically that creates tense conditions and magnifies the situation in the interest of monetary gains for their healing service. Furthermore, all this means that traditional healers who use certain material objects such as bracelets to protect clients from disease do sometimes add an emphasis to achieve good results. However, there is a difference between traditional medicine healers whose power is attributed to God or natural spirits, and witchcraft whose belief is to do harm, or to wish a person harm.

According to local people in East and Central Africa whom I consulted, witchcraft may be inherited and sometimes individuals may not know that they possess the power until the power shows itself unexpectedly. There are also ancestor cult healers, who could be classified among the night dancers who claim to posses the power of calling departed spirits. While considering the traditional beliefs of ancestor spirits according to African stories, these are spirits in natural objects and these beliefs are shared by many African societies.

However, celebration practices may differ according to cultures; for instance the ritual celebrations for birth, naming, legitimacy, initiation, concussion, war, hunting, rainmaking and averting epidemic disease. Farmers in eastern India, for example, have sent their unmarried daughters to plough fields naked in a bid to embarrass the weather gods to bring some badly needed monsoon rain. Witnesses said that the naked girls in Bihar state ploughed the fields and chanted ancient hymns after sunset to invoke the gods. Villagers have vowed to continue this practice until it rains very heavily. In 2009, India suffered its worst start to the vital monsoon rains in eight decades, causing drought in some states. (The New Vision, 31 July 2009).

Just to cite another example, Edwin Nuwagaba narrates the Ugandan traditional Convention for Community Development in Rubaga, which from outside may seem like any other business at first glance. They repair cars, sew clothes, have a school and a community bank, hold training sessions to teach maths and science and run a large security business. But step inside, ask a few questions and a deeper spirituality becomes apparent. These are the followers of Jjaja Ndawula (grandpa Ndawula), a spirit that has shown its followers a new way: a path of miraculous healing, religious rituals and intellectual empowerment.

A few weeks later, having asked Omulangira Ssuuna (prince Ssuuna) how he came to name his studio Maureen, the artist led me to an area in Rubaga, the base of abasamize (traditional healers), spirit worshippers. (Sunday Vision, Article, Sunday Life, July 2009). Maureen, as I found out, is a spirit that most members of the sect take on for their businesses. You perhaps have heard of Maureen Security, which is hired when there is an international artist in town. It is one of the businesses they own. I was introduced to the leader of the sect, John Musoke Sendawula, a short, dark-skinned man in sandals, who has drawn over 2,000 members to the sect. His followers refer to him as Jjaja (grandpa) because he is the intermediary for Jjaja Ndawula, the chief spirit.

Other spirits or guardian angels possess Sendawula and other members during rituals. Every shrine there has a different spirit that inhabits it, like Jjaja Mukasa and Jjaja Walumbe. The spirits sent him to Kongogye at Nakibinge Omulwanyamuli, Jjaja Ndawula's grandfather's place, where he was sworn in by the spirits.

We finally arrived at the central shrine for all the spirits that these people have tapped into all their lives. (Sunday Vision, Article, Sunday Life, July 2009).

It therefore necessary to argue that for so long the African church has not taken the trouble to look elsewhere for how Christian churches are related to traditional religion, such as Haitian Voodoo, which is a variant of the word "hoodoo" and is also called "rootwork" or "root doctoring".
(http://wwww.erukies.com/site/articles/views/5). This is a folk magical tradition from Central Africa in the Congo region in which roots, leaves, minerals and the spirits of the

dead are employed to improve the lot of the living, often including the reciting of Psalms and other Biblical prayers.

These are all signs that the African religious tradition is not anti-Christianity, but could complement the church ministry only if it can be welcomed by the church to be modernised, as a means of purification. Rootwork also incorporates Native American herb lore and European and Jewish magical traditions. During the turbulent period of paganism in Europe, an ex-Roman Catholic seminarian wrote books in which he purported to reveal ancient mysteries and occult law. However, he drew on theories of magic and the kabbalah, which is an ancient system of Jewish mysticism.

Also, after decades, ritual celebrations and traditional ceremonies still play an important part in Aboriginal life. Small ceremonies, or rituals, are still practised in some remote parts of Australia, such as in Arnhem Land and Central Australia, in order to ensure a supply of plant and animal foods. These take the form of chanting, singing, dancing or ritual action to invoke the Ancestral Beings to ensure a good supply of food or rain. The most important ceremonies are connected with the initiation of boys and girls into adulthood. Such ceremonies sometimes last for weeks, with nightly singing and dancing, storytelling and the display of body decoration and ceremonial objects. During these ceremonies, the songs and stories connected to each of the Ancestral Beings are told and retold, some being "open" for women and children to see and hear, others being restricted and cloaked in "secret-sacred", only for the initiates to learn.
(http://www.aborigineals.culture.comac/religion.shtml/).

Therefore, the question of people's belief was paramount and still is very important, which raises a number of issues as to whether the use of draconian measures had resolved fears. The Aboriginal religion, like many others, is characterised by having a god or gods who created people and the surrounding environment during a particular creation period at the beginning of time. This form may be a particular landscape feature, an image in a rock art shelter, or in a plant or animal form. (http://www.aborigineals.culture.comac/religion.shtml/).

If we consider African traditional religious experience, there are similarities with the Australian Aborigines and the Native American Indians, which are also being rediscovered today. And yet evidence drawn directly from their experience shows what people believe and how culture has persisted in its existence.

From an observational point of view, culture survives because of its "elective affinity", its psychological fit, with the demands of daily life. The evidence of this is that African traditional religious beliefs have struggled for their survival for the last decades without official recognition by society. In order to find appropriate mechanisms from both a religious and legal point of view for safeguarding the public, it is firstly important to identify the difference between genuine traditional believers and greedy imposters who use witchcraft practice, which in reality has nothing to do with traditional religious beliefs. There is an urgent need for Africans to find a remedy, considering the fact that African cultures, historically, were demonised in general and denigrated, as if they did not have important tradition in their heritage and beliefs that had sustained them for centuries.

The situation is more precarious than before Christianity and the concern for people in society is that if this situation is not wisely resolved, it might add up to the long-range survival of other unknown dimensions. The aim is to examine Christianity as a prominent feature of society and practice in Africa. There is need to demonstrate that while traditional beliefs occupy a marginalised position in terms of public recognition and practice relating to healing, there are difficulties with the technical, rigid and sometimes harsh operation of missionaries in some parts of Africa that led to controversies surrounding the level of bias and pattern of conversion among converts, which differed in many ways to the Christian faith and behaviour.

It is a recognisable fact that the church in society is fully engaged with people on Christian faith issues; however, on the other it has had less influence on moral behaviour issues. The church in Africa seems to have been hooked for the past few decades on doctrinal issues, which are the reasons why the church still insists on treating traditional beliefs negatively. This is all this seen as a problem of the influence of past doctrine and its source is that the church is less concerned with people's culture where Christianity in Africa has not reached people's lives. Despite that, in Europe and the rest of the world they do realise where in the past the error lies. So often the African church's failure lies in not accepting responsibility and not looking around the world to compare with other similar areas that have moved on from the same problems, or other religious initiatives, to join hands to see how they have integrated their own traditional beliefs, which are necessary for accomplishing self-liberation; for instance, learning from the Latin American experience of integrating Voodoo.

I have argued in my first book, *Testing Times, Globalisation and Investing Theology in East Africa*, that the power of God to redeem people operates largely, not exclusively, through people's culture in society, as an ongoing incarnation of the spirit of Christ in the lives of many people who have offered their lives to the service of following Christ. The Christian church cannot remain forever in the state of transplant or imprisonment in the foreign culture that is operating in Africa; it must truly become an African centre of worship in African understanding and in the community.

Consider the statement by Luke: "Now, will God not judge in favour of his own people who cry to him day and night for help? Will he be slow to help them?" (Luke 18:7). This is suggestive of the fact that Christ was concerned with the plight of all people in their environment and still is today. On the other hand, Luke 10:40-42 says that when our concern for serving Jesus exceeds our need to be with Jesus, we are in danger of focusing on the lesser thing.

The hardest thing to do for most believers is to sit and listen. Let me make no bones about any African church's action to impart religious change from the point of view of the superiority of the West. This has meant that the final religious decisions in Africa are still deemed subservient to the doctrinal permission of Rome or Canterbury and any decisions taken without permission from those two headquarters would be treated as a perilous attempt to divide the universal church or the Anglican Communion. In this case, all doctrinal matters are still decided either at Rome or at Canterbury, the position argued as still being a sign of submission to the master's wisdom or discernment.

This has not yet recognised and does not allow the African church freedom of choice to embrace the traditional beliefs, which are regarded as evil by European culture. There is instead an insistence on keeping the African church in a perpetually submissive position, which virtually maintains dependency. The lack of choice raises another important issue: when the European or Western churches embrace and integrate the increasing rise of a homosexual culture, when it comes to the decision, African church's objections are out of the equation or referred as the voice from Africa, which suffers from a lack of appreciation of Western culture.

If that is not a colonial mentality, I don't know what else to call it. It has recently been described by the Archbishop of Sudan as seriously harming the church's witness in Africa and elsewhere, opening the church to ridicule and damaging its credibility in a multi-faith environment (The Church Times, 28 August 2009).

Hort is more relevant at this period, arguing based very firmly on theological convictions of how to live a Christian life in a practical way. Hort and Westcott believe that the doctrine of incarnation and redemption has practical implications. It is argued that the theological concept of God's incarnate operation includes the sociological connotation of the "The Lord's Supper", which is the sharing of the material resources of this world. (Matt. 26:26-30; Mark 14:22-26).

The whole essence of the theological concept of incarnation is self-sacrificing love in the search for the right relationship. Thus, to have a relationship with those you wronged in the past involves giving support to those who seek to change and repair, which implies a positive attitude to social values and the environment. In other words, it is the Christian way to express God's will through the incarnation that brings heaven and earth together.

Some errors may be due to logical inconsistency and are mostly easily correctable once seen, but they are not always easy to spot. Others are due to the long-term influence of traditional devilish assumptions and a gradual shifting through time and are much harder to correct, requiring vigorous ironing out of perceptual categories and evaluations of priorities into a societal contextual bed of logic.

This is very important as it is the incarnation or "embodied" character of Christ that cannot overlook human concern, to leave out the physical and social conditions under which people actually lived. One should be aware of the fact that Paul, a founding father of the early church and the most successful missionary who ever lived, confessed in Corinthians (9:20-22) "To the Jews I became as a Jew, in order to win Jews; to those under the law I became as one under the law -- though not being myself under the law -- that I might win those under the law. To those outside the law I became as one outside the law - not being without law toward God but under the law of Christ – that I might win those outside the law. To the weak I became weak, that I might win the weak." (Romans 3:7). "If through my lies God's truth abounds to His glory, why am I still being condemned as a sinner?" (Philippians1:18) (see http://www.messiahtruth.com/response.html).

In every way, whether in pretence or in truth, Jesus is proclaimed and in that I rejoice. The veracity of everything that missionaries stated and taught is called into question by the fact that these quotes are found in the books St Paul himself authored.
(http://www.messiahtruth.com/response.html).

St Paul represents the work of Christ as the creation of a new humanity, one which Christians "put on" like a robe in the baptism, when the old nature – fallen, corrupt human nature – is put away. This is Paul's conception of the Church as a newly created humanity in Christ, both eschatological and incarnate. (Romans 8:29; Galatians. 3:28). This seems to be an emphasis that derives from the doctrine of Christ entering human life and thus giving worth to all that is human. Christ's incarnate life made clear God's sovereignty over the earth and implies our positive attitude towards it. (Cfr. Hort, A. F., [1977]. Just Men, London: Epworth Press, p. 400).

In the midst of conflict, it would appear to suggest that an understanding of the love of God and stimuli in the environment and individual cognition might help to control and improve habits of responsibility. Lerner defined responsibility in this way: “the ability to observe ourselves and others in interaction and to respond to a familiar situation in a new and different way.” (Lerner, H. G., [1990]. The Dance of Anger, Wellingborough: Grapevine, p. 17).

This begs the question of when Africans will stop being treated like babies, fed spiritually on traditions and cultures that are irrelevant to their own spiritual needs, for even as babies they object that the food doesn’t have a natural taste. Furthermore, the church should ask when Africans will be saved from dependence. Is it because the church cannot think and discern God’s saving grace for it? This should not mislead us into suggesting independence of mind operating in isolation from the universal church; rather, it means being treated on equal terms.

It is argued that the rationalisation of incarnation acted for a universal church and did not act in isolation from the universal salvation context within which Christ’s actions occurred. On the other hand, the idea of incarnation informs the long relationship between humankind and God’s revelation principles of individual response to God’s knowledge, denial of which is fundamentally myopic in that it ignores the nature of social phenomena and consequently has to find ways of excluding that nature from its gaze.

However, what Christianity in Africa so often seems to overlook is the fact that Christ did not come to abolish culture but to fulfil it. If the Christian message in Africa is to be seriously conceived, then the interpretation of God’s enlightenment or revelation to human minds has to be recognised in the ways in which revelation is a step towards knowledge of God and the social world and, through such knowledge, a step towards some form of human salvation or liberation is achievable. It is on this side of relevance of the cultural context that the African church is still lagging behind. Therefore, in the view of the rationality of incarnation, I would imagine that when Satan looks at the church, he is aware that the church in Africa has this potential and consequently Satan works hard to isolate the rest of the vital richness of its culture and religious traditions to keep tension in society and hinder human salvation.

If the universal church chooses to maintain the past in this way, it forever risks losing relevance to society. Not all generations to come can continue to live under the pretence of being saved while they are not. There is one great bridge that the church must cross before it can effectively meet the conditions for world evangelism. The universal church will have to realise that the African church's teaching in society requires urgent overhaul from missionary concepts to become relevant practical and theoretical in consideration of the European mind.

The African church needs to reconsider the objectives of its mission during the conversion, to urgently address a response that can cater to uncertainty and risks that are deeply intertwined. Otherwise, the certainty exists of greater risks where so often the Christian nature of the message becomes apparent in many ways that are less effective in society.

However, if the church chooses to maintains its irrelevant previous bias, the present resurgence of belief in ritualistic sacrifice highlights a worrying situation that threatens people's security. A willingness to engage more constructively in response to societal issues is wholesome, though if nothing is done to explore the possibility of translating traditional practices in the church, the church will always remain foreign to its own people.

Durkheim is still relevant here. In *The Elementary Forms of the Religious Life*, he examined Australian Totemism as the simplest and most original form of religion and claimed that people's beliefs rest on a specific experience whose demonstrative value is, in one sense, not one bit inferior to that of scientific experiments, though different from them. This is roughly what the sociological approach ought to mean: the totem, the symbol of common origin, becomes the object of a believer's veneration and awe, because it is supposed to provide such sanctions. Durkheim observed that Totemism was thus the origin of Australian Aboriginal religious worship in their environment. So a "traditional religious experience", if we choose to call it this, does exist and it has a certain foundation – and, by the way, that is why religion varies from society to society. (Cf. Durkheim, Emile, The Elementary Forms of the Religious Life, London, Allen and Unwin, [1915], pp. 147-19).

The assumption of leadership obligations is an important element in pastoral care. This is a particularly important matter, bearing in mind the nature of numerous problems faced by people in local communities. It is therefore not surprising that traditional healers' clinics echoe what often African churches have forgotten, that there are many other churches who have embraced traditional religious models, such as Aborigines in Australia and Voodoo in Latin America that led in radically different directions.

As children grew up they used to undergo a variety of rites of passage, which initiate them into adulthood. Boys would be subjected to practices such as circumcision, subincision into the urethra, blood letting or tooth pulling. Girls would be ritually decorated and subjected to partial seclusion or food taboos. Tokenism was also important to the Aboriginal world view. In a way it represented the mythic or living beings who were seen to provide the means to access the spiritual powers of the Dreaming.
(http://www.aborigineals.culture.comac/religion.shtml/).

There is further evidence that still supports traditional practices that are actively practised by various communities without church acknowledgement or recognition and are still regarded as evil; for instance, in Buganda (Okwalura Abalongo) there is a twin celebrating ritual and among Banyarwanda (Okulya Obumyano) an equivalent to a birthday party in Western society. But the church ignores these functions and always responds at times of crisis by being baffled about what to do about the situation, which results in it antagonising individuals by describing them as possessed by evil.

Most of the worry about the domination of traditional beliefs stems from people who think that in this seemingly zero tolerance policy towards local beliefs, the ascendance of Christian beliefs to the pinnacle of historical power implied the dominance of colonial multilateralism in competition with capitalistic ideological influences. A number of communitarian civic groups in Africa that have shouted themselves hoarse about the trampling of traditional beliefs from the time of abolition to the present day, also cite the resurgence of ritualistic murder that is moving fast into society. The fear is that the implications of fake ritualistic murder seemingly point the finger at the church's objection as a lesser concern than integrating African healers into Christian teaching as a way of dealing with human rights' issues.

The challenge to African church leadership is that if politicians can go into negotiations to find a peaceful solution with their opposition, why can't African church leaders make the effort to think about integrating the traditional healing and beliefs that are their heritage? Long-term projections indicate that traditional healing beliefs will continue to challenge the African church in society, if nothing is done to look at traditional belief very seriously.

All factors most strongly associated with the influence of the past so often disarm the church when it comes to its own church members' spiritual needs. Furthermore, it is argued that the situation will continue until the church has crossed over the river Jordan and left the rest to follow in search of the living truth. The root cause of the crisis is not a problem of traditional beliefs as such, but the misuse of traditional beliefs and their abuse by unscrupulous fake individuals who hide in the guise of traditional beliefs, to which the Christian church is not willing to offer a remedy.

Chapter Nine

9.1 The Discernment of the Healing of the Holy Spirit

Let me emphasise that Christ's resurrection in the power of the Holy Spirit gives the church hope that Christians have a foretaste of his kingdom here and now and that through the church's ministry Christians shall receive his love, strength and healing touch. What form that healing touch will take, humans cannot tell. Most Africans, though, still believe that God created medicine out of the trees and shrubs in Africa, but wise white men developed them into sophisticated medicine to disguise the fact that healing powers and medicine had existed and been practised in all societies before European advanced medicine.

So far, there is abundant evidence of human healing in every society throughout human history. Evidence of these claims can be traced to the early church Fathers, for instance from Irenaeus, Origen, Justin Martyr and Tertullian to Augustine, all who have practised divine healing after the time of the Apostles. Pope Innocent is described as anointing and praying for the sick as a right that every sick believer ought to receive from the church. What is significant about healing, both in the Old and the New Testament, is that it requires faith on the part of the sufferer. (Matthew 9:2; 29:8-13; 15:28). The Bible does imply faith in God's healing power.

The early church's healing ministry was continued through the commissioning and sending out of the twelve. (Matthew 6:7-13; Matthew 10:1-5; Luke 9:1-6). Also, the Acts of the Apostles and Epistles provide clear evidence of the continuation of divine healing throughout the apostolic church and James (5:14-16) placed greater emphasis on healing the sick through the prayer of faith. This illustrates that faith helps the faithful to carry through a prolonged illness or disability; a recovery more rapid than expected is all that is his. Christ demonstrated this at Nazareth due to people's lack of faith and in Matthew (17:20) a healing was delayed because of lack of faith. However, in Africa it seems that the church's caring for the sick was restricted either on the grounds of lack of trust, or doubts about offering pastoral visits to the sick, practical friendship and intercessory prayer for troubled ones. This is the practice for some churches, especially missionary-oriented one, in which rather than enhancing their power to heal the pastoral, the focus is levelled at friendship.

Yet, in my view, it was from this period that the African church's healing ministry was sanctioned for modern medicine alone. The Christian mission seems to have had a double mission, to save Africans, but at the same to disarm African society of its ability to develop its own ideas and beliefs. In doing so, the church did not even fulfil its imperative for spiritual or physical healing as commissioned by Christ: "I tell you the truth, anyone who has faith in me will do what I have been doing. He will do even greater things than these, because I am going to the Father." (John 14:12).

That is why the pastoral church congregation's prayer has always included the provision for worshippers to intercede for sick people for whom they are concerned, but the church fails short of recognising its spiritual gifts if it fails to put them into full use for healing both individuals and human relationships. Jesus Christ commissioned his disciples to "Go into the entire world and preach the good news to all creation." (Mark 16:15-16).

On another occasion, Jesus called them to him and spoke to them in parables: "How can Satan drive out Satan?" (Mark 3:23). There is not much confusion about what Jesus is saying in these verses and it relates to all of us. When we share Christ with others God allows us to gain a deeper and greater understanding of every good thing in Christ. But the missionary church lost sight of its mission as it was handed down through Christian tradition, to recognise contextual openness in a changing society. In the view of modern psychological trends, the African church's role became simple postal visits, which lacked commitment to renewal in the Holy Spirit. Therefore, this calls for the African church to re-cultivate fresh what the New Testament teaches about its healing ministry. The church in Africa is still separated from society with regard to its ministry, for it only produces the Christian faith of double standards.

So far, recent research evidence reveals the instrumental role of conversion as mostly being aimed at the creation of fear in converts to Christianity, leading them to reject their traditional beliefs as devilish because preachers dramatised the fear of hell, which played on congregation's minds. Stressing the Christian truth as "the only way to heaven", presuming that the traditional religious beliefs were empty and that there was nothing in them (especially the determinants of their value in society), remains doubtful, despite its bias to African beliefs. This may sound as though I am a convert, which is not the case.

Brian Schwetley observed, "Furthermore, I wish to argue that the church has to recognise the fact that almost the whole ministry of Jesus Christ on earth was spent according to the New Testament healing of the sick and casting out demons, which vividly demonstrated the coming of the kingdom; and his charge to continue that ministry as the purpose of God for this world." It is therefore argued that it was necessary for the missionary church in Africa to propagate interpretative approaches for converts' understanding of God's righteousness as vital for the church message. Therefore, the righteousness of God comes as a gift, which we do not merit. (Rom.3:24; 5:15-17).

We can look at the ministry of healing as a gift and it is following the idea of equality and fairness to re-address the distortion of facts about local beliefs and practice. This distortion is the very subject under the forensic understanding of fake healers under the stimulus of the profit motive. This is surely the prevalent culture of misleading falsehoods against traditional beliefs and is why it is important for the church in this situation to re-examine the content of healing rituals to provide formal equality with the substantive quality of the treatment of traditional healers in society.

The critique of the danger of reductionism seems to have divorced itself in the real world and presents a dynamic state and cycle of being and well-being, a model of teaching that illustrates the need to accept people as they are in their society, with spiritual, mental, institutional and political life all contributing to the total person. The folly is to have preconceived, stereotypical ideas about going to Africa and to act as if they are entering a space or a forest where nobody exists and impose new structures, culture and religious beliefs.

It was totally wrong to assume that other humans have no ideas, beliefs and culture within their communities and yet colonisers and missionaries could see the evidence of social harmony where people lived with each other, within the material environment and with God. In fact, at the risk of being premature in judgement, at this stage to introduce alternative beliefs suggests that the model of Christian belief that was imposed illustrates someone who comes with a saving message when people are converted and becalmed by material needs, but not necessarily spiritual. The model of the present church reveals how little was taken in at conversion and how revisiting traditional beliefs can help to remove prejudice and bias, to understand what was forbidden as evil and treated as dangerous.

Given the rehearsed history of Christian conversion methods during which so many initiatives indicate mixed motives, including collaboration with the colonisers, this is the reason why there is a need to bring to the surface what has been kept for so long in the dark, reflecting reformed values and attitudes to health and healing in society as a right of freedom to find out whether the traditional beliefs were evil or not. This is when the church can fully know to what it is objecting, bearing in mind that for thousands of years traditional religious beliefs had existed in society before any other faith and yet had sustained and guided human lives.

Disillusioned when Arabs arrived in Africa, Africans became Muslims and when Western missionaries also came, Africans embraced everything from beliefs to culture and lifestyle. As noted earlier, the most current overpowering wave is the need for the church to consider the formal ways by which its message is disseminated to local African communities as a whole.

In a sense, it even humbles Africa as a continent to fail to develop its own beliefs, and to choose to discard its own revelatory concept of God is argued as a mistake. Look at Japan, China and India, for example. All these societies have their own beliefs, but are also open to other persuasions. In the case of Africa, there was a use of sheer dominance. It is hard to imagine how foreign religious philosophies and theologies could easily be authenticated as the word of God when the indigenous believers were indicated for extinction, or forced to operate undercover; a reason why traditional religious belief still struggles to find a place in its own society.

In general, the church needs to end the demonisation of traditional healers and be aware of the context in which this healing is vital, reversing what happened during the missionary conversion period, which was totally out of context and disarmed local people of their knowledge and the natural manifestation of healing ability or spiritual gifts. Healing is a manifestation of God's kingdom and forgiveness and the gospel shows that the kingdom is better understood as the announcement of God's reign.

Instead of burdening converts with a European style of living, the church seems to have missed a vital point of announcing God's reign, conversion representing the tradition, social and cultural backgrounds of converts to the God whose power to heal and spiritual redemption was to fulfil Jesus Christ's promises to make all things new rather than predispose people's beliefs. Christian conversion is argued as the reduction of the gospel to merely personal salvation, narrowing conceptions of what to believe where people were called to do little more than sharing some facts about Jesus and inviting others to agree with these facts.

If we turn to the Old Testament and to Christ's teaching, the Bible presents two basic views concerning healing and sickness. It is a new age in practice, which may have confused the conversion exercise. Looked at from this angle, the missionary church was a reduction of the gospel to make a form of salvation. This has led to disparity in society and failed to enhance the purposeful understanding of how Christian values promote human dignity.

In the healing ministry of Christ, faith was a dominant factor, but it is arguable that the effort of missionary conversion concentrated at masking the important values of society, tradition, beliefs and cultural backgrounds, which could contribute to people finding faith in Christianity. If it is viewed as a universal church, diversity in theology is needed to reverse past ideas of excluding anything that was not known to Europeans, for contextual theology pursues a wider vision of Christ's mission and advocates infrastructures suitable for the twenty-first-century society in Africa.

In order to facilitate social and political systems that contain a wider range of broader opportunities for citizens in chains of command and bureaucratic ladders, the issue needs to be borne in mind that colonial rule and missionary influence were not just a product of their own charisma or powers, or of the disorder caused by the confrontation between wanting to be healers and allowing other sources of healing.

This was much more the product of ideology and politics, making an "easy target" of an earlier political agenda rather than competing with unknown groups over residual doubt about their authority and the source of their power. Before the Christian arrival, traditional healers had ministered to the sick, protected the possessed from evil spirits and healed broken relationships. In my view, the church in the love of God and people can restore the traditional spiritual charisma related to spiritual gifts (inborn in traditional healers). These are manifested without any connection to human abilities, but need development and enhancement for use and should have been considered in the sense of individual gifts of the Spirit, received with thanksgiving and yet with the wisdom of discernment. (Cf. 1 Corinthians 12:1-11).

I will further argue that in every society God is not distant and that those who exercise gifts of healing in society need to be assessed on their authenticity and to be helped by the church. To be recognised fully by the church for their development, they are endowed with gifts in fulfilment of God's purpose of healing the church, in the same way as defined in the World Council of Churches' report of its Christian Medical Commission for members under supervision by church leaders. The object of the church and traditional healing must be progress towards health and wholes; whether physical, mental or spiritual in location of pathology or disorder.

The healing ministry, like the traditional healing in the past, has to be deliverance; release from evil spiritual influences operating in a person, or hindering the response to God's saving grace. This is where the argument comes from that the traditional healers' shrines should not be demolished or demonised; the healing practice must be encouraged to develop to avoid projecting church members' personal internal codes of behaviour and placing unreasonable expectations on other people.

Spiritual gifts can often become more effective if those who exercise them learn from others and accept training, but the charisma of healing is manifested in a person to equip them with experience of the power to heal. These spiritual gifts complement healing ministries, even in developed countries, especially in hospital chaplaincy. Hospital chaplains are recognised and respected and the usual courtesies are observed by hospital staff when they perform their healing ministry on the admission of patients.

Therefore, African churches have to encourage those with gifts to come forward to admission in local churches for training and mutual support and the benefit of the Christian church. Everyone involved in the healing ministry needs to have a sound grasp of the healing theology on which the Christian ministry is based. So far, the persistence of traditional beliefs and ritualism has quickly become evident and increasingly for African churches there is a need within the church for a healing church to become part of normal everyday life.

For this task to be done effectively, the church should work within itself to assess church members' views in an honest, open way, which seems to have been expressed in many ways and must not be purely consciously regarded as criticism, but seen as mainly the African formulation of knowledge about their tradition and God. Firstly, look at the whole issue of contextual theology in partnership with the Bible in the way the Old Testament God (Yahweh) alone was the source of healing, just as the traditional religious belief considered by African people as the God of life and the source of healing. Deuteronomy chapter 32 verse 39 portrays God as the direct dispenser of sickness and any disease as punishment for humankind's sin. (Cf. Number 12:9-15; Chr. 21:18-19; 26; 16-21).

In systematic theology the harmony of God's justice and love is treated primarily under the doctrine of Christ's atonement. In this process of healing, God forgives the sins of the justified on the basis of Christ's atoning death, so that Christ's death (the price paid for our sins) is a reward for us through his obedience. Therefore, the healing of spiritual sickness is prominent in the Old Testament, clearly narrated in Job and the Psalms stories and yet the motive on which Jesus Christ based the teaching accepts sickness as a consequence of the corrupt nature of humankind caused by original sin. (Romans 5:2-21).

Secondly, in the New Testament, because of faith's integral part in divine healing, wholeness is salvation in which all these words embrace what God achieved through the incarnation of Jesus Christ. In Jesus Christ he shared in his life's suffering and death on the cross and he can draw close to people in times of suffering, which means that suffering has a higher purpose in human lives.

In fact, it is not surprising that there are misconceptions about suffering. For example, in John 9 we find Jesus refuting the misconception of suffering when His disciples point to a man born blind and ask, "Who sinned, this man or his parents?" Jesus answers frankly, "Neither this man nor his parents sinned, but this happened so that the work of God might be displayed in his life." Jesus redirects their attention by pointing forward and upward with a new and different perspective.

Not all suffering is a direct result of sin. Pain has a higher purpose in human lives, which is to reveal God's glory. Suffering is meant to refine us. (John 9: 3 NIV). It is under these circumstances that society will have to realise the fact that not that everyone who goes to traditional healers necessarily enjoys going there; many go to traditional healers out of desperation.

However, Christ's death, resurrection and ascension into heaven vindicated the truth of the gospel. After the resurrection he commissioned his apostles to preach that gospel in the power of the Holy Spirit, so the church doctrine must emphasise a God who loves, who heals human lives and who is a God of justice. The early contribution of the Christian mission was to emphasise healing ministry in the world; we might say that is what the church's mission is all about.

In terms of reference to church leadership today, if we look at the situation critically, there are signs of self-defeatism, which shows stray Africans are living under submission and are easily convinced by new things and that we prefer theologies and philosophies developed elsewhere. I have recently even had Africans in Uganda who had been converted to Judaism, Hinduism and other schisms.

Through its sermons the church could make believers understand the Bible in a more culturally sensitive way. However, Francis Wijsen rightly argues that Western logic, which is based on the Aristotelian "law" of non-contradiction, is universalised too easily. Durkheim (in *The Elementary Forms of the Religious Life*) argued that the simplest and most original form of religion includes mythologies represented under many different forms. (Durkheim, Emile, The Elementary Forms of the Religious Life, London, Allen and Unwin, [1915], pp. 147-19). This is clearly the case with Gadamer's "fusion of horizons" and the "theory of communicative competence" of Habermas.

(Wijsen, F., and J. van Slageren, Missiologie-beoefening in Nederland en België, in: Wereld en Zending 27 [1998/4], 25-34).

Ideally, there is a need to identify the falsity of the distorted ideas of traditional beliefs as superstitions is not to exaggerate the repressive apparatus constantly supported by mythologies, as the indoctrination was in its essence as much characterised by lack of reason and lack of the appreciation of local values and respect for their concept of God that made local converts suspicious.

It is argued that no matter what changes were introduced into some of these revelations that have distorted their originality, the key to understanding is the extent to which conversion and colonialism colluded with Christianity. Under this influence, the attitude was born that African people who are illiterate are predominantly traditional religious believers and their concept of God was a revelation of a backward society, which had to be abolished. Therefore, converting the (heathen) inhabitants was both to civilise them out of their ignorance and save them from famine and disease.

It is certainly fair and possibly accurate to say so, but there are bound to be some areas that remained free from distortion and thus are common to many African spiritual needs. This is why many years later, African converts to Christianity began to compare Christian teaching about the revelation of God, trying to discover parallels with the African traditional religious concept of God to see the European influence of the Bible or the influence of Judaeo-Christian thought.

The criticism here is that to bring change does not mean to wipe out what existed, because the fact is that whether traditional religious beliefs were bad or good, they did not deserve to be distorted and demonised rather than modified. If Christianity was sufficient, methodologically speaking, it could have reformed traditional beliefs and practices, which does not mean to destroy, but to help make perfect. In effect, the changes that were made in the name of Christian morality in conversion were being irresponsible to society and, indeed, were extremely destructive of the norms and social arrangements that had existed as moral restraints on society. The lack of acceptance of people's cultural, religious concepts, social arrangements and differences and not treating Africans in a manner appropriate to each individual argues that change needed to be normalised and embraced. Yet what was embraced had not been felt and fully understood as both lacking and desired in society. For instance, take the example of when roads and public highways were constructed in Africa: there was no need for a campaign for using them. They were an obvious necessity for people.

Bishop Sangu once said at the fourth Synod of Bishops in Rome in 1974 that "too many innovations are the work of missionaries, who, disregarding the great traditions of the continent, wanted to change things after their own ideas." (See "Wesen Und Wahrheit Der Religion", p.166).

In this case, it is arguable that the good work of missionaries missed the point as a result of a failure to try to see the positive benefits of the diverse backgrounds and life experience and to obtain insights from local people's point of view. However, missionary work evidently started from its own premises, with the attitudes of its cultural social order transmitted in conversion, which needs urgent attention and calls for local cultural consciousness to retrain those who mount the pulpits to preach, to put right the distortion of people's beliefs and culture.

The predominant church approach from the theoretical assumptions of the missionary teachings used in church preaching still hangs on the past biblical interpretations, which stem from too much of the former and too little of the latter. Today, the peculiar dilemma may well be for the church in Africa that there are long-held assumptions about traditional beliefs, which must be confessed and that either fear or ignorance may be holding church leaders from engaging with traditional medium men and women to make grand proclamations of their commitment. The challenge to the church is to respond without a repeat of the condemnation, but having to talk in an appropriate way to people who need genuine action, love, support, help and commitment where so often social responsibility fades into oblivion.

The church's response to this challenge is more complicated, with both problems of being misunderstood by church members and yet an opportunity for a role of caring to resolve the past distortions of traditional beliefs. The church has to realise that its role in society is caring for humanity in a holistic way, but you cannot care for someone by avoiding, or not dealing with, conflict or the anxiety of people in the church in general. It may be that the appropriate first response is to listen and learn and to reflect on what needs to change in order for the church in society to be become caring and supportive.

Secondly, there is an aspect of traditional believers' experience of healing powers, which are sometimes described as a gift. In some way the epidemic of corruption in society may have produced fake healers in a wake of economic pressure leading to numerous social problems, which has an effect on Christian communities as well.

Thirdly, there are many things that churches could be doing in terms of facing the issues and experiences that are producing a resurgence of traditional beliefs: helping to educate society, creating awareness of fake healers (including traditional healers) and challenging corrupt behaviours where people abuse their beliefs and practices.

The central mission for the church is to use a cultural body of knowledge and language that does not replicate the past to isolate traditional beliefs and believers and is thought to be inclusive and relevant. It needs at least to end the blindness of denying the existence of traditional beliefs through correcting the way that past cultural values were embedded in society. The church must realise that traditional beliefs are posing a challenge and are here to stay. For the church to be effectively excluded from the new age of society and to realise the fact that it was a great mistake to keep denying and doubting the role of traditional beliefs in society, as yet a continual denial offers no practical solution for moral deterioration. An impartial theological truthfulness is urgently required from African church leaders or theologians. Ironically, some converts and missionaries agree with this urgency for African church theology. Maybe through diplomacy, romanticism or possibly naivety, church leaders in Africa continue to teach the denial of the African divine revelation of God in the context of Africans' own thinking.

In traditional religious beliefs, unlike Christianity, it is noted that the concept and doctrine of divine beings and entities elevate both men and women to the same level and role, as among Africans, where religious symbolism in traditional religious beliefs is both male and female. Thus it was easily conceived by African Christianity when the Christian church opted to ordain women to the priesthood without objection and opposition; where objection occurred it was more to do with outside doctrinal influence. African women for centuries had qualified to serve as healers, exorcists, witches and sorcerers and still officiate in offerings and sacrifice, though there are some high level rituals in most African traditional ceremonies that are only led and officiated by men.

No doubt traditionalist believers have a profoundly strong argument to demand equal rights. For instance, for a long time they have opted to remain silent on the polygamy issue. If the church can take the trouble to commission an independent survey, it would be surprised to discoverer that among every 100 church members, three quarters are polygamists or concubines and frequently consult traditional healers. As if it were not a cultural problem to try to distinguish between what was regarded as essentially Christian and "merely" European culture, it is essential to go beyond cultural boundaries to ask what had determined human action before. Christianity persistently preached against traditional religious beliefs and practice, but there was evidence of the contrary. It is in my view that the weak link between the church and societal reality is a cause of the ineffectiveness of Christianity in human lives.

It is therefore argued that wrong elements of society searching for wealth have moved into the secret ritualistic practice to deceive people. Traditional healers were forced by Christian conversion to live under the shadow of the traditional beliefs and practice of secret ritualistic healing. Therefore, against this background, the genuine Christian identity still seems to be in search of its ground and to be caught in the battle lines of identity drawn with earlier beliefs. Of course, in the conversion period converts were convinced that outside the church there was no salvation and without it life was less propitious.

As Christianity divided into rival churches, it was often believed that the church's mission consisted also of the evangelising. It was believed that the appropriate targets of mission were "heathens" of various sorts. But considering the theological confusion and traditions, some converts began to doubt who was right and who was false, whereas, through observation, another group taught that salvation was through faith, in baptism and for good works.

During the conversion period there were contradictions about salvation, as one Christian group taught that converts were saved by grace and argued that through the design of the atonement, Christ as a sacrificial lamb was for everyone and all would be saved. In the end, each of these ideas led to confusion where these teachings sounded similar to African traditional religious glorification of God. Therefore, there was a misconception that salvation was perceived in society as a focus for changing people to serve a new European God.

Thus one can argue that if the church does not change in the long run, it will be changed. I will be quick to add that the church in Africa has to stop living in pretence and being ignorant of the reality, as if monogamist marriages were the only means of salvation. If the church can look back to Old Testament times, or around in the world community of faiths, does this mean that all these populations who are not Christians are destined for hell? Let's call a spade a spade and agree that hell and purgatory are petty doctrines that were simply developed to create fear for eternal disbelievers, but in this case we refer to believers in God.

Does it mean that there are no more deadly evils institutionalised in Christianity that exploit human lives and corrupt people's minds than polygamy? The African church's negligence in its misjudgement of the functionary role of societal arrangements raises a serious question, which suggests a need for fundamental Christian reform to restore trust and confidence.

Of course, an African cultural problem that has to be tackled as it has in Western Christianity is that Christians in Africa have shown solidarity with their own gay and lesbian communities. It is the Christian responsibility to realise that people don't simply wake up and accept strange cultures, but they must be recognised by society as part of its beliefs and culture. There is no way you can impose a culture on another culture and it be accepted. Christian teaching in society needs to be carefully examined by open-minded people to root out church teaching whose persecution of traditional believers goes beyond the church building.

Where old identities were replaced by new ones they developed around the assumption of patterns of new beliefs and new cultures, which weakened the local community's unity. The reasons for suggesting integration of the old in the new is to create an open forum for religious dialogue, which seeks to repair broken bridges over the loss of the African true identity and the stigma of traditional beliefs and to analyse how African values were falsified.

Cautiously incorporating beliefs and culture evidently remains critical, because it is very difficult for the Christian faith to provide equitable access to development opportunities where the church still maintains its judgemental attitude referring to traditional practices as devilish, does not find an end to discrimination and prolongs a hostile relationship. Very often those who try to step outside the lines of a paradigm shift lack the meaningful language to do so and it is argued that success will depend on the adoption of what politicians, actors, philosophers, sociologists and mathematicians have long had to develop: some sort of meta-language in an attempt to talk over and about what is taken for granted as common sense.

Studies conducted over several decades have documented the far-reaching changes over generations, especially concerning the religious dialogue that is required between Christianity and the traditional religions. A positive role is to find methods of learning how to use these different and rich religious practices for people's own purposes to internalise the representations they use and create meanings in the formation of their own understanding and interpretation of their world.

Whether it is accepted or not, cultural and psychological variables determine and predispose certain metaphysical beliefs. Through the Israelites' relativism of their history and the nature of saving power in their history, the God of Israel is revealed as a God of righteousness, who acts rightly in all His works and judgement. (Gen. 18:25). Therefore, the old concept of righteousness is closely linked with God's judgement. (Pss.50:6; 143:2).

This is why, while Christianity is important, there must be a truly justified reason why the African church does not seriously appreciate the culture and revelation of God to legitimise its own traditional beliefs as part of self-emancipation. God judges equitably; and does not forsake the righteous, and the judges of Israel were commanded to act accordingly to his example. (Exod. 23:7).

In the context of Christ incarnate, church teaching is perhaps crucial and we must argue that the church appears to have put an emphasis on Puritanism, which produces differentiation. It is this message that was seen by African people as the reason for abolishing their cultural practices, as if it was aimed in particular at establishing new religious structures and boundaries. As such, it is contrary to the grace of God, which transcends all boundaries in order to bring all humanity into one in Christ. In the opposite way, missionaries chose to pick some portions of the Bible and in some instances ignored others. The choosing of New Testament salvation thinking is simply a hangover from European culture and the missionary failure to fully seize on the Gospel of grace can be observed in other areas, of which slavery is an example.

The crucial point remains, however, that the church's purity rules historically have tended to exclude some from the community of believers and potentially from the grace of God and this plainly excluded traditional believers, since the biblical teaching is known as God's macro story of redemption. On the other hand, the Old Testament forbids contact between the "unclean" and the "holy" (Lev.15:31); and anyone who is defiled, whether deliberately or not, cannot take part in sacrificial worship. (1Sam.20:26). This should not be seen as depriving the Bible of its spiritual dimension in terms of the necessary biblical interpretation, in this case citing an example that represents the African contextual revelation of God.

9.2 African Experience

In what sense may truth be designed as a value or an end in itself? This question is generally believed to date from the time just after the exile from Israel, when the Jewish community was struggling to re-establish itself and there were great dangers from external pressure and internal conflicts. (Cf. Wijsen, F., and J. van Slageren, Missiologie-beoefening in Nederland en België, in: Wereld en Zending 27 [1998/4], 25-34).

In order to avoid getting caught up in the theological differences that may arise from definitions, it could be argued that the intention of the constructive idea of truth as a value was simply to draw attention to the importance of acquiring knowledge. For the sake of clarity on truth, the designation of the appreciation of one's inherent moral and cultural pattern of values may give profound satisfaction to the contemplative mind. This is further argued as a long-term strategic idea of dominance based on theories of superiority to give the power of knowledge to rule Africans.

Such ethnocentric theories were the methodology during colonialism and the missionary period and applied the concept of black genetic inferiority to degrade black beliefs and culture. What is overlooked in this type of church persistence on missionary teachings is recognisable from the start, as they seemed to have had preconceived ideas about their mission to the colonies. This is seen as the reason the missionary denial of an African revelation of God is argued as having been part of the agenda of a European concept aimed at promotion of sweeping changes through Christian conversion, without a proper assessment of what ought to change.

If they had weighed up the advantages and disadvantages, they could have either reduced the peril or not endangered society in the long run. But the trouble was the one-sided claim of revelation with its biased, preconceived ideas on the basis of which traditional beliefs were distorted by Christian missionary doctrines imported during this period of colonisation.

On the other hand, we can't help viewing missionary activities from the inception of their mission in Africa as operating under assumptions of change, control and domination and these three will be discussed throughout this section. This reason is that there seems to have been a hidden agenda of a mixture of the control and dominance ideas of colonial ideology, which is suggestive of how neatly colonial ideology was incorporated in church doctrine to intoxicate converts with negative messages about their heritage.

It is even sensible to argue that the missionary messages transmitted through conversion subscribed to the colonial policies and ideological theories that led the church to consider it appropriate to abolish traditional religious beliefs, and why they could not accommodate or redefine traditional religion to integrate it in church teachings and worship as elsewhere. Obviously, the denial of any removal suggests that the missionary process of inquiry required sober minds and it is seen as the required task of the church today to trace the underlying assertion or assumptions, but not factual historical causes which may be a combination of different factors. One of these is the assumptions used in racism as "people who are fundamentally different from one another", creating superficial differences that require to be transcended in society. Kimball, quoted by David Roach, argues that it was inaccurate for Christians to claim that one must believe in divinity through a foreign culture to have a correct understanding of God. (Cf. Roach David July 2003).

The use of differences deliberately undermined other people's beliefs and cultural values, but what suits one person may not suit another. It is therefore argued that the Christian church's role today is to develop contextual biblical teaching using common knowledge of the people, who benefit from sending the right message to the right address; people who are there and talking to them with regard to their own situation and requirements.

In retrospect, it is incredible that the inconsistency between the legitimating Christian practice and accumulation and speculation was invisible in a society that was formerly true to the values of mutual respect, caring and love that Christians have learnt from Christ. The view of Christian growth and benefits is worth summarising here. Firstly, how do I know that God is personal, someone to talk to, who personally reveals His nature through Christ? Through the Cross, humankind has a way straight through to God. Biblical teaching helps in understanding and growing a reverence for God, who is constantly ready and real in human struggles for salvation. As people encounter the God of Scripture who establishes and keeps his covenant promises with His people, we see something of God's majesty.

However, in Africa the fault lies not with traditional religion, but rather within historical strategic instruments of change used in the colonial era, which were put in place to abolish every unfamiliar cultural practice and people's beliefs. It is this notion of being agents of change that reinforced superiority theories in a situation where people were weak and fundamentally different in cultural perspective; the missionaries were probably prevented by their own culture and beliefs of superiority from allowing the integration of traditional religious belief and their development. Some of the models followed by enthusiasts for conversion to Christianity were dangerous to society and fed into unrealistic expectations. As such, they helped colonialism to implement its ideological conceptions against the will of people who were concerned about everything of value to local communities being done away with.

Nevertheless, engaging in a debate on the proposed sequence of localising traditional beliefs is not going to be easy. Of course, the local sequences of culture have doubters and advocates such as Brian Schwertley, who argues, "You need to ask yourself seriously: Should I trust the salvation of myself and my family to a church which changes its doctrine to cater to the surrounding culture (e.g., Vatican II), when biblical doctrine never has and never will change? Should I trust my place in eternity to a church which explicitly denies the biblical doctrine of salvation (e.g., Council of Trent)? Are you willing to read the Bible and obey what it says, even when it runs contrary to what your family and friends believe? Jesus said that you must love and serve Him more than your own family, even more than your own self." (Lk. 14:26). (CF. Council of Trent, 25th sess. [1563]; Baltimore Catechism, sec. XIV, no. 181, p. 129; cf. the Council of Trent, 25th sess. Heresies of Rome, as quoted by Woodrow, p.71;.Schwertley Brian, p.1).

Nevertheless, Leonard argues that when talking about a pluralistic environment, critics invariably quote John's gospel: "I am the way, the truth, and the life", which is fine, but if we're going to be literal about that, then let's trade literalism and read Matthew 25, because in Matthew 25, there's a suggestion that on that great getting up morning, the "ones who are welcomed into the Kingdom are those who fed the hungry, clothed the naked, visited the sick." And in doing that, the text says, even when they didn't know it, they were Christians. (Cf. John 6:44). (Roach David, July 2003).

However, whether the church admits it or not, these denials are often closely related to instruments of colonisation that forged a conversion philosophy to enslave or dominate and control African colonies in several spheres of life, leading to a loss of will to develop their traditional beliefs and their own salvation and move out of the dominant colonial shackles of powers. (Cf. Joseph Zacchello, Secrets of Romanism. Neptune, NJ: Loizeaux Brothers, 1948).

We could examine some important Roman Catholic doctrines in the light of the Bible and determine if these doctrines are in harmony with, or contrary to, the clear teaching of God's Word. Because the Roman Catholic Church believes (as does the author) that the Bible is the inspired, infallible Word of God, all good Roman Catholics should study the Bible for themselves and abide by its teachings. As Pope Pius XII stated, "To ignore the Scripture is to ignore Christ." (Schwetley Brian, p.1).

The object of the scriptures is simply to reinforce the obvious, but well-hidden fact, that considering it necessary to abolish people's beliefs and culture was based on the introduction of a superior religion and culture, which leads me to conclude that the approach was totally wrong as it had a longlasting effect on African society at large. And since then, the evidence of this has been the relationship between the traditional beliefs and the church, which has continued (and continues) to be ill defined.

When it comes to the question of assessing how African traditional beliefs and practices were demonised and are still distorted to the present day, it becomes impossible to think of reform and alternatives to traditional healers' current practice. In the chapters that follow, I will therefore primarily use interchangeable phrases such as bias, stereotyping and prejudice towards African beliefs, ideas of God and cultural practices.

What needs consideration is the apparatus applied by the missionaries. Firstly, the theory of doctrinal change played the role of negating influences and domination in the way traditional religion was treated as devil worship or satanic powers of darkness, which the Christian church maintained in its teaching was related to the mythology claims of truth monopoly and seen as determined by the functional role to change from the so-called darkness into light (redemption) of pagans.

Secondly, even after independence Christianity in Africa maintained the same teaching whereby the church in Africa refused to baptise children whose parents were either not married in the church, or owned traditional religious shrines. This illustrates the fact that the methods used could have contributed to later developments and were responsible for the weaker commitment to the Christian faith.

The fact that those who had access to missionaries also had access to such benefits created a relationship between religion and material products. While others used baptism as an incentive for social services, if the child was not baptised, he or she could not be offered a place in a Christian schools and several other social services were often denied on the grounds of not being baptised. As a result, individuals who needed these services denounced their traditional beliefs, those who practised healing as mediums were forbidden to practise, and husbands in polygamous marriages were forced to separate from their wives, or were excommunicated by the church. These converts became distanced or semi-detached from the society in which they lived. This caused enormous pain to families who were separated from their children and wives they loved and who had committed no offence, just a value set by the rules of having “a wife of the ring”. (Taylor, J. V., 1958).

It is painful and embarrassing to think that the church would separate families, yet it was required if people wanted to become a true follower of Christ. The reality is that it would have made a great impact to accept the converted rather than for the church to push them out. So the church’s teaching could have welcomed God’s holy intrusion into a convert’s life and encouraged submission to God and in their Christian performance, rather than spending more time splitting up families.

Drawing on the methods of conversion, the approach still reflects an earnest endeavour to develop more effective weapons to erase African identity. It was soon realised that individuals needed some social support for their conversion, so the “salvation of souls” approach was supplemented by the expansion of Christian services such as education and European modern medicine. In practice this meant transplantation of European culture to the mission countries. In these services, Christianity gained greater influence than religious belief at this period, when it owned hospitals, schools and church teaching missions financed by missionary societies abroad. Both point to the influence of financial gains, since even after independence financial support continued from missions abroad, with grants and donations creating a dollar culture for continued

Christian influence in spiritual awakening influence in Africa.

Conversion and baptism were accompanied by the tokenism of privileges for civil employment: to obtain employment, the colonial administration had imposed conditions for providing evidence that people were baptised and married in the church. Furthermore, Kofi Asare Opuku observes that although the agents of the missionary enterprise have changed, the assumption of superiority persists, albeit in modified form, in the evangelistic work of fundamentalist groups, some indigenous African churches, as well as the mission-founded churches. (Kofi Asare Opuku in the Baobab Tree of Truth: Reflections of Religious Pluralism in Africa, ©2000 World Council of Churches).

It was most recently apparent that some African theologians realise that due to the forces of history, the masses became more educated, at least to an extent. Yet converts were set against their own communities from the moment of conversion and were regarded as traitors to their own customs, cultural values and society. Relevance to their own culture was extremely limited and as for going to the heart of the social order, the emphasis of the Christian church's teaching was on the denial of traditional beliefs.

Even after independence, Christianity in Africa pursued the official line of teaching under which the social system was financed and supported by grants or donations, which created a dollar culture in which the superstructure of religion was nurtured and maintained. The attitude of many church leaders was to seek prominent positions of leadership in society while resisting the integration of traditional beliefs, which objectively eats away at possibilities and is a major influence to those who listen to them and admire their status in society.

In those examples when it is assumed that religious beliefs are a "natural" form of human relation with the Supreme Being, the issue of concern was how this could be communicated to society. It is indeed very difficult to avoid the conclusion that the Christian conversion followed the European cultural and social order whose influence extended across the entire practice of Christianity, paying so little relationship to the real world of converts. It is a sad reminder of the distorted missionary dominance of some humans that the most absurd prejudices continue to exist, but suppressing traditional beliefs is not the answer. That will only succeed in people masking their true sentiments and will make martyrs of those who are persecuted.

Where two different visions of the centre of inquiry exist, condemnatory preaching should be confronted not by the church's censorship, but openly by the outraged public, who can freely express their justifiable condemnation of ritualistic murder purely originating from the abolition of traditional religious beliefs, which had nothing to do with claimed truth.

The church needs to realise the truth of the old adage that we can dwell on the past, we can learn from the past, but we can't live in the past. The consequence of understanding the past will have a wide influence on missionary teaching. Huge masses of people were converted to Christianity, sometimes by persuasion or witness and occasionally by coercion. Note, for instance, Charlemagne's repeated baptism of the Saxons. (http://www.interfaithdialog.org/reading-room/the-problem-mission-and-or-dialogue.html/1/10/09).

For instance, basic flaws in the methodology of conversion presented entirely outside cultural values, which demonstrates how little consideration there was of the issues people were facing. At the start, it looked like a great waterfall running into every corner of society, but the most crucial point was that there was little realisation at the time that it had led many converts to live a double life.

For converts who had families, it was hard for them to abandon their families, especially leaving children without care and they had to prevent their wives from turning to prostitution. This is why conversion had a double effect. An action that has two effects, one good and the other bad, may be permissible if the good effect is the one that is intended and the bad effect is merely an unwanted consequence of achieving the good effect. However, in this sense polygamy was justifiable in African culture; the economy was almost entirely agrarian. In this context, polygamy was viewed as a social necessity in order to ensure continuation of society and to provide for the needs of the many women who might otherwise never enjoy the status and benefits that accompany becoming a mother and a bearer of children and are thus a vital link to the ancestors. Wars between groups often resulted in the reduction of the male population, thus females usually outnumbered males. In fact, culturally unmarried women risked social humiliation without a husband and children and so the system sought to provide for the needs of everyone in society.

African polygamy, it is usually argued, at least sought to shoulder extra social responsibilities as a man progressed through life, in contrast to the version of polygamy currently found in western countries, wherein the modern serial polygamist divorces his wife and marries others in succession, all the while seeking to avoid his social responsibilities by shirking his alimony payments and striving to dodge child support payments whenever possible. This practice has become so ubiquitous that it presents a challenge to the western legal system, which has become overburdened in its efforts to track down "deadbeat dads", and must create new laws to cope with the new societal acceptance of cohabitation without marriage, such as "palimony" laws. (Ian D. Ritchie African Theology and the Status of Women in Africa presented to the *Canadian Theological Society*, 25th May 2000).

Perhaps there is a general truth about social psychology in desperate circumstances: people are more likely to regard the institutions hostile to their own society with a lukewarm reception, particularly if it is widely believed that the institutions are responsible for their circumstances. In Ephesians, Paul lays out of the foundation of marriage as being rooted in mutual love and submission: "Wives, submit to husbands as to the Lord" and "Husbands, love your wives, just as Christ loved the church and gave himself up for her." (Ephesians 5:22, 25, NIV).

Nevertheless, note also that Paul begins this chapter with the charge to "Be imitators of God", another reference to the disposition described in Philippians chapter two. If our attitude is to be the same as that of Christ Jesus (Romans 6:4), then consider how Jesus responds to his frequently unfaithful bride, the church. Despite the undertaking in the baptism, which means crucifying the old, this even today is unlikely for church members. However, for converts in this desperate situation, some gave wholeheartedly to the conversion, but the majority of converts were unable to do so sincerely to an institution that seemed so exploitive. Some at best gave sullen and pathetic allegiance out of no choice.

The accounts of most surviving African observers of this period show that they experienced internalised conversion with suspiciousness, which was a product of the need to keep a look-out for signs of trouble, potential danger and culture clash. For those poor souls who walk in darkness, there is no chance of assuming the self-denying character of Christ; but for those whom Christ has made alive, there is the all-sufficient well of grace. It is to Christ that the Christ-follower must go with his "irreconcilable differences", not to anyone else. But it is arguable that it is only Christ who reconciles the unrighteous with the righteous and it is only Christ who can reconcile.

However, the stereotype (bias) became a self-fulfilling mission, as converts with a new culture led them to denounce their own culture as evil and to self-claimed freedom from the past; a vicious cycle of deviance amplification. The process of conversion needed to develop a finely grained biblical interpretation associated with what was meant by the cognitive, affective and volitional elements of the personal life of the real social world, so that the Christian mission could have had that fundamental local characteristic of Old Testament anthropology, the awareness of handling the culture, local beliefs and daily living of a wide range of many different contexts, without losing the Christian teaching in any encounter.

It is furthermore necessary for missionaries to realise that people's thinking is being evoked in the environment they are in and that they are not only a body plus a soul, but a living unit in a vital culture and they are a psychological being. In the physiological world, the stereotyping of others is the subject of many critiques. Therefore, signs of stereotyping are used as a religious tool to detract people from suspiciousness; since then they have become an endemic process marked with a cultural flow down to the unreal world in the Christian view, where it is unnecessary to divide people and continue to polarise people into different camps.

Jesus Christ once cautioned his disciples that if a country divides itself into groups that fight each other, that country will fall apart. (Mark 3:24). Such divisions have existed for so long and continue to drive people farther and farther away from each other, dividing families and communities as the fruits of Western impact on African society. (Cf. F.B. Welbourn, 1965:145).

In the real world of an African, it was vital to realise that every group has a culture of its own, but not so that no comparisons could be drawn, or where even the same form of culture different concepts could be found. Many presuppositions – at least concerning religion – are based on theories formulated in the past. What Christian conversion needed at this period was often ignored by the fact that to change lives you need first to understand people's tradition, culture and their beliefs. Arguably, this made it psychologically even more dangerous for converts.

On this issue there was a striking shift in the prevailing view among communities in various types of social conduct. It was a period marked by a cultural shift where polygamist wives were forced to be abandoned by their husbands through the church's emphasis on New Testament monogamist marriage. Generally speaking, the battle lines drawn between earlier converts who emphasised drastic change argued that it could have been avoided through assimilating tendencies among communities. In this aspect, consideration of local beliefs and culture was a powerful endurance factor in social life.

Let us try to recognise some home truths in the conversion methodology and have an honest debate about the misconceptions over Christian converts' experience, because there can be no double lives in the truth. Of course, in the eyes of missionaries with their Victorian moral Christian values, it sounded odd to live with more than one wife. But what we should not forget is that polygamist marriage had played a number of important roles in these societies; particularly in an agricultural society without welfare (social security), polygamist cultural marriage prevented hunger and prostitution. A man who had several wives and a number of children was highly respected in society for his success in the community. This is why the general consensus is that family breakdown across communities today is a factor that be attributed to the changes and that its avoidance could have played a key role in preventing antisocial behaviour in local communities. Furthermore, it is arguable that societies in Africa at this period of conversion to Christianity were sleepwalking into a future disaster when a culture of monogamy was introduced. Prostitution was introduced out of these new arrangements, while it was inevitable that men found it hard to separate from their wives and children and were forced to live according to a double standard.

A list of rules to follow left converts' minds dominated by European cultural thinking, likes, order and routine, blanketed with religious contradictions. There is some comfort, I guess, in being able to assess converts' commitment to Christianity and performance according to a set standard of values. Obeying these rules was a sign of doing OK and following the right steps in righteousness. But, as far as one can argue, there is one big problem with that line of thinking. It tended to redirect converts' focus from what really matters: the condition of one's heart, not public exhibition.

Jesus identified this as a problem with a group of religious people called the Pharisees and it didn't make Him happy. In fact, He reserved His harshest comments for those people whose insides didn't look anything like their outsides. That makes us wonder if the Pharisees were well intentioned. Did they really want to serve God and thought they were by following the rules? Or was it more of a power play to gain respect? Either way, Jesus split open their pretty packaging and revealed the ugliness of their hearts, just like He rebukes us today.

It seems that God continually brings believers to the end of their endurance, both emotionally and physically, to reveal the truth about the human heart. What is revealed in those moments of conversion pressure is usually something that needs consideration, like self-interest, insecurity, exploitation or manipulation.

It is arguable that being split apart isn't pleasant. It is therefore the inconsiderate approach of the process of conversion that undoubtedly reveals the truth that this period brought rapid revolution to a society that was unprepared for both positive and negative, but massive and sweeping social changes. At the same time, society was modernised and industry erected in the form of new communities, where unmarried young men from rural areas moved to urban areas in search of employment; they stayed away from their families longer because they indulged in other relationships, since there were plenty of available separated (freed) ex-married women. It was a situation that subsequently and unknowingly had introduced official prostitution into society. If the church wishes to restore moral values, it has to start from here. The condemnation of prostitution is an empty phrase if it is not accompanied by an appropriate solution to what went wrong from the start of the Christian advent in African society.

Chapter Ten

Contextual Theology

10.1 To Develop a Pastoral Theology

In earlier chapters a distinction was drawn between bad and good missionary teaching that failed to appreciate the nature of traditional beliefs and culture. The task here seems to lie in an exploration of what kind of theology is most needed today. This suggests that modern society needs to respond on various new challenges, which to an extent have blinded the church so that it does not see the actual danger in the real context of sin. Karoli Ssemogerere rightly observed that churches "that combined their ministry with serving as apologists for the regime through receipt of gifts and offering of political support are struggling to reach their flocks consistently." (Karoli Ssemogerere, article, Daily Monitor, 17th September 2009).

Therefore, the rejection of the fundamental premise and case for objectivity in the church's mission is that to an extent it has weakened its evangelism to certain communities or, in other words, it is restricting its own mission in the world. In my view, the immediate need for the church would be to assess what kind of theology can respond especially to these questions: (a) the fear of insecurity; (b) how to end corruption in society and (c) the question of abolished traditional religious practice and the hidden culture that has prevented the church from accessing all the above areas and has led to it hiding behind a few Bible verses to evade reasoning.

It is, therefore, arguable that until the church can engage society in the facts that face people, it will not be able to fulfil Christ's mission to the world. Whether or not many people object to the idea of integrating traditional religious beliefs into Christianity, the disagreements will not remove the fact that these same people were deliberately divided on the grounds of particular interest. Informed Africans were worried at these developments that maintained outside cultures, imported beliefs and local beliefs, which kept one generation apart from the other without integration of the past into the present.

It is therefore argued that if nothing is done and church teaching continues to exaggerate differences, it is predictable that in the long run the church will defeat itself and gradually church teaching is likely to become less effective and irrelevant to certain groups in society. There are already groups of people who are puzzled and wondering what is happening in the church, with fake churches preaching and glorifying wealth rather than Christ and yet there has been no firm reaction from the church, which the public sees as Christian inaction. This is what has turned society itself to feel suspicious about churches, which seem to offer instant conversion in a highly charged, emotional atmosphere and leave others to pick up the pieces.

What the church needs to do is first restore the distorted teaching on demonisation and respond to worries about the prevailing culture, which needs to hear the church's message that Christ came into the world to save all who believe in God. The African yearning for God would identify them with Christ and would lessen the hold of the despised African beliefs in God before the advent of missionaries. This sounds like a good approach and doing so would help to heal the past and restore in the present the validity of traditional religious values, as well as improving the church's image, which is so often portrayed as not caring about those with divergent views.

The reason why for so long mission churches in Africa have avoided looking closely at society and congregations to discern their needs, is because they have a fear of the increasing human tensions and confusion of so many in our ever-changing society. Considerations such as these have led many to despair of a search for alternative salvation, especially when the church, instead of helping towards their needs, opts to condemn them. All this self-defeating activity has to end. The church needs to realise and put emphasis on developing a theological framework that caters for these challenges, in which it can consolidate various needs and bridge broken relationships in communities to restore people's trust, to reduce fear and to promote moral values.

So far, the consensus is that the church needs to prioritise theology that appeals to the human predicament in society, instead of maintaining its negative condemnation of what it seems not to understand. The best way is to stop shying away from its responsibility to help society by finding out what attracts certain people to ritualistic practices, as a way to heal the past and address the grievances of traditional religious believers. At the same time, it needs to develop the level of its theological concept towards salvation to ensure it is relevant to people's environment and social organisation. In fact, traditional African prayers individually and collectively do combine human love with God's love and human will with his will, so it is vital to translate traditional religious beliefs into theological diversity. Another way of putting the same thing is to ask whether theoretical relativists have ever really considered the heights and depths of African traditional religious virtues in society.

An important role for the church is to acknowledge people's customs and traditional practices as harmonious with biblical teaching, for instance in healing practices. The church has to take seriously the warning of Christ against superficiality and concentration on externalities. (Matt. 15:19).

Let us consider a situation where the social order is not upheld. Any repressive regime that uses force to suppress the feelings of the people does not only violate the social contract, but also calls for public abhorrence of the same and total withdrawal of their trust. Try to imagine a wise rationality in society where people have socially contracted moral norms and governing customary rules within institutions that protect them while following their wishes, pitted against people who arrive and condemn every rule and belief that has had meaning and protected society for centuries.

Since out of the heart proceed evil thoughts, these are the deeds that are evidenced in ritual murder. As a last resort, the church needs to recognise the African tradition and Christian worship, which for centuries has always laid hands on the head of someone who is sick. As far as the church is concerned, it only intercedes for the sick and customarily addresses the Father through the Son and in the power of the Holy Spirit. This action in the church originates from the Old and the New Testament, which is why in many instances it is similar to the African approach in traditional healing, when they call on the ancestors; fathers, mothers and spirits.

Alexandere Kimenyi in Rwanda noted that Christians' intercessory prayer, in which the church refers to God, is similar to the familiar "Supreme Being" and so they drew freely on such ideas in the process of elaborating their conception of the Supreme Being. (Kimenyi, A., [1989], pp. 47-48).

It was a justification for people's belief in God that they had so many words to describe His existence. David Roach quoted James Leo Garret Jr. saying that names and titles of God are indeed important, but the reality they represent or that associated with them is even more important. (Roach David, July 2003).

In Kinyarwanda, mythological names are symbolic and represent God as He is seen, or felt, in the real circumstances of daily living. In fact, missionaries held misconceptions about African traditional beliefs and the African concept of God, because wider evidence proves that God had revealed Himself/Herself to people in similar ways; for instance, the Akans of West Africa have the same "high" reverence for God as the Banyarwanda (Imana), Gikuyu or Kikuyu (Mogai) and Baganda (Katonda). He is commonly referred to by all these people as Akans (Nyame) from West Africa. While in contrast in Katonda, we find Butonda and Mukasa Lubale owe Nyanja knows everything on land and at sea.

Historically speaking, all divine revelations are arguable as proceeding symbolically from a conception of the one God, when He is considered omnipotent and omniscient. The Akans have several "praise names", which vary according to His numerous attributes. Even with human distortions throughout history, some parallels are bound to exist. If God is universal, God is also perceived as an active being who manifests Himself through what He does. (http://colanmc.siu.edu/BAS495/students/chris/ghweb.html).

For example, Africans use various names and attributes for God. These names were used while praying to the Supreme Being during times of worry and need. Christians in Africa still use them, especially when making supplications for the health of someone who is ill. Issues arise, however, over whether the accommodation of earlier beliefs constitutes a new basis for their importance. A lasting belief rested on how traditionally valuable they were and still are, especially at celebrations. Regarding this issue, there has been a steady increase in the use of such names as Nsengimana (I pray to God), Nsengeyunva (I pray to the one who listens), Habimana (God exists) (Kimenyi, A., [1989], pp. 47 – 51) and Ryangombe, which is a "praise-name" of the ruler of everything that is.

From names like those above and from proverbs and other sayings, we may conclude that Africans had a concept of a personal, invisible and living Supreme Being, from whom all life comes. In this respect, there is evidence of persistent traditional belief. According to African mythological stories, God conversed with people long ago. (Loewen, Jacob, Vol.16n. 4, July-August, [1969], p. 147).

Therefore, in Kinyarwanda, it is argued that he withdrew from them because of their wickedness. This is evidence that a belief in separation was very much a guiding principle and was part of people's restraint in their daily conduct to resist bad decisions, to catch the eye of the public and to observe their actions and what they do and say to others. In fact, there are many stories in Kinyarwanda about the separation of God and man, which explain death as a crucial element of traditional religion.

This is why the need has risen to assess how Christianity in Africa guides society to help people make decisions that may affect them and assist others to live a better life. This chapter wishes to develop the argument that societies should not judge sacrificial rituals as if they were a failure of one group of people, or to call them names. They should rather be seen as a collective human failure caused by individuals' greed for wealth and power.

Interestingly, despite the fact that these societies are living in an extreme moral crisis, there is no evidence to suggest that human sacrificing is being committed for the consumption of human flesh. However, human history reveals that society has always been like that; humans have always quarrelled with each other. This accords with Malinowski's assertion that "we must start by knowing ourselves first and only then proceed to the more exotic savageries." (Malinowski, B., (1938) in Facing Mt. Kenya, p.vii).

Other kinds of violence include homicide, on which the data is abundant and striking. The other major challenge posed by the decline of violence is how to explain it. Payne suggests one possibility: that the critical variable in the indulgence in violence is an overarching sense that life is cheap. The European form of violence in the past involved religious inquisition, physical torture and persecution to save the souls of unbelievers.

As a matter of fact, a more contagious form of violence is that sanctioned by society or those in power when used in the form of punishment, which will be argued as violence born out of rationalising justice, duly sanctioned by society, impartial and under the control of law enforcement, in restraint of unlawful violence such as mob justice and in benevolent constraint of the insane, using pathological analysis. In this respect, there is even evidence of persistent traditional belief stemming from African mythological stories, which depict how God conversed with people long ago.

The next sets of comparisons explore the effects of bad leadership on people. People conceptualise their societal leadership as a consequence of the structure of Christianity in Africa and the politicians' role and effect in society. Looking at some of the ways people behave, allows us to see people as copycats of leadership in society. In-depth analysis of the leadership role in public service and the moral nature of our leaders in society, as well as the implications of the theories of public service, show whether ethical judgement is a natural and fair view.

African societies are still catching up with the cultural functioning mechanism in order to compete in production and for efficient services. The inherent problem is that developed societies are ever advancing to a more sophisticated modern technological culture, which is one of the processes that tends to disarm African society and to keep it lagging behind. This is the dilemma that not only allows, but insists upon a continuing manipulative culture of corruption. On the whole, if the leadership is productive and efficient, it follows good policies to stabilise society, but if it is bad it poisons society and is a danger to the population.

It is worth underlining that if leadership makes it convenient for people do what their leaders do, such as engage in corruption, it also makes it commonplace that subjects lose their sense of responsibility to one another and community values. This is a poisoned relationship through the bad example of our leaders who are supposed to fight corruption, but are themselves hell bent in corruption. It is therefore arguable that such leadership has both positive and negative connotations. On the negative side, the manipulation of corrupt leadership to serve particular partisan ends has unfortunate consequences. The public expects leaders to lead by example, but when they see the opposite conduct, it becomes the norm in society.

There are millions of young, able-bodied people without a legal income and physical activity to occupy them. The question arises of what society expects them to do. Man is a member of a species of bipedal primates in the family Hominidae (taxonomically Homo sapiens, Latin: "wise human" or "knowing human"). DNA evidence indicates that modern humans have a highly developed brain and are capable of abstract reasoning, language and introspection, as well as being capable of solving problems. (Cf.http:en.wikipedia.org./wiki/human-being#Evolutionary-studies/28/4/09).

This means that society has to realise that necessity is the mother of invention and there is evidence of this each time new inventions are made. For instance, in South

Africa, Nigeria, Kenya, Uganda and other countries, there have been constant reports of organised gangs of youths who waylay travellers by using logs to block vehicles before they force the occupants onto the public highway to surrender all their belongings, either by day or night. There are reports of burnt-out schools and gangs of thieves using tools and guns. All these are symptoms of a poverty culture, which explains the manipulation of natural phenomena through either religious beliefs or other criminal innovations.

What is certain is that this is a cry for help characterising a corrupt society, which has led people to engage in illegal innovations out of desire for self-enrichment. It is a symptom of a wider crisis and overall a moral decay in society, which has led to a wide range of immoral and unethical behaviours, such as pretending to heal the sick when people are not traditional healers, business and company directors who cheat on income tax and pilfering company supplies for personal use. As a result of a wider immoral influence, people resort to forging everything from academic transcripts to driving permits and passports, whilst others impersonate government officials in order to bribe or steal. I will go further and argue that human sacrifice itself is symptomatic of people with a poverty mentality who believe in wealth accumulation as freedom from that poverty.

The broader interpretation of human conduct and purpose can refer to Weber's idea that work is not just necessary to earn a living, but morally good in itself. (Weber, M., [1930], p.80). The Protestant ethic (Puritan tradition) of the sixteenth and seventeenth centuries saw good work as evidence of godliness and poor work as an insult to the Almighty. The actual belief or theory was used to persuade people who have good habits and attitudes to accept discipline. However, in our society the bad habits are in the form of Isaiah's typology of ungodliness, which starts from the top and goes to the bottom (Isaiah 6: 1-6). Nevertheless, the trouble with this approach is that it is one way. The reason Christianity in Africa often sends its messages to the wrong addresses is because it continues with small thoughts of traditional beliefs and great thoughts of its own beliefs.

Furthermore, if Christianity is to liberate society it must first create a dialogue to develop a policy of communication with traditional believers and the mediuma, priests and priestesses in order to find a common ground on which to speak at a range of events, conferences and meetings to promote understanding of the service being offered by traditional healers and the importance and reasons for their persistence. The church leadership will have to commit itself to a sound contextual theology in whatever capacity it adopts. It is a commonly held opinion among African scholars and other "third world" theologians that Western logic, which is based on the Aristotelian "law" of non-contradiction, was universalised too easily in colonialism. This is clearly the case with Gadamer's "fusion of horizons" and Habermas's "theory of communicative competence".

10.2 A Dialogue with Traditional Beliefs and People's Culture

Nonetheless, it seems clear that the only way for the Christian church to influence society is to secure the confidence of traditionalists. This is unlikely until dialogue between the church and African tradition religion is established through the use of hermeneutics, summarised in four points:

1. In classical hermeneutics, the aim is ultimately to understand oneself. It is an individualistic enterprise. In

contrast, African hermeneutics has a communitarian approach.

2. Classical hermeneutics is focused on harmonisation. Intercultural hermeneutics recognises differentiation, the other as a stranger who is to be done justice.

3. Classical hermeneutics is seen as instrumental: the reader takes possession of the text and makes the text his own property. Intercultural hermeneutics is relational.

4. Classical hermeneutics is mainly based on a propositional understanding of truth; intercultural hermeneutics is based on the existential contextual meaning of the truth.

The principal point of the church's dialogue with traditional beliefs will be to open channels of understanding the past, to allow cooperation and openness as a process of discovery of the values in traditional beliefs and healing of the misery caused by the distortion of the past influence on society. The focus of the dialogue will be to explore African heritage and to discover new areas that might be sensitive for both sides. Each participant will be treated with equal respect and their views listened to and analysed without bias or prejudice. Where differences of opinion or theological interpretation may surface, participants agree to disagree on principle; finding a common ground for the interpretation for traditional healing is safer and will eradicate imposters who exploit the public, in order to restore confidence in society.

The whole discussion has to be grounded on finding ways to heal past fears in society and to discover and iron out any misconceptions and misunderstandings to improve communication. The theological debate must rather be treated as a measure to regulate rivalry between healing groups to engage in human affairs, which is not only acting as a pastor, but as a means of God's response to people's fears of the powers of darkness and hatred. It is now seen as desirable in the African church to fully commit to examining people's beliefs to develop a contextual theology that integrates traditional beliefs in the changing role of Christianity in today's world. This is argued as necessary, especially in a society where various brands of Christianity have had an influence on the lives of its population.

On the other hand, an important historical feature that is notable among these groups is how all traditional religious rituals offer gifts to invoke spirits or ancestors. J. Mawinza observed that it is helpful to distinguish between worship and veneration, as traditional beliefs respect ancestors' role in the clan life of the living. (J. Mawinza, "The Human Soul", TMP. Kipalagala, p.138).

However, ancestors are not worshipped, but venerated; this was pointed out by both Kenyatta and J. H. Driberg. Kenyatta suggested with impressive clarity that the Kikuyu (Kenyan people) do not worship their ancestors, but hold communion with them, although their attitude towards them is not at all to be compared with their attitude to the deity, who is truly worshipped. Driberg further added that the Latin word "pietas" "probably best described the attitude of Africans to their dead ancestors as to their living elders." (Jomo Kenyatta, "Facing Mt. Kenya", London, 1958, pp.265-266; J. H. Driberg, in Secular Aspects of Ancestors-Worship in Africa", supplement to the "Journal of the Royal African Society", Col. XXXV, N. 138, January 1936).

Furthermore, in many examples, the deities of the Aborigines are regarded as the direct ancestors of the people living today and so they are "Ancestral Figures", "Ancestral Beings", "Ancestral Heroes" or "Dreamtime Ancestors". Here, the one term "Ancestral Being" is used to describe these deities. Ancestral Beings taught the first people how to make tools and weapons, hunt animals and collect food; they laid down the laws that govern their society and the correct way to conduct ceremonies. (http://www.aborigineals.culture.comac/religion.shtml/).

In the Voodoo religious belief, there are a few spirits or groups of spirits that have a particular relationship with humankind, such that it is not unreasonable to say that anyone might approach them with some confidence if a few basic forms and preferences are known. Among these are Papa Legba Atibon, the gatekeeper of the spirits, Danbala Wedo, who is said to own all heads and is the oldest ancestor of all life and Papa Gedeh, who gives voice to the spirits of the dead. For instance, H. Melsen described the ways the Nyakyusa tribes turn towards God as numerous (Melsen, H., in his Ms. "Dieu", p.28), and seemed to agree with J.S. Mbiti's observation of Abaluyia, Chaga and Meru as people who sacrifice to God by prayers, blessings, greetings, wishes, thanksgiving, oaths and curses, name giving and songs. (Mbiti, J.S., [1975], p.178).

Again, when we consider the languages and oral traditions of most African indigenous cultures, especially the mythology around the creation and separation of God and humans and all the stories of the beginning, there is no doubt that an andocentric society was in existence in Africa for a long time before the arrival of Christianity. It is not surprising that J. Hendrick and Melsen assert that in the past African people invoked God more often than nowadays and acknowledge that even in modern days at the occasion of sacrifices to ancestors, God is invoked first. Traditional beliefs and rituals have been ignored for so long and yet still exist and thrive in urban areas, but are more active in rural areas for the reason that generally the church in public tends to show a negative reaction towards the practice of traditional beliefs as backward practices, but when individuals are drawn into crucial questions of life, certainly many are challenged, including Christians, to turn to traditional healers.

The recent resurgence of traditional religion does suggest that the revisionist embodiment of questions of human conduct is important for Christianity in Africa to be available to support and live in communion *(koinonia)*. Also, there is a need to support those who have already fallen victim by offering them spiritual guidance and advice on how to make moral decisions without the church judging or condemning them; spiritual guidance is required for Christian growth. Likewise, the Roman Catholic saints are all very approachable to anyone who asks for their help, such as St. Anthony or St. Michael. (http://wwww.erukies.com/site/articles/views/5).

The only difference identified is in the types of gifts offered to the spirits. However, it all depends on the group or tribal rites; for instance, among the Banyarwanda they use milk or local beer, either made out of sorghum or millet and the Baganda still offer on some occasions a white chicken, local-made beer, money (Ensimbi Enganda) or a spotted or non-spotted goat or cow.

What is significant about the gifts is that each type of food and drink is the very food consumed by those offering presents to the spirits, which indicates that the spirits demand presents they had used in their lifetime. This creates differences between various cultures, which again are based on environmental factors. Of course, ancestors or spirits would not request for whisky, lager or a cake, due to the fact none of ancestors ever tasted these things; in most cases every ritual depends on particular environmental factors and customary needs.

In another contrast, Voodoo rituals are elaborate, steeped in secret languages, spirit-possessed dancing and special diets eaten by the Voodoo priests and priestesses. The dark side of Voodoo is used by participants to summon evil spirits and cast hexing spells on adversaries. The priesthood of Voodoo is held by both men and women. Key items are used in the many rituals of Voodoo. The two parts consists of ti-bon-ange (little good angel) and gros-bon-ange (great good angel). The gros-bon-ange is the body's life force and after death the gros-bon-ange must return to the cosmos (ibid). Gifts are required to invoke gods and ancestors for clients' special needs, such as seeking guidance in marriage, childbirth, rain for the harvest, protection for fishermen (Lubale Mukasa w'Enyanja) going to war and safety from ill wishers. However, for the sake of clarity and not to confuse this with the Christian concept of the Supreme God, I will use "god" to describe the supreme being of traditional religious believers and "God" to refer to the Christian Supreme Being.

The church in Africa needs to support people in society to see God in their own daily living, a God who is ever present in all their needs and who guides those who put their trust in Him and who know and revere God truly. It should offer teaching dedicated to biblical tradition and cultural themes of showing the God who is partly universal and African from Scriptures to depict God's mission among African culture and traditions.

Practising biblical teaching helps us overcome our misguided ideas. As African people study biblical teaching, they are led to joyful submission to God and to abandoning also helps inoculate Christianity in Africa against doctrinal controversies.

So, Christian teaching helps to maintain the continuity of logical argument for consistency of the Bible's mission for salvation for all by God incarnate. It is further arguable that the method by which the church can nurture individuals' right attitudes and spiritual growth is to engage their culture and beliefs in society; to divorce them from it, is seen as a failure to put culture and biblical teaching together in the form of a jigsaw puzzle.

Chapter Eleven

11.1 The Concept of God in the African Context

Returning to the question of the interpretation of the natural revelation of God, even in its straightforward form, it is far from dead and still flourishes in local African communities, especially among traditional believers. Although the different form of Christianity introduced in missionary days encouraged analytical penetration and detailed information, it seems to have acted as an ideological façade whereby a shared African concept of God, core assumptions and the social reality of God were ignored or denied any development.

The missionary view can then be contrasted with the revisionist position on these same issues to infer that the religious legalised a new religious institution, not a new revelation of God, but people's culture, tradition and new liturgy embedded in specific practices of worshipping, with new rules and beliefs that were irrelevant to people. This is seen by local people as not only eliminating some of the unnecessary contradictions of religious beliefs in African society, but also reducing their ritualistic incidence.

This is because the irrelevant Christian messages embedded in European culture and values disseminated through constant church preaching were not rooted in an African psychological and geographical environment. This in the process has led Christianity to direct contradictions of cultural and customs, which the Christian convert role mandated them to perform from a different ethos.

An issue that requires urgent consideration by the church is to assess whether it is true that before the missionaries' arrival, Africa did not have any conception of God. If Africa did not, was traditional religion a satanic revelation? If it was satanic, then we might as well say that it is how it was intended for an African to be; if a loving God can choose to reveal Himself to certain groups of people and fail to reveal Himself to others, then it is still an unresolved problem. Does it mean that a black person was created by Satan? If that is not so, how could God create an African and then fail to reveal His true nature and the purpose of His creation? If God did not reveal Himself, then it would be like a mother abandoning her own innocent child at infancy.

The way colonies were treated reflected a belief that racial characteristics are fundamentally biological in nature and are thus transmitted to succeeding generations. However, the concept of race today is discounted as non-biological and without validity, which highlights the colonial belief that black cultures were incapable of holding any truth because of deficiencies within the black culture, which could not lend itself to success.

This negative dominating stereotyping prevailed in Europe and America during this period and was used to degrade the black race and its culture as deficient, putting the dominant culture into the practice of beliefs by institutionalising Christianity as the only religion that holds truth and salvation. The historical assessment tool to be used is structured with underlying assumptions among extremists who harboured beliefs that whites were superior, a belief that stems directly from the notion of preconceived ideas of superiority and explains the overruling of the authenticity of the African divine revelation of God.

Kofi Asare Opuku adds, "The fundamental questions as to whether God acts in other people's histories and what those histories tell us about God, as well as whether history is the only arena of God's self-disclosure, remained unasked and unanswered." (Kofi Asare Opuku in the Baobab Tree of Truth: Reflections of Religious Pluralism in Africa, 2000 World Council of Churches).

History demonstrates the large amount of ethnocentric theory that illustrates the kind of superiority framing a set of attitudes and behaviour towards people of other races, based on beliefs that races are distinct and can be graded as "superior" or "inferior".

The search for an answer may be facilitated if one simple rule of objective search is observed. Those who believe that the rest of the world has to be fitted into the narrow terrain of shallow prejudice have never considered how people from different cultures prevented the advancement of their revelation of God concept in their own knowledge and religious practices. The reason they decided to legitimise their cultural parameters at the time was that those at the receiving end of colonisation were much more deferential of other social strata.

It is arguable that the use of "race" concealed a much more complex theory developed around this period and promoted by many European academics, politicians and missionaries that people of a particular race, colour or national origin were inherently inferior, so that their identity, culture, self-esteem, views and feelings are less valuable than the Europeans' own and can be disregarded or treated as less important. It is therefore argued that these theories were used to interpret the Bible in a way that protected colonial interests, prohibited other groups and undermined everything that had been valued by society.

Let me say upfront that I don't think traditional beliefs are to blame for the crisis in ritualistic murder in Africa. The use of racist theories presents a state of objective knowledge in order to keep one group in a permanent state of subordination and reject anything that sounded either politically, culturally or religiously as a sociological mode of colonial control in African society. This laid the blame on traditional religious practices and led to firm control of local beliefs as heathenism. Violence was perpetuated against African beliefs, yet for that particular society God had for centuries guided them to develop the knowledge of God in their own culture and tradition. Therefore, it has to be recognised that those cultures have different interpretations of life and the world surrounding people, in a similar way that Aboriginal stories relating to Ancestral Beings are an intrinsic part of Aboriginal belief and everyday thought.

As one moves through the day, walking past a particular rock or creek, spearing a particular animal, catching an iguana (large lizard) or collecting other bush foods, the Ancestral Beings who created these places and things come to mind. Even making tools and weapons will bring to mind the myths and legends of the Ancestral Beings who taught the Aborigines these skills.
(http://www.aborigineals.culture.comac/religion.shtml/).

However, to advance the alternative argument of the African mythology of creation, likewise, the myths in Genesis chapters 1-11 are a certain way of recognising oneself, which may be a symbolic narrative or rationalisation. African myths have the power to move men and women to heroic action based on their beliefs, whether true or not. And a myth is not supposed to be logical and may be contradictory with another one, because a concrete symbol permits only a partial approach to reality. The myth is a realisation of one's environment and one's explanation of fundamental questions. It is sometimes a mythological integration of human function compared with past and present experiences and harmonises the past and prevailing situation, or in times of peace or crisis.

Therefore, each society has its own creation story, has performed specific activities in the Creation Period and has played a specific role in relation to laying down the laws for people to follow or in creating the landscape. This information is contained in the body of songs, dances,

stories and paintings for each clan or tribe and is revered during certain ceremonies. In this situation, what is required is a theological discourse of open debate on the theological issues surrounding authentic traditional healing as an accomplice in the prevention of people's achievement of self-identity, which was embedded in their traditional belief.
(Cf. http://www.aborigineals.culture.comac/religion.shtml/).

As the pattern of violence against traditional beliefs denied any room for examination to assess possible ways to develop in the early conversion period, it is argued that the biblical basis of this approach was heavily based on the European empirical theory of revelation. In actual fact, the claim of truth was not a new invention, but was a familiar one in Africa, which is the crucial reason that claims for the truth in African society demand religious debate.

The distortion occurs in the previous treatment of truth, which made it quite clear that the basic position was relativist, one sided and biased, overlooking other sources of the truth. The use of truth claims promoted discrimination and denied the right to any rational truth and were argued as one course of conduct to restrict the knowledge and revelation of God.

The church in African society needs to work out how to include biblical and other sources of truth or revelation as a means of repairing the degradation of African truth, revelation and belief. One could say that because it is true that Socrates was a man and all men are mortal, then Socrates was mortal. (Ewing, A.C., 1961, Second Thoughts in Moral Philosophy, London: Allen & Unwin, p19).

The major criticism of the philosophical objective of basing all arguments on a poor creative process, would appear to have been avoided if the hidden agenda of colonial ideology and its genesis were instituted matter-of-factly in reference to the colonial set-up.

With colonialism came racism. Society was thus carefully calibrated: society had the whites, indigenous peoples and others. Race determined to which school the English colonialists' offspring went, where the Asians studied, what was left for the children of African government workers and where the rest of the local settlers in the town lived.

This separation defined where they lived. The whites resided in the more beautiful (mostly hilly) areas, referred to as the white residential areas. They stayed near the airports or water (possibly for security reasons). The white quarters were no-go areas for anyone. As for truth, conventional values were adopted to reduce the influence of reductionism and deny African society any room for its ideas and beliefs to develop. To restore a more relevant culture, differences in diversity were promoted, in which conflict had, for so long, been seen as a hindrance to development and as the source of people's suffering. What the church is called to teach today is suffering in love, which means safeguarding not only Christianity but pastoral care for salvation.

This is a challenge and call to the church to cross the River Jordan and suffer in love. The need to stand firm and preach the full truth, not the half truth, under the banner of the universal question of revelation raises a number of issues that need consideration before drawing any conclusions. Nonetheless, returning to the issue of reconciling traditional beliefs with Christianity, today it is seen as the only way to heal the past. It argued that the church in Africa, in the process of healing the past, has to analyse the situation relating to certain commonalities of the Old Testament outlook. Old Testament teaching has a strong connection with African ideas of sacred worship.

The sacred usually produces the double reaction of veneration and fear, because it becomes imbued with magical-religious powers. Accordingly, under the traditional interpretation, if sacred worship is not approached in the right way, the sacred becomes dangerous, whereas Christianity is characterised particularly by the fact that it realises a living synthesis of the sacred and the good. In a way Christianity has to become truly a belief owned by people in society, has to develop as the background pattern of understanding where believers are coming from. This can help the African churches to cope with adjusting to the Christian expectations and tensions that confront people in society.

11.2 Approach to a Local Theology

Although this topic is very extensive, it is often argued by Africans as of paramount importance to obtain a theoretical construct of the contextual framework of the church's teaching. At present, it seems to lack concentration on contextual relativising, rather than maintenance of missionary teaching. It needs to bring its teaching home in a fresh way. For instance, it is important for Christianity in Africa to re-examine the meaning of ethnic diversity, to determine whether it is God's creation and to discover if He has a reason and purpose for it. It is therefore vital to look for a theology that can talk to Africans clearly in a way that acknowledges ethnic diversity as being useful to society.

For Christianity in Africa to act as salt and light in society, it will have to re-invent instruments of change to reverse the past and lay firm foundations in the society in which it is situated. In other words, it is a process of contextualising the gospel to meet the social situation in all of its uniqueness, which informs the thoughts and actions of individuals.

However, another human being might possess some part of the truth that others have not yet received. This leads to the immediate, self-imposed question: “How do we proceed with those who claim absolute and exclusive truth?” The phrase “social or structural sin” is worth mentioning in the context of African theology, in order to understand that what happened to African society has made people act in ways that were perhaps not unexpected by the Church. As argued elsewhere, people learn their attitudes, values and views of reality from the societal structures within which they are born. On the whole, it is true to say that deteriorated moral values and social responsibility broke down any sense of common citizenship, which in its extreme form eventually drifted into committing what society had forbidden as taboos.

The argument for the deterioration of human values calls for society to be determined to be faithful to traditional values, as a church that serves God must move away from being manipulated so that it does not lose its sense of truth and follow a wrong path. (Loewen, Jacob, Vol.16n. 4, July-August 1969, p. 147).

Thus, like the theological notion of “Ubuntu”, the focus of African theology must be on “Ubumwe” or “oneness”, combining past experience with traditional Christian doctrine to examine what went wrong in society, to explain why people acted contrary to expectations by failing to protect each other as they would from the Ubumwe point of view.

Edward Farley argues that the everyday contemporary experience of ordinary people has theological meaning and significance. However, producing a just solution is often at the expense of further inroads into the establishment of restorative theological doctrine. There is a clear need to remember that missionary doctrine was not originally formed in a vacuum, but in response to the particular needs and cultural climate of the time.

Therefore, Christian teaching in Africa today is not a formula or rules set in stone, irreversible and immutable, but a response to people's needs, religious beliefs, society and culture. When Christianity in Africa starts to consider its methods and approach, that will be the time when its theology begins to help people in their own everyday situations. It is argued that the new theology will function as a guideline to restore the framework of societal values and expected responsibilities within communities as part of the reconciliation process. First and foremost, according to Christian leadership in Africa, a redefinition of a theology of national unity is needed. (Mbanda, L., [1997]. Committed to Conflict, The Destruction of the Anglican Christianity in Africa in Africa, London: SPCK, p.135).

Since Christianity in Africa is described as a dynamic body, it is ever changing, sometimes very rapidly, in response to new demands in an effort to provide the best possible solutions to contemporary grievances or demands.

Moreover, some moral judgements in the Bible are actually brought into question by the Gospel itself. The acceptance of slavery is a case in point. No Christian today would argue that because both Old and New Testaments accepted slavery as normal, we should only seek to regulate and humanise it. In fact, we need to be clear about the moral issues. Questions are not settled by appealing to factual evidence, they are argued out through a complex interaction between morals and principles, which are treated as given and factual information, which enables people to apply those principles.

So far, examples have been cited in various areas such as in Latin America, where life emerged in areas referred to as "base communities", which had been rejected by missionaries. This is similar to the African church's rejection of the inclusiveness of African traditional religion and culture. In this case, one argument uses the Bible to emphasise the objective presence of the word of God, not merely in, but as the written word of the New Testament. Another prefers to underline the discernment required by the reader about rules, profuse in the Bible, which give rise to most of the fears about African church reform.

This is therefore where the question of context arises, because the Bible is rooted in particular concrete historical situations, in which prophets and lawgivers and apostles dealt with people and problems of their own time and formulated norms and rules for their own society in the light of mostly unspoken principles.

It is the role of the church and it should be a concern in African society today to save thy brother and sister, which is a prophetic call and was laid down on believers. For instance, the African church should seriously consider the salvation of those who were rejected because it was believed they worshipped the devil. In the book of Creation, when God said to Cain, "Where is Abel thy brother?" Cain replies, "Am I my brother's keeper?" God says, "The voice of thy brother's blood crieth unto me from the ground." (Genesis 4).

If we contrast the two states of affairs, there is no comparison between Abel who was a murderer and traditional believers who are practising the faith of their ancestors.

What is needed is justice, since God is shown in traditional beliefs and in Christianity alike as being opposed to all forms of injustice and exploitation. If we examine African customary and biblical laws, both set out God's nature of love and justice. This calls for a structure of thought about society and its culture, which is not fully integral to the African church's teaching today. In some respects the church is still tied to European missionary cultural society. So, today, African societies are still subject to distortion and divisiveness, which disadvantages those who were liberally defined as evil, underlines the injustices of missionary teachings and demonstrates that the church's attitude today towards African traditional religious beliefs and practices is still evil.

What we say of the God of justice and mercy challenges the perception of the notion of judging and rejection of other people's revelation and reflects the theological understanding of God's presence in all generations and societies. (Ephesians 2:8-18).

Yet it is argued that affirmative action comes from listening, understanding, appreciating others' points of view and trusting their beliefs and values as important for them. All these points suggests why missionaries should have learnt from Christ's example and how he related to sinners, those possessed with evil spirits, mediums and those rejected by the religious establishment of his time. Therefore, the church needs to listen to the voices of people searching for spiritual help outside the church; in fact, the missionary push for change could become the reform of a new Christian spiritual practice.

If the church takes time to understand the African problem and chooses to engage with the African people, it would be like somebody breathing new life into church beliefs and practice. This lessens the confusion over the specific role that Christianity in Africa can play in a moral recovery. Furthermore, the process of reconciliation requires repentance and for both the church and traditional religious practices to end their hostility to each other. Assessment of theological differences may offer a better understanding of how Christianity works and how traditional religious practices are performed to help people to choose the strategies and tools best suited to the goals they hope to achieve. In this view, Christianity may show

how seemingly irreconcilable differences can be harmonised.

Also in consideration of religious justice and equality, evidence also shows that there are some rituals that elevate womanhood over manhood, as reincarnation and some mortuary rites. In African traditional rituals, only women performed the most important part of the rites. In general, religious experience extends the highest form of spirituality to men as well to women to participate equally in any form of organised religious experience and realise the human element of the ultimate goal of equality in worship of God.

The rules that promote the behaviour of the Old Testament may be seen to fall into two systems based on quite different principles. The first system governs by an understanding of people's rights and duties in relation to each other, to society as a whole and to God. This is a justice principle. The Ten Commandments are a sketch of that system and suggest that Christianity in Africa should explore the process of contextualisation of the Christian message to restore its membership of responsible Christians in living and caring communities. It is important to create an understanding of what is normatively human, in the hope of dealing with the current needs of divided communities.

The other system is the theological concept of devilish preaching, although it is not a systematic theology, as to a large extent the New Testament's righteousness or justice is seen, first of all, as an attribute of God's being (one of the moral and communicable attributes) and then derivatively as universal attributes of humanity in God's image. It is therefore closely related to God's holiness in every society. It is very important to recognise that the concept of God's truth rests firmly within people's moral law in their culture and traditional beliefs, as well as the expression of their moral holiness in daily living. As an earlier examination of conversion implied, this is the key to understanding how people feel, which is expressed by those who join independent congregations. Similarly, each day the Lord adds to their group those who were being saved through their healing acts, as in the Apostles' time. (Acts 2:47).

Thus, the main factor mentioned by respondents was the need for a theology related to people's situations. This is why the inculturation of a vibrant, homebred, true African Christianity is necessary in order to meet the spiritual needs of Africa and to deliver the gospel effectively to the people. As a matter of fact, this is just a rediscovery of the theology of the "seminal word" of the early church. (Cf. A. Roest Crollius, What is so new about inculturation?, in: Gregorianum 59, [1978], 721-738; J. Waliggo et al., Inculturation: Its Meaning and Urgency, Nairobi 1986; Anglican and Society, Report on World Conference, Geneva, WCC, September 1997, p.210). It is therefore essential to take the people's faith and locate it within the teachings of Christ.

The Christian mission in the world has always been to make the Word flesh (John 1:14), which is precisely the aim of inculturation theology. Schreiter, in *The Faces of Jesus in Africa*, quotes Pope John Paul in his encyclical "Redemptory is Mission", where he addresses the practicalities of inculturation. The action or mission of making oneself agreeable, or simply to please, shows compliance with, or deference to, the wishes of others, obligingness, courtesy or politeness to people. However, inculturation considers the whole community, not just a few experts, since people reflect an authentic "sensus fidei" of which we must never lose sight. (Schreiter, R. J., [1992], p.vii).

The leading role of the missionary is not without its critics. Bishop Muzorewa, addressing the All African Conference of Churches in Harare, Zimbabwe in 1990, drew a link between liberation and inculturation. He criticised the negative role played by missionaries when they chose to please the fellow colonial Europeans, who were oppressing their converts rather than opposing them. (Muzorewa, G. H., [1990], pp.190-97).

Throughout this chapter, I have argued that such an approach would help the church in Africa endeavour to be faithful to the culture of the people, to the human spirit and to what God says. It also becomes necessary to revisit the Bible.

The presuppositions people start with are very important so far as the development of dialogue is concerned. If the church starts with the assumption that traditional religion is worshipping the devil, then the relationship with traditional religious believers are likely to be distant at the best and hostile at worst. St Paul had this in mind when he said, "I have become all things to all people, that by all means I might save some."

Certainly the uncivil, rough and rude speaker will please no one and none will listen and take in what is taught, whether the gospel is true or false. No doubt there is a time when plain, outspoken condemnation is required; this will certainly not please, but it will be respected, especially from one who is always gracious in the way the truth in conveyed. This argues that God calls people to move away from how they feel they need God's salvation and to where God wants them to be saved in the future, and people are constantly reminded by God again to move on. This is why people read the Bible in different ways, not as a fixed and unchanging law, but as a fallible record of where previous generations got where they were and in their understanding of the nature of their relationship with God.

To advance this idea further, society's way of thinking and forming religious convictions is very near to the mentality of biblical people, especially the mentality of the

Old Testament. The need for the inculturation of theology is based on misconceptions created in the early days that the present Christianity in Africa can be located in its environment in order to start from this way of thinking, from people's convictions and from the ways in which their convictions are formed and expressed. In addition, this need for the inculturation of theology explains the historical background of society.

Dickson Kwesi asserts that people's way of life is the means by which they comprehend reality. (Dickson, Kwesi [1984], p. 3). His assertion parallels previous suggestions that it is difficult to see another culture if one views it through one's own culture, especially in communication. Evans-Pritchard adds that cultural translation is supremely difficult and that it is perhaps even impossible to understand another reality without becoming a part of it. (Evens Pritchard, E. E. [1965], p. 7).

The key point is that a state of inward transformation and growth is rooted in an attitude of receptivity, wrongly described as passivity, if people are to be moulded without contributing to the process. This is what appears to have happened during conversion, when local culture and beliefs were treated with contempt as if they did not exist and as if nothing had happened before the missionaries and colonial rule. In this case, the new theology in society may be described as a way of life or a value system. The aim of this analysis therefore includes theological contextualisation, using familiar language and symbols in a given situation, recognised and practised in nearly every civilised and uncivilised society throughout human history, all of which is necessary in order to reach people in their own context.

The issue of language is particularly significant. The use of the verb "to create" shows how important this is, as language lies behind the concept of the creation and the communication of the Genesis story. The first thing that

Adam did after he was created was to name all the creatures. John's gospel states: "From the beginning was the Word, and the Word was with God, and the Word was God." (John 1:1–2).

The uniqueness of words is summed up by Lenski and Nolan, who argue that "without words and other symbols, human societies would differ little from the societies of other primates, for they would lack their most distinctive feature." (Lenski, G., Nolan, P., and Lenski, J., [1995], p. 20). James Woodward and Stephen Pattison reinforce this argument by stating that the capacity to be able to reflect on and articulate something of the theological significance of human experience is highly valued in theology. It is implicit for this argument that it was time for Christianity in Africa to respond to the voices of its people and the church's leadership to interpret the meanings of the myths and symbols that shape people's views of themselves and their world. (Cf. Woodward, C. Vann, [1971]).

Another concern is the style of worship, which is still foreign to Africans, although a few congregations have made slight alterations to the liturgy. Louise Pirouet reasons that those who had found a Christian faith could have been allowed to use gestures and symbols of their old religion to express their Christianity, without implying a mixing of religions. (Pirouet, L., [1989], p. 105).

Indeed, traditions of piety, Keswick teaching and the search for the "higher life" all influenced missionaries who worked in Africa. (Woodward, C. Vann, [1971]). This hunger for a deeper experience of God in one's life was a deep undercurrent leading to the missionary teaching of Christian outbreak. (Woodward, C. Vann, [1971], p.9).

Rubenstein and Roth observe that, in practise, this was achieved through a variety of theories of exclusiveness. It is "important to keep in mind that Luther's attack on the Jews is not an isolated phenomenon, but arises out of the monotheistic common to all of the religious traditions rooted in the Bible." (Rubenstein, R. & Roth, J. K., [1987], p. 60).

Down the centuries, there have been groups in all the major world religions that have made such claims. Islamic fundamentalists may be the most obvious today, but there are many Christians who claim a similar monopoly on truth, just as missionaries confronted their converts with claims to absolute and exclusive truth.

It is also important to consider the influence of Protestant Evangelicals, who tended to identify good practice and Christian morality with the accepted behaviour of nineteenth-century Western society, with its Victorian values of absolutism and claims to exclusive truth, which led missionaries to demand that converts should abandon their own cultures. Nonetheless, it quickly became evident that for the missionary task to have been done effectively, the wider gulf in influence between the "two forces" of colonialism and Christianity, which were sharply manifested in the nineteenth century, needed to be hedged around a conversion in which converts had to abandon their culture and tradition, simply succumbing to a new form of slavery that was not a feature of just religion.

Thus, whatever missionaries conceived at one level, they could not have made sense of the world in the same way as the converts to Christianity. It was impossible for missionaries to see through traditional religious eyes without conversion to the people's ways of seeing the world around them. It is argued that this is required for integration and, if they had not integrated, they would otherwise only be observing other people's reality; until it was internalised it could not be real for them. The same applies to Christianity. It is not real for people as long as they lack a vital aspect of comprehension; it will always be observed from other people's reality. It will remain incomplete until African Christianity affirms and accepts that the truth can be discovered elsewhere. If Christianity in Africa does not do so, it would be as if it was turning its back on its own greatest discoveries. The new emphasis is on including the positive elements of the older terms, but going beyond this in order to consider the new challenges of theologising, as well as offering pastoral care.

Christianity in Africa's burden of recovery and rehabilitation during the first phase was shared between local churches in communities, NGOs, local associations such as Widows' Associations, Youth Associations, Co-operatives and the government's Department of Rehabilitation. At a local level, the department was only supposed to play a facilitative role, leaving the beneficiaries to participate fully in caring for local needs. The technique of eliminating an eliciting stimulus, which prompts undesirable behaviour, is widely used in clinical psychology. For instance, if the church in society can examine the history of Christianity, it will soon discover that some of what is called Christian traditions were pagan practices; for instance, from Jewish culture, even in the early days.

The Christian church fathers believed strongly that they had established the best tradition and they were certain that canon laws, worship and liturgical decisions were always followed and that they had embodied the most appropriate solution for the future of Christianity in Africa. These issues sometimes led to controversies and schisms as time passed and other churches with different cultural needs referred to themselves as the East and West churches.

Many other factors caused the East and West in Africa to drift further apart, partly because the dominant language of the West was Latin, while that of the East was Greek. Soon after the fall of the Western Empire, the number of individuals who spoke both Latin and Greek began to dwindle and communication between East and West grew much more difficult. With linguistic unity gone, cultural unity began to crumble too. The two halves of the Christian church were naturally divided along similar lines; they developed different rites and had different approaches to religious doctrines. Although the Great Schism was still centuries away, its outlines were already perceptible.

So far, the Christian church in Africa has not realised the necessity to respond to issues surrounding traditional beliefs and indulging in controversial satanic practices. However, this has created the current crisis of human sacrifice and it is arguable that the church cannot afford to sit back and wait or continue to spread and distort people's beliefs. Fresh evidence discounts the assumption that matters concerning beliefs will just go away or disappear and it continues to believe this; the church again is getting it wrong.

If the church can recognise this much, the church leadership will have to recognise that the other person or community or traditional belief is not simply going to go away. They are not just going to be defeated and silenced. For the foreseeable future, they are going to be there, recognisably doing something like the church is doing. But yet the church can't pretend, as it would like to. On the other hand, I am quite aware that traditional churches prefer to go about their work without drawing attention to challenges to establish the beliefs of the Christian devout. In some churches the attitude is to expect continuous tensions; in my view it is illogical not to look for rationality and coherence.

The fact that it continues to deny links between its own heritages, despite evidence throughout the history of Christianity in African society, demonstrates how the ambiguous role of the church developed in cultures and traditions that are riddled with contradictions. In its recent

Assessment of Research Quality, the Association of the Universities in the Netherlands noted the danger of "an overly introspective Eurocentrism" in doing theology in the Netherlands and called for more "involvement with extra-European issues." (Wijsen, F., and J. van Slageren, Missiologie-beoefening in Nederland en België, in: Wereld en Zending 27 [1998/4], 25-34).

If this is what Christianity in Africa thinks, it beggars belief. Instead, a realistic approach should engage Christianity with people's cultural beliefs and tradition through consciously identifying what is possible, given the fact that Christianity links the Holy Eucharist (Holy Communion) with Christ's sacrifices on the cross and, remarkably, depicts Jesus Christ as the sacrificial Lamb of God who took away the sins of the world.

Relevance can be gained for Christianity in Africa by integrating people's traditions, like the Jewish tradition was integrated into liturgical worship, which was purely the Jewish sacrificial ritual of the early church reconciled with Christ's death to symbolise His act of death (redemption), which was done once and for all to pay the price as a ransom for many.

In the view of the above argument, the church in Africa must emphasise the doctrine of Christ's sacrifice on the cross and resurrection, which are a convincing act of love demonstrating truth. As matter of fact, the resurrection of Jesus Christ is the very capstone in the arch of Christianity. This provided the truth even to those who doubt His resurrection, but Christ appeared to numerous other individuals as well, providing "many convincing proofs" of the resurrection. (Acts 1:3). Christ in His resurrection body was even touched on two occasions (Matt. 28:9; John 20:17) and challenged the disciples (Luke 24:39) and Thomas (John 20:27) to feel His wounds.

This is rather more convincing than other church doctrines and it is noteworthy that after examining the evidence for the resurrection of Jesus Christ, Greenleaf suggested that any cross-examination of eyewitness testimonies recorded in Scripture would result in "an undoubting conviction of their integrity, ability, and truth." (Cf. http://www.iawwai.com/EternalLife.htm/4/2009).

Despite those who claimed that Jesus' body was stolen from the tomb, by the Romans, the Jews, or the disciples, we know that the Romans would have no reason to steal Christ's body. Besides, if the Jewish leaders had stolen the body, they could have later openly displayed it to prove to the disciples and indeed the world that Jesus was not really raised from the dead. Not only did the resurrection of Christ transform the disciples from cowards to lions of the faith, but His resurrection still continues to transform lives today. Because Christ lives, the Scripture says, those who trust in Him will live also.

Christianity in Africa today calls for the church to go to traditional believers with due humility. The church is ever reminded not to be like the Pharisees, proclaiming its good deeds before everyone, or like the Good Samaritan, but to do something about the underlying causes of the need to discover a way to integrate what is African.

If Christianity in Africa is the instrument of Christ's mission of redemption for all humankind, it will have to meet people where there are, in their fallen state, in order to save them. Society is crying for help and appealing for Christianity in Africa to open the window of opportunity to traditional religious beliefs and culture to liberate it. The reason for adopting such an approach is to give Christ's mission in African society a high priority, where Christianity will be able to communicate and challenge the latent activism in society at large and to channel its energy, worries, faith and hope into building communities and in service of the Lord.

The basic cause of the need for reform lies in the twin pressures of people's beliefs and societal culture and for the first time the church needs consciously and seriously to revisit history to discern the background on which the missionaries laid the foundation of Christianity in Africa, to see the danger of bias against values which for centuries had shaped and developed people's ideas, community and faith and offered hope.

The point of revisiting history is to clarify the culture and tradition, which have risen in the issue of human sacrifice, and yet there is no way the church in African society can deny that Christians celebrate Holy Communion or Holy Eucharist, a Jewish ritual sacrifice which is thousands of years old. For instance, the only newspaper in Germany that often screamed the accusation of ritual murder in Jewish faces, was *Der Sturmer*, which caused it to be under constant attack by the Jews. However, *Der Sturmer* was not stopped for several years and wanted to fulfil its mission. (http://www.thewatcheerfiles.com).

However, if we try to see the current situation regarding human sacrifice from a macro-sociological perspective, this openness will force open channels of communication that will engage society in the issues surrounding traditional beliefs. They will thus free find compliance and how to administer healing practices to clients without causing public fear.

Nevertheless, it is worth giving credit where it is deserved, given the generosity of some governments to allow the freedom to practise traditional religious beliefs, which was a positive decision that indicated the desire to pull traditional believers along the developmental trail.

Regarding the rights of traditional healing practitioners, these challenge the church's teaching to seek to undermine the efforts of a large number of dedicated missionaries' work in Africa. Nevertheless, the church needs to allocate space for a discussion; there is a need for the church and traditional healers to collaborate in a dialogue to forge a joint effort at examining acceptable practices of healing. The significance of this is to bring everything into the open to scrutinise who is who and to weed out fake elements and satanic influences. The main intention of this is to enable genuine traditional healers to be differentiated from dangerous scammers who have led society to the present crisis of human sacrifice.

Properly interpreted, the traditional religious belief will yield an understanding of how it can share with Christianity to reduce the tension in society and superstitions about the former. This is why it is proving hard to identify the fake healers perpetrating ritualistic murder, whose tricks operate to the advantage of hidden beliefs as disguised backgrounds for such people coming forward for church services, such as religious weddings and taking pastoral steps to help newly wedded couples to cope with the traditional hidden beliefs of the vast majority who live in both camps. This ministry encourages each member of the congregation to consider carefully and look beyond their own circumstances and needs, to put their problems, challenges, weakness and suffering into perspective and to seek healing and closer relationships through and with God, for themselves and for other people.

As a whole, the above questions need to be taken seriously by a society in which order is constructed to understand what has led some people to self-destruction and to highlight the social pressures that modern living places on poor societies. One of the aims of this book is therefore to assess whether church leaders in Africa do believe that traditional beliefs have a sense of purpose and how many church leaders realise that society is on the edge of very real despair. Of course, church leaders see and have in many ways expressed concern about the stress placed on individuals in these situations, which needs to be faced and eased by politicians. But does society really believe in the human sacrifice that has caused unnecessary human suffering? If it does, is there any theological justification for human sacrifice in modern society, or does it stem from a lack of rationalisation?

The question begs answering of why there are some systematic social arrangements and some interactional social situations that seem to work against people's interests concerning the improvement of behaviour. So far, expressed especially in interactionist perspectives, this tends to have the view of Janus. Janus was a Roman god, the guardian of gates and doorways, who had two faces looking in different directions. Interactionist perspectives tend to look two ways, both at the patterns of society stressed by macro-sociologists and at the work and negations that individuals accomplish in keeping society going, as stressed in micro-perspectives. (Broadfoot, P. [1979]. Assessment, Schools and Society, London: Methuen).

In an agricultural society, the supernatural is manifested in spirits and underpins events and processes in the microcosm of the local community's organisation and its environment, while the Supreme Being underpins events and processes in the macrocosm in the African world or in heaven. Yet in the modern society there is no mention anywhere or any interpretation of the meaning of human sacrifice; the only mention of relevance that points to past culture is of the belief in night dancers, who have powers to communicate with spirits and wake dead bodies, following them to their homes. It is also said that night dancers do this to eat their flesh, not for ritual. There is also a traditional belief that long past ancestors' spirits helped relatives by intervening in their daily affairs when consulted.

If we look closely among Bantu traditional beliefs, ancestors' spirits are considered to be part of nature. Therefore, a belief in spirits is open to fake claims. For instance, in Luweero district, police arrested 14 cult members. The resident district commissioner, Geoffrey Kyomukama, said the cult was operating illegally because it was not registered. Kibwetere was the cult leader, who was accused in 2000 of murdering over 500 members of his cult in Kanungu district who believed in demonic worship, which is totally contrary to African ritual celebrations, in which there is no description of human sacrifices.

The evidence shows that such beliefs survive because of people's "elective affinity", or psychological fit, with the demands of their environment. In fact, there are many stories in Africa showing beliefs about the separation of God and man, which explain death as a crucial element of traditional religion, symbolising the separation of humankind from God the maker. The only explanation of the current development of human sacrifice is that it is a sign that both the former bad and good elements still exist in the form they took before the abolition of religious practices by the colonial rule.

A veneration of evil spirits is also a clear signal that these cultures have not developed further since the abolition period, given the fact that they continue to function as private beliefs pushed to operate underground in communities. The mission, entering the field in the shadow of the colonisers, was part and parcel of the radical changes that this new political era brought to the indigenous population. The missionaries represented the powerful religious arm of the colonisers and, yet, they had the naive policy of not becoming involved in politics, but concentrated on evangelism, as observed by Scheer. (1995:326).

Today, as we understand society, it is absolutely ridiculous to think about the nature of such a policy. A policy of non-involvement by definition has the effect of perpetuating and strengthening the political status quo. That is why the wonderful effect of the revival was confined to personal relations, but never changed the inherited subordinate position of the Hutus under the Tutsis, for example. This policy did change, however.

The next stage in mission theology came about when Christians in Africa came to the conclusion that they had to do something about the injustice and oppression of the majority by the ruling minority. Significant numbers of Christians became "the voice of the voiceless" and took the side of the majority of their members. They pitted their (moral and international) power against that of the ruling class. In the end, this led to reforms and eventually a majority government. In the process, they made enemies, because, as Scheer (1995:326) says, "Local people's loyalties in traditional culture were personal, not ideological. Parties were more like gangs. They divided the Christianity in Africa."

However, the church did reap some short-term benefits. More correctly, the church leaders were rewarded. They developed a close relationship with the political rulers. However, what seems to have resurrected the traditional beliefs is that the political and economic climate relaxed towards traditional beliefs, which facilitated their continuance. Therefore, it is arguable that these developments are in a way a challenge to society to assess what has caused this new drive, which is contrary to the past traditional ritual celebrations, yet leads to a lack of stability and peaceful means of living today.

Chapter Twelve

12.1 The Social Implications of the Resurgence of Ritualistic Sacrifice

Of course, there are valid reasons why traditional beliefs keep resurfacing in traditional rituals and the implications of this are argued as still linked to the past, from which in the last fifty years two dimensions of social developments in society have gradually emerged. Firstly, the long-term suffocation of traditional religious beliefs is a form of a challenge to church teaching in African society today. Secondly, the restoration of cultural institutions to an extent provided confidence for the resurgence of traditional religious beliefs, which have a wide influence and are recognised by innovators in an uncertain economic climate.

The situation seems to have fuelled and added demands to consult traditional mediums or witchcraft in search of protection. In order to identify the source of ritualistic murder, it is then necessary to assume either of the two possibilities of fake dishonest ritualistic sacrifices, or truthful genuine traditional healers and seek all evidence that may verify or refute the assumptions. Since these two possibilities are contrary to each other, it makes little difference which one may be assumed to initiate the analysis.

One needs to investigate the background of conversion to Christianity in Africa and the extent to which such a background could have resulted in the faking of ritualistic culture. In a way, this reveals the damage and negative extent of abolishing traditional religious practice, which was argued as a source of individual disparity. At the same time this pushed beliefs that had been long harboured into secret operation to evade the church's negative teaching against their practices, as evil and superstition have led to the faking culture.

For so long the church has ignored or failed to grasp the damage its actions would cause. This is why recognising the benefits and strength of the integration of traditional beliefs with Christianity is important and can be a good thing for the church. Indeed, this is often cited as one of the satisfactions of young people who attend new independent churches that use an African cultural approach in their worship and teaching. The traditional cultural relationship with Christian teaching can be difficult to establish when Christianity in Africa is continually moving away from the past to modernity. But further research will be needed to clarify the issue, since there is every disincentive to accommodate these cultures.

Analytically speaking, it will require the church leadership to overhaul past distortions before there is positive encouragement to take this route. One needs to have more confidence in the traditional beliefs, rather than modernising Christianity in Africa. Technological and globalisation theories have been an especially great influence in relation to the rapid-changing experience for some people, which is mixed, both highly positive and negative, as the cutting edge of the process is, in poor societies, frankly exploitative of the poor.

It is also true that in the last few years people in the West have experienced rapid changes from modernity to post-modernity. The positive side is the rise of modern science, from the background of Christianity and through the development of the Enlightenment. This has made possible an ongoing technological revolution, which has had impacts on many aspects of our lives. Equally, of course, the enormous impact of these changes was regarded as a means of freeing people, literally, from ignorance.

On the contrary, this so-called freeing was driving them from communitarian living to the other extreme, to the point that so many youngsters have embraced individualism. The individualistic perspective is simply "human nature" and as such almost led to an exaggerated emphasis on autonomous individualism. In a sense, this has turned out to be false for some and has instead led to an over-dependence on setting restraints in incipient communities. Of course, abolishing a system in which people cared for one another, which was once the African way of living, has unquestionably created the absence of that community setting and has turned many kinds of human conduct and behaviour rebellious towards once accepted community norms and values. To the great apostles of economic freedom, the rejection of the old order and the meaning that was attached to is important.

What is very clear is that the agenda of globalisation worldwide and the revolution in technology has led to rapid changes, which have brought wealth, mass production and a wider selection of goods for sale and facilitated many activities, although another effect for many people has been to accumulate greater economic pressure. Modern living has also long exploited both positive and negative outcomes corresponding to the decline of Christianity in society.

Fake traditional healers are generally driven by the influence of monetary gains, but they give the impression that what they do is special to demand from their clients extraordinary things, such as human organs to present to the spirits as a necessity. Many so-called traditional healers are charlatans and constitute a danger to social life, economic development and health. They will claim to do anything to convince their desperate clients to obey the spirits' desires. This has turned out to be the experience of victims of both modernity and rationality, which have made some people highly exploitative.

Power is about speed and global influence, such as global commercialisation, but as mentioned this has created in African society a type of McDonaldisation, a commercialisation in the romantic fantasy world of pop singers, film stars, celebrities and new fashions of materialism, together with the psychological manipulation of normal people who take size 12 clothes; all this has put pressure on young people, whose wish is to acquire material goods. In this respect, equally religion has likewise been radicalised and commercialised in the globalisation transformation that has been taking place in terms of how to win over people's minds through the use of media and pop-type music, like that played in modern churches. The resurgence of sacrificial rituals seems to have derived from both the fake magic healers and obsessed individuals who wish to acquire wealth when other factors pose a threat to the continuity of their lifestyle.

On the other hand, the late-modern lifestyle situation is characterised as being the source of double-edged beliefs in two ways. Firstly, people, especially the modern generation, have lived under the shadow of one foot in the new official religion and the other foot in the old camp, which is seen as an alternative. Indeed, this is indicative of a broader and more pronounced trend, wherein the performance of the Christian moral function has come to be less relied on and has been weakened by wider influences. With regard to the rest of the wider influence, many find it easy to blame the changes that were introduced by the West, often owing to resentment at its perceived arrogance.

Conversely, there is a similar erroneous mentality among African countries who claim that they have not contributed to the moral deterioration in their political corrupt dealings with the West, suggesting that they should exhibit solidarity to eradicate vices and restore moral values. Those who seem to have misunderstood what is happening still water down the reality of people's thinking and actions. This limited segment of fanatical and misled religious believers in a certain section of society has to be assisted to make an internal assessment to take account of recent phenomena.

Given the role that traditional rituals had played in society, Max Gluckman rightly throws light on the past when he observed that such thinking highlights the fact that the Christian church did not take the performance of rituals seriously; where they tried, rituals were interpreted in terms of the symbolism of the West. (Gluckman, Journal, No. 4, December 1945, p. 224.)

According to the importance attached to one's beliefs, the rules governing ritual practices, like in many other social groups, were passed to children by family members, either verbally through conversations with elderly people during meal times, or children's attendance at ritual celebrations. In this manner they acquired knowledge that was a normal part of cultural education in terms of knowing who you are and what is acceptable and not acceptable for that culture. Also, having been given these outlines, it was manifest that if rules were to be effective, they had to be accepted and legitimated by the elders, and anyone who acted to the contrary was warned of the danger that disobedience would cause to anyone who did so. More significantly, Neckebrouck argues that no faith harmonises itself with people's situations and requirements; however good the faith may be, limited choices have to be imposed on an unwilling society.

Victor Turner points out that crisis and fear can encourage a sense of communitas and the use of fear as an aspect of ritual is developed by Harvey Whitehouse in his study of male initiation rites in Papua New Guinea. The invocation of fear in initiands is a powerful way of inscribing meanings on the body and mind at its most receptive and vulnerable. (quoted in Bowie, F. [2000]. "Ritual Theory, rites of passage and ritual violence". The Anthropology of Religion, Oxford: Basil Blackwell, 151-85. ISBN 0631 208488, p.153). This is indeed true and is supported by the recurrence of other similar incidents, which are evidence that a lack of remembrance of what God has said has an effect on people's lives.

I will therefore go further and argue for the need for a listening ear to what traditional religious believers say. I will go even further to cite examples of how society has been working against its ethical values and to analyse the production of the most violent films, which portray humans being sacrificed and bewitched for other people and families to gain personal desires, including riches.

The Christian church and traditional religious leaders must engage in a constructive theological dialogue with all stakeholder, which provides room for openness and assessment, in order to grant permission to harmless practitioners to practise their beliefs openly and to identify fake ones to reduce the danger towards their clients. In this view, it is now paramount for the African church to initiate religious dialogues to reducing the large horizontal inequalities, which it is essential to eliminate, as they are a source of conflict in belief.

It is hard to talk of democracy, if we consider that colonial rule and the introduction of changes by Christianity were one-sided in favour of European culture and leadership. But there is a need for open-minded approach to dialogue between traditionalist healers and Christianity in Africa. A distinctive theological debate is urgently needed to construct a contextual dialogue of a church talking in clear language for society, focused on deterring the scandalous culture of greed, which seems to have consumed human nature and the moral fibre to resist temptations out of a hunger for accumulating more and more.

Unfortunately, governments do not often have the capacity to bridge the gap between local fears and people's beliefs in society. Comparative pastoral theology is not to be confused with comparative theology, which is the study of religious traditions other than one's own and their theologies. This is argued as getting to know people in their local communities, such as the missionaries in Africa taking the initiative to discover what it means to live together. The aim of the initiative is to provide a focus for the reconciliation, which is currently being developed around issues of people's broken relationships.

Christianity in Africa has termed this concept the healing dialogue; it is the prime vehicle for examining and raising major issues concerning the situations in which people find themselves. It was intended to transform people's lives through learning and discovering how communities handled social problems in the past, such as acting collectively to eradicate poverty.

It is an idea to look into the past to confront challenges by sharing what they knew as a means of sharing a communal spirit to form a focus for a common destiny. It is argued that part of the deficit of present-day theology in African society is its inability to connect meaningfully to meet people's needs. (Maluleke, T. S., [1997], Missionalia, 25:1 April, p. 339).

It was even conceded by the respondents that it was foolish to begin talking about religious commitment before addressing fundamental problems, such as how to find food or employment. This illustrates a situation of despair in a country where unemployment is chronic among villagers and health is poor in refugee camps. The need for pastoral support springs from a deep concern that Christianity in

Africa should not lose sight of its ideals. In William Temple's pastoral view, "The only real cure for unemployment is employment. In other words, the country is challenged to find a social order which provides employment, steadily and generally, and our consciences should be restive until we succeed. Christian sympathy demands this." (Temple, William, [1976], p.35).

However, the experts and conflict resolution practitioners tell us that for dialogue to bear fruitful results, there must be an ideal condition or conditions. There must be trust, faith, humility, respect for each other and a spirit of give and take. On the other hand, dialogue is incompatible with arrogance, patronage, manipulation, fear, hostility, exclusion or a superiority complex. Furthermore, for dialogue to lead to reconciliation, every participant must have an equal chance to contribute and question any subject on the agenda. Likewise, every participant in the dialogue must have an opportunity to contribute ideas without the constraints of the church hierarchy, status and protocol.

Similarly, for genuine dialogue to take place, there is a need for transparency and openness and a dialogue framework that spells out who is allowed to participate and how the decisions of the dialogue are to be implemented. The agenda must be clear and every participant must be afforded an opportunity to contribute.

Given the above guidelines for an ideal dialogue situation, it is ironic that almost everybody is proposing dialogue over the crisis in human sacrifice without considering the chances of its success. For example, the opportunity for religious traditionalists openly to express their grievances and to contribute their views in dialogue has never been recognised by the church leadership as necessary. However, the church leadership needs to stop the blockage for this debate to happen. The opportunity to conclude the matter of religious grievances and prejudices in opposition to traditional practices must be allowed to be implemented as a process of reconciliation.

On the question of a conducive environment, the theological dialogue must include outside influences in the process of change in relationships. The dialogue participants, who are supposed to manage a dialogue agenda, have to analyse together the system of abolishing traditional healing and why the church looks at traditional religious supporters with contempt and often characterises them as an institution of witchcraft, or superstitions and comprised of self-seeking individuals.

On the side of traditional religion, practitioners hold the view that African society is still under occupation by European influences and Christianity is still seen in society as an inappropriate belief that does not meet African needs. Christian belief is characterised as being like the relationship of colonialists to former colonies. This compels us to ask how dialogue can succeed when each party feels that the other party is representative of colonial influence.

Another question to ask is how church dialogue with traditional religious groups can succeed when there is no respect for each other in the anticipated dialogue. Given that the Christian church is characterised as against traditional religion, the point advanced here is that the past missionary teaching abolished society's confidence in traditional religion. How can dialogue be seen as attainable with an institution perceived to have no religious moral value or legitimacy in the eyes of the church leadership? How can a successful dialogue be conducted between two groups when one group does not accept the principle of religious integration and unity in diversity?

I agree with Welbourn, who sees theological dialogue as a means to bring traditional beliefs into the open and remove the secrecy cloud, which he argues is part of the reason for including traditional beliefs in Christianity. He gave the example that the European church practises exorcism as a regular part of its ministry; therefore, the African church must recognise that there can be no sin in holding the same healing practices as most of the people of the Old Testament. (Welbourn, F. B. [1965], p.103).

The need here is for a theology that provides a forum for discussion of various issues across a number of past and present religious matters in communities. The aim is to establish common ground for how to assess valuable religious elements of traditional religious practices, which require further negotiation before they can be integrated into church teaching. The church should even recognise the fact that there will always be long and short-sighted people who agree with, and are opposed to, the idea of a Christian dialogue with so-called devil worship.

As a matter of fact, it is the church that can help society to shed darkness on the fear that was created by missionaries out of a bias against African culture and beliefs. The church will have to establish a joint community faith centre to search for how to erase past missionary distortions, not just as a one-off type of research, but an ongoing study to examine a number of issues surrounding the abolition of traditional beliefs; for instance, to examine herbs and shrubs used in purification ceremonies by professional medicine stakeholders and religious theologians to assess the beliefs and claims behind sacred places such as trees, stones, hills and rivers used in initiations and other ceremonies, and many other sacred places associated with traditional beliefs.

For example, a few places in Uganda like (Katonda we Butonda) Nakayima and Kiganira, traditionally take children born near the river (Timba) and name them either Settimba (boys) or Natimba (girls). This is the place where my surname originally comes from. If they were born on a hill (Kabugo), they were named Kabugo (boys) or Nakabugo (girls). This happened in many other places in different African countries.

Therefore, there is a need in our educated population to ask and find out the meanings behind African mythological explanations of all these traditions. Also, from the view of a sacred history, the church has to take the basic messages and teachings of revelation history as a foundation for formulating a credible theology of society, rather than blindly failing to develop African theological connections with a modern society such as China.

I will go further to ask why it always needs to be anthropologists from Europe or America who tell us about our own tradition and culture. In contemporary society, Temple's argument is more patently relevant to the economic situation than when it was written. It is quite clear that many people need to hear of a God who can liberate them from this state of bias, allowing them to see that their situation could lead to one in which all people find themselves in God's mission for salvation. This is not illustrative of the preaching of the gospel; it is a demonstration of the reality of God's love.

As Ian Linden states: "Indeed, the starting point for the thinking of the Peruvian theologian, Gustavo Gutierrez, was precisely the disjunction between the Christian message and an experienced reality, that of the Latin American poor. 'How is it possible to tell the poor, who are forced to live in conditions that embody a denial of love, that God loves them?' His implied answer was that this message would be a lie if God's love, and thus the Christian Gospel, were disincarnate, not about changing the world of the poor economically, socially and politically." (http://www.sedos.org/english/liden2.htm/12/8/07)

With reference to today, the quest for a contextual theology illustrates the significance of the need for African society to share the love of God and involve itself in evaluating the immediate issues of everyday life. Indeed, it is the task of Christianity in Africa to show people the means by which to move forward and to assure every ethnic group that living in such an ethnically pluralistic culture is part of God's design to manifest the purpose of His Kingdom. (John 11:52).

The assumption is that a devotedly pluralistic culture would develop a theology based on normative teaching about politically sensitive issues, explaining that differential politics causes suffering and dehumanising conditions for both the oppressor and the oppressed.

It has been said that there is a need for the church to explain its doctrines and symbols in order to create an inclusive platform for all in society. It has also been argued that the "truth monopoly" and the doctrine of Christ incarnate do not justify any culture as superior to others. Giving prominence to one truth is argued as tantamount to missing the point that God's revelation is regarded as symbolic and there is a need to go beyond human geographical boundaries in order to arrive at the everlasting love God has for humankind, which He has created.

It is this everlasting love, even when humankind is in the darkness of sin, which is implied in the nature of God. For instance, Ryangombe's historicity is comparable to that of the Israelis (Yahweh) and this concept of Yahweh is of cultural, rather than cosmic significance. The title is a respectful surname (as in the Old Testament); therefore it is argued that Yahweh of the Jews was very much a god of Gihanga in Kinyarwanda (creator) character. Yahweh was interested in the welfare of the Israelites, took their side against other nations and expected certain behaviour from his people if they were to retain his favour.

Another argument is that of Old Testament sacrifices, which have their origins in paganism's attempts to keep the tribal gods content. (Genesis 22:1–14). It is argued that it is through this environmental background that Yahweh called the Israelites out from the familiar security of family, clan and household gods, to the insecurity of a desert journey (Genesis 12:1–16). Successive generations are socialised into it, but not as passive or manipulated learners. Likewise, Gihanga is a god who plays a part in Africans' daily affairs and in the living faith. To some, including those who have little or nothing to do with active membership of Christianity in Africa, He is real, His presence is near and His care is certain.

A belief in Christianity is not necessarily a belief in Christianity in Africa. Yet Christianity in Africa is an important element of the Christianity that is believed in and is said still to be trusted. However, it is never identified with Christianity as such; it is "only human". If Christianity in Africa is believed in, it has to exist and operate in society as a vehicle of Christian unity, support all people to direct them to Christ's way of living as witnesses to His virtues and appeal to non-Christian believers. Richard Gray called it "a problem of historical perspective", asking "In order to become a Christian, must the African cease to be African?" (Gray, R. A paper originally submitted to the conference on "The Anglican in a Changing Society" held in August 1977 to mark the quincentenary of Uppsala University).

Moreover, this did not mean that the disappearance of traditional belief was imminent; rather that converts adopted the culture of the missionaries, at least on the surface, to become "Black Europeans" rather than Christians.

All of this could have contributed to the state of confusion surrounding the meaning of Christianity. This meant that to be a Christian involved a number of things, including the abandonment of traditional culture and preaching of the gospel, which they had been taught in foreign terms. It was even stated by findings that converts were encouraged by revivalist missionaries to despise the old ways, which created a crisis among converts. I believe that this crisis has a similar effect on our church members today, in the fact that converts were expected to act based on the demands of their new faith and to be detached from the local community. The whole network of informal interpersonal relationships ceased to play a determining role in the systems of mutual aid, welfare, recreation and economic production and distribution. They were manifestly detached from positions of functional relevance to society and decisions about the communities they had belonged to.

On the other hand, Africans were used to the belief that wealth brought with it certain obligations to help the less fortunate, as well as the opportunity for status, prestige and approval by providing feasts and demonstrating personal generosity. In fact, I agree in particular with an argument of Richard Harris, that these were contradictions that caused confusion in the minds of many converts. The implication of their actions and the probable long-term consequences were that when converts tried to relate their new belief to the traditional concepts that wealth and success were, naturally, signs of the blessings of God or of the ancestors; it was their way of making sense of conversion. (Harris, Richard, (Ed.), [1975]. The Political Economy of Africa, Cambridge, Mass: Schenkman, p. 99).

When trapped under these contradictions, converts reasoned that by accumulating wealth beyond their personal needs, as the Europeans did, they could then acquire prestige through the redistribution of the excess wealth. However, the converts continued to see missionaries living with what they saw as unimaginable wealth, preaching the message of Christian charity and love for one's neighbour, yet giving away very little.

The question of "Who is my neighbour?" challenged missionaries to share the common life in Christ. In this respect, many elderly converts stressed that such practices were often connected with conversion, but many findings saw this move as dangerous and deluded; it appeared to them that the new order relying on private wealth was prone to corruption.

The new cultural order is eventually seen as a breeding ground of crime and disorder, due to its rapidly altering the very institutions that had created real worlds for people (Interviews at Gahini mission, July 1998). Liberal criticism from Popper asserts that such change demanded a realistic construction of that which people had been active in creating, as opposed to that which was imposed. (Popper, K., [1945; 1], p. 7). This confirmed that an individual's perception of what they can do is largely formulated on an abstract sense of the prevailing situation. Therefore, if the missionaries' good intentions were to be understood by converts, they clearly had to be given enough time for both the actions and the message to be digested.

Mario Aguilar argues that it was also essential for missionaries to have considered the importance of identifying what was necessary for change, through consideration of the implications involving converts. Where the converts' ways of living had to change as a sign of moving on from the past, the point argued by findings was that at the same time, missionaries were using messages that were often misunderstood by convents. (Aguilar, M. I., [1996]. Nos. 148 – 150, p. xii.).

The critical voice raised against the procedures argues that to insist on change was not necessary. Harris agreed that the missionaries' role must have seemed rather confusing to converts (Harris, Richard, (Ed.), [1975], p. 100). Indeed, in a sense it is true that under such conditions converts faced startling differences between what they observed and what they were told. The situation can only be understood through what Southall observes as the Christian missions being colonial forerunners (Southall A., [1961], p. 3).

It soon became clear that neither the universal franchise, people's beliefs or the colonial movement had succeeded in making much of a dent in the monopolisation of a culture in society that was relatively strange to people. One way of silencing those who were apparently opposed to the principle was to use the argument known as the "civilising mission", which suggested that a temporary period of African dependence or tutelage was necessary in order for the "uncivilised" society to advance to the point where they were capable of sustaining liberal institutions and self-governance.
(http://www.seo.leeds.ac.uk/entries/colonialism/11/9/07).

We can thus argue that despite the positive sound of universalism, it was taught and developed in European or American cultures, derived from Eurocentrism on the world, which could never be accepted, for example, by African people through the cosmos-vision of indigenous peoples, nor by more universalistic Christians. In this globalised world, theology and politics are intertwined, obscuring a poor approach to local needs and the aspirations of people in the colonies, making it ineffective.

Rather than bringing greater insight and sensitivity to the philosophy of Christian universalism and not treating different cultures and traditions with bias, it had its own limits that were specifically to do with European cultural influence, affecting the deepest level of the local environment's cultural practice. Assuming that Christianity was a universal religion should not have detracted from the accomplishment of a universal equilibrium Christianity, which can manifest itself in different ways in different times and cultures, while remaining essentially unchanged.

It is further argued that in the first instance, universal equality was a Christian obligation, concerned with equality for all people everywhere.

However, the universalism required was not cultural uniformity, but the salvation of humankind in his or her environment, through the interpretation of salvation in his or her own culture and from the wide teaching of Christianity that portrays Christ as not just a Man, but the Man par excellence who came for all mankind; the Man in whom we are all to be united in a universal brotherhood, in whom all diversities can exist in unison. Moreover, Christ is God.

On the other hand, from the local perspective of self-determination, this argument made sense of linking the structure of society and the structure of thought, suggesting that people should learn ideals of values and forms of morality drawn from Christ and society. In fact, this dilemma presents a significant difficulty to the heart of any effort aimed at defining morality by reference to an external authority. I will quickly add that conversion showed regularity rather than idiosyncrasy of what social scientists often call values. It is arguable that the notion was a sociological solution to the problem that Western philosophical forms of values and moralities are often seen as outdated, where new forms could be advanced as society develops.

The controversy here is that the morality implied in the nature of the proposed varying values imposed on society is open to debate. The symbolism in a society can serve as a criterion or standard for selection among the alternative orientations to what may be called a value. For instance, love, tolerance and justice are values for Christianity that forbid bias and prejudice, but where these two are restricted, then claims for truth fall short.

On the other hand, it is also important to note that universalism had nothing to do with Christian spirituality, even though it was often treated as such by agents of cultural change. Furthermore, findings argued that missionaries brought not only the seed of the gospel, but also the soil, the flower and the flowerpot. (Interviewing elderly Anglican members at Gahini mission, July 1998). It was these aspects that showed a lack of awareness of local beliefs and thoughts, which could have contributed to this idea of universal culture. Since there was no completely universal perspective of policies, all human thoughts and beliefs were limited by structural bounds.

It is argued that human recognition does take place in the midst of countless cultural variables. Subjective universalism at the time could have encouraged openness in the Christian mission and in colonial dealings with Africans. In assuming a level of communication, but knowing that the provision of adequate information is not a guarantee of successful communication, the question is whether or not the message is relevant and transparent to the receiver.

I wish further to argue that the messengers of the gospel paid more attention to their values and the message than they paid to the receiver. In other words, contextualisation involves valuing other people more than ourselves and our cherished methods or culture, regardless of others' backwardness or lack of development. It was this type of détente campaign against anything not (European) Christian that has influenced African church leaders to ignore their own revelation of God.

Christopher I. Ejizu comments, "While it is true that the traditional religion still has considerable influence in the life and culture of many African peoples, it no longer enjoys exclusive dominance and control over the life of the vast majority of the population. The prevailing social and political order in most parts of contemporary sub-Saharan Africa resembles more the state of affairs in European countries." (Christopher I. Ejizu, African Traditional Religions and the Promotion of Community - Living in Africa).

But it was not fashionable to oppose the menace of cultural dominance during colonial rule. However, it is arguable that Christian ethical morality could have helped church leaders voice their feelings in making rational decisions, enabling missionaries to formulate well-developed strategies that would function in a reasonably integrated fashion. Increased consciousness of these cultural variables is generally identified as significant at this period of Christian conversion and this is why it is argued as the sensible universal revelation, which raises the issue of finite human understanding, through which God's love and self-disclosure are visible.

Furthermore, the denial of people's culture and tradition is an example of political colonialism denying common experience that has a legitimate place in the contextual theological scene and that there are signs that such approaches must be reversed in the contemporary Christian church, especially in Africa. (Cf. Burdon, C.R., 1964, "Theological Expository Times", February Issue, p. 12).

People live today in the presence of greed, indifference and corruption and when they see that their situation is as severe as it ever was, it is clear that what was claimed about conversion is not true. If it is viewed in this way, a church theology of religious diversity is needed to develop the idea of inclusiveness in a local context and for the church to pursue a wider vision of Christ's mission suitable for the twenty-first century in Africa.

By pursuing this mission, the church is not only searching for a way forward towards harmonising traditional believers, but this is seen as the best option for a functional role for the church; it only calls on the church to act as steward or caretaker of God's world. The church arrogating to itself a sort of judgemental God to assume a superior and dominant role over other beliefs, is seen as a crisis of rationality.

I wish, therefore, to conclude that to examine the latest resurgence in traditional religion from a psychological approach is as essential as doing so from a social-anthropological one. Since psychological fears echo the rationality crisis arising in contemporary society, they encourage wrong initiatives, for instance of immorality, which would include lying, cheating, killing, stealing, defacing another's property and other similar forms of deviant behaviour.

This takes us back to consider the previous question of power as imperative control; the probability that a specific command will be obeyed. The notion needs to be seen in the light of the methods of Christian conversion, which undermined the question of choice, often never considered by the church, but often used to exclude and judge traditional beliefs as evil practices. However, a number of issues emerge out of "truth" claims that restrict the omniscience and omnipotence of God's knowledge. For example, what about those who died before the arrival of Christianity; are they all for damnation? Many never came to know God before the advent of Christianity in Africa, in which case they died without the knowledge of God.

Of course, a good evangelist may argue that because of the fact that there was no one to convert them, or bring them to Christ the Saviour, they were therefore destined to damnation. However, I would argue that they were all judged by either their consciences or God's grace. If we believe that every human being is created by God, then God has control over creation in every generation and power in all spheres of life to meet the needs of His creation, under the theological concept of omniscience, the process that atheists often fail to acknowledge; God's temporal knowledge of all past, present and future events. (PS 16:198; PT 97).

John Macarthur rightly argues, "Is it because I chose God, or is it because God chose me? The construction of the Greek verb for 'chose' indicates that God chose us for himself. Statements defining God's sovereign choice are related to a call for the reformation of church wealth, corruption and abuses of beliefs that are not in the Bible to cause controversy, as if God's election means that sinners don't make decisions. The doctrine of election demonstrates God being God, exercising divine prerogatives. In this case, it will be a shock for some to find that God didn't choose everyone for salvation." (Macarthur, J., 17th March 2009).

The experience of many African societies has shown that missionaries, as noted before, were over-optimistic when they thought of conversion subjecting people and society to a position of religious subjection, which would need church interpretation to bring out the meaning of humankind as God's image. The church was created to see things from this perspective from day one and, from generation to generation, God's message was disseminated, which is why it is believed by many in society today that God existed in African society, even before the arrival of Christianity.

To retaliate against the moral judgements in the Bible, missionaries were bound up with particular social structures and ways of understanding society that were not African. The appropriate response is not to assert the biblical rules regardless, but to ask how they must be re-interpreted to fit and talk to people in their situation and for them to receive them and understand their full meaning. Here the policy of conversion and teaching is seen as opposed to the mission of saving and protecting souls. In general, when pioneering missionaries from all denominations erased social values and replaced community arrangements, they effectively lessened the bonds of society's functioning.

The ultimate objective of the message of the theological context and the whole history of communities and the conditions in which they lived is that their tradition and cultural values had held them together in the past and offered them solidarity, leading to a well-developed division of responsibilities as part of the customary care, love and duty to their neighbour.

All knowledge was set in relative terms and determined by these arrangements for facilitative divisions of labour or bonds that had united and existed for the common cause. In fact, it was unheard of for neighbours to sacrifice a neighbour's child, as happens today. In most cases, human knowledge and behaviour were predisposed to habitual responses by given sets of tradition and cultures, which were treasured by those involved as the glue that held the community together and any individual who was suspected of abrogating customary law, was dealt with by the community. Anyone who either molested a child or caused any harm to anyone was either banished to a far land, or else the whole family subjected to isolation, as punishment of one offender affected the whole family. This deprived families, for instance, of seeking a marriage in the community until the family requested pardon and was restored through a ritualistic ceremony for cleansing.

Considering all these developments, over the years there have been changes in African society, which argues that the foundation of the Christian faith in Africa undermined all those values that had held Africans together in the past as moral restraints. When church missionary teaching insisted on degrading what, for all intents and purposes, was wholly non-spiritual in nature, it abolished every existing belief and value and they had to be abandoned. Nevertheless, what missionaries had not taken into account is that the removal of such beliefs and cultural values had deeper implications, because they were the bonds that had united people. They failed to realise that their removal eventually would lead communities into disintegration, immorality, corruption and lack of communal responsibility.

People are not only physical or spiritual, but also cultural, traditional in mind, soul or spirit and all these values had a functioning role in community activities that brought together people in society. A good example is that of the Hutu and Tutsi, whose cultural and traditional arrangements facilitated a livelihood of co-existence based on historical immigration with different level and qualities of powers of self-determination and self-transcendence. Hence, their knowledge was not time bound, but they were not allowed to act as agents responsible for their own actions.

From a historical social perspective, the analysis is still valid. It is argued that this is a form of social organisation in which there is a minimal division of labour and individuals are united by a collective conscience, usually in religious form, which evolves into organic solidarity. Thus, it is argued that these bonds embodied the society until influences reversed that order.

Communities had a common experience of a communal way of life at their heart. A valid argument for this theory is that it was simply common sense that the division of labour such as among the Uburetwa had economic advantages. In relation to the values and objectives of the system, it is also argued that both missionaries and colonial administrators owed obligatory service to society as a whole and not just to their own interests. This may also mean that their failure was their lack of recognition of value and purpose. For instance, hunters, gatherers and pastoralists had differences in their division of labour that also brought them together to develop and provided a service that complemented different groups' needs to create a feeling of solidarity.

This point resonates with the observation that missionaries needed to recognise the difficulties associated with change, when people needed to be given the opportunity to decide what might be the most appropriate and realistic path they should (or must) take. With reference to the theory of exclusion, when making changes it is important to remember local people's cultural experience. In this case, the historical societal structure that was known to people was important to them, so missionaries needed to recognise the social arrangements. For that matter, the missionaries' approach to society in Africa was seen to be one-sided and influenced by their determination that society and people had to change, as a sign of conversion to Christianity. In short, this insistence meant that missionaries only saw their role as being to achieve conversion and to save souls. In this case, the best approach was to allow people through their cultural influence and creativity simply to dispose of undesirable traditional practices and beliefs.

However, if one follows the emergence of this real possibility of collaboration, it retrospectively invalidates the missionaries' decision to undertake a joint venture of changing or abolishing people's thinking, beliefs, social life and its organisation. To persevere on this sort of mission, no matter what faith is being taught, requires that the society in which the success is achieved be irrevocably changed for better or for worse, and often in ways that are quite destructive and possibly unforeseen. Such cross-cultural understanding is equally indispensable if one seeks to communicate to those of other cultures in terms of their own revelation of God, thoughts about salvation and language describing God. In other words, these were the best ways of grasping what they were abolishing.

Nevertheless, in my view Africans were deliberately cheated out of their concept of God by the abolition of African beliefs such as demon worship. This Westernised version of influence is argued as illogical because it ignored meanings where the logic of reciprocity can also work the other way round, such that the current destructive behaviour points to past undeveloped practices of ritualistic sacrifice. It is important to add that Christian moral duty required tolerance and competence in handling the process of change. However, according to people's views today, from their interpretations of meanings related to naming their children, indigenous names had deep meanings referring to God and creating closeness to God. It is further argued that such expression is necessary for the full flowering and fruiting of spiritual growth. There are also complications caused by the public seeing even religious leaders who are supposed to be society's consciousness, but choose closeness with corrupt leadership.

Nevertheless, being wealthy must not either condemn or be regarded as an evil thing, but what is treated as evil is the means by which the wealth is acquired. If the means are straightforward and acceptable, there is nothing wrong; being wealthy in that case is morally neutral and it is socially useful for communities and nationally to achieve societal needs and to create an environment that helps to meet the population's ability to participate with equal opportunity in national development. The notion of wealth being morally neutral is important for any society where it is argued that the bad dominant culture of corruption and a given action are right, if a particular situation they promote may be regarded as community ends. This reduces people's ability to treat one another well, without values or respect for human sanctity and the motive turns to achieving more and more wealth.

One may then ascertain that a lack of moral foresight comes partly from this attitude. Of course, money gives people access to an immense number of means, which is the purest example that the loss of rationality rests on an untenably narrow conception, which fosters an uncontrolled avarice that feeds individualism and idolises wealth as if is an end in itself. It is, therefore, this external influence that has led many into a belief in - and obsession for – wealth, which has eventually turned people away from values of caring, love and service for one another and has led many to think less of others and more about the pure accumulation of wealth.

However, social integration is achievable through objective culture – the development of universal values and meanings that begins with societal expectations. The growth of such a culture extends human freedom, but constricts the integrity and depth of the individual life. It is further argued that human beings are the crown of creation and are given power to overcome nature and that nature serves them. This is seen as bad if the sense of development contains the kind of greed, wealth worship, immorality and unaccountability that set Sierra Leone, Rwanda, the Democratic Republic of Congo, Ivory Coast and Liberia on fire. Unaccountability saw all sorts of despicable people emerge on the African scene, further destroying the continent. Therefore, restraining yourself from an extreme negative life on earth is fodder for good life in your next incarnation. The metaphysics aside, accountability, as an antidote to corrupt practices, hugely defines progress.

American economist John Kenneth Galbraith said, “Hard, visible circumstance defines reality.” The reality of the campaign for African accountability is that it has not been addressed from the point of view of African culture, which is perhaps the key source of corruption and in which dubious wealth tends to embed within individuals a lack of honesty and integrity. This conception and trend in affairs has been seen as the result of a myriad of factors, which are over-arching for individuals. Individuals will take all means, whether legal or illegal, to endanger other people's lives in the name of acquiring wealth. However, this is the bad sense of creation, which is characterised by traits of corruption, immorality and disrespect of human rights or integrity, when people's very soul is mortgaged to wealth.

This is why it is difficult in many parts of Africa for the new order to break through to the fore after countless years of the disintegration of the post-colonial system of leadership within African society, which has largely not been taken through to its logical development. Therefore, the African struggle for stability and development still has a long way to go from the shackles of colonialism. This is why in many ways people have ceased to have self-control, and the way they acquire success, caught up in the contradictory culture of aspiring high for acquiring wealth in dubious commercial systems, has been the concern of this book.

I will be quick to add that there is no greater scourge that affects the proper functioning of any economic system than corruption. The evaluation of the fulfilment of duty in liberating development affairs is the highest form that the moral activity of the individual could assume and, according to Weber, it is God's calling to save that has the same value in the eyes of God. (Weber, 1930:80).

I therefore want to put forward some of the priorities that communities have identified as an essential next step in the long and arduous need for Christianity in a specifically African context and that a pastoral theology might liberate the disadvantaged, unemployed and homeless. This should be shared among mainstream Christian churches in Africa in the form of an Ecumenical action forum for Christian involvement in the eradication of the moral crisis and wanting to share with others, who have the same concerns, to put them into action.

An ecumenical approach will be all important in thinking about and dealing with the whole of society. The breadth of the problem must not be neglected: the shape and configuration of homelessness will vary in different parts of society and there are many angles to the problem e.g. the psychological stress of poor families in slums or single mothers in rural areas.

Chapter Thirteen

13.1 The Quest for Making Things Better

This chapter looks at ways of safeguarding the public and harmonising rational relationships between Christianity and traditional healing beliefs. The argument for harmonising the two in consideration of the African heritage is seen as an important foundation for Christianity in order to stabilise African religiosity and uproot the historical bias on which the Christian rationality model was based. The research conducted on much of the missionary teachings of Christianity in Africa has found that there are cultural remains of missionary teaching designed to facilitate ideas of change, which still undermine any development of local culture in favour of Western culture. It also shows that no effort was made by the leadership to reform Christian teaching in Africa, especially to re-address the assumed cultural superiority of Christian beliefs to suit the present need for rights of expression of all faith groups in society.

The purpose of this is to move forward rather than lagging behind in every sense of development, to the extent that Africa fails to develop its own culture and identity. It is argued that in this sense development has to start with people's thinking so that they can embrace development. I will therefore concentrate on how to improve the situation, rather than spending time on incriminating those who hold different views or traditional religious beliefs. The idea here is to improve human relationships so that religious communities can launch new developmental programmes, or expand existing ones to tackle issues surrounding the corrupt culture that has led to the human sacrifice crisis, so often portrayed negatively as associated with the existence of traditional beliefs in society.

Abubaker Semmandrwa neatly summed up the current crisis as follows: "The mind clings to events that baffle, watching them like a movie over and over but without the power to choose a different path! Sometimes you may think that you have seen it all but something creepier, spookier comes up." (Abubaker Semmandrwa, in New Vision, 20th March 2009).

Indeed, it is this situation that has left so many people in a state of confusion and anger, lacking knowledge of what to do, with other populations living in fear and those who are terrified to the extent of migrating out of their birth places (villages) in search for a safer haven. It is therefore imperative for the Christian church in Africa to continue a pastoral, sensitive role and where possible to extend a theology whose focus addresses the beliefs that have given rise to the present crisis in order to discern the truth that lies behind these beliefs.

Regarding human sacrifice, the Christian church in my view has the answer to the problem, because it was abolition that pushed traditional healers into hiding, creating the problems in the first place. This is why the church in society today needs to join together with all religious groups to re-examine a range of issues concerning the eradication of human sacrifice, which relies on the prevailing corrupt culture that often serves the same purpose.

The church itself has to develop a theology that offers hope and assurance to traumatised populations who fear the unimaginable havoc created by the lynching of any suspects of sacrifice and theft, which has led to further loss of life. The church has to provide support to the population to cope with the loss of their beloved ones, so that they feel that the Christian church is with them in their suffering. I am sure the church does this very well in Africa, but it has to do more than comforting; it has to work out a way to protect them from any further menace of sacrificing fellow human beings.

The first task for the church in response to this question is to re-invent a listening ear to what people in society say and the values held by distinctive groups; those who never attend church, those who attend sometimes and those who attend nearly every week. This is to highlight the danger of not listening to what society believes in and wants to advance. I am quite optimistic that if the church approaches traditional beliefs with an open mind, it will soon discover that most of the ideas of distortion and demonisation are just a superficial sign of the societal disintegration that has unnecessarily led greedy people to speculative and fake magic or traditional healing.

What I have called "engaging with society" is scrutiny of what is evil and what is not, so that evil can be discouraged and what is not evil integrated into Christian teaching as a means of establishing a system that ensures the stability of the social order and religious harmony. Contextual religious worship and teaching takes people back to their roots, which speak with innocence and directness and which have much appeal in our cynical age.

Of course, the bias against and past hostility to anything that was not European undermined the development of local culture under the guise of introducing a superior culture, which contributed greatly to the persecution of traditional religious beliefs and risked creating conflict in communities. The moment one group appears to be favoured at the expense of other groups, they will claim to have similar needs and, if denied, will have to result to fighting for their rights.

The traditional believers have spoken volumes by the sheer determination of their persistence to be rich, which is evidence that using draconian measures is not the best approach and does not provide a healthy environment or public safety.

The fact of the argument remains that whether other religious groups like traditional religious beliefs or not, they will still exist, even without their approval. Rightly in this view, the Kenyan government was the first officially to acknowledge their existence and accord them recognition. The right move was to adopt Masai traditional religious leadership as a religious presence in the parliament and official functions and implies a response to the contextual situation that follows the discourse theory of co-existence in diversity. The failure of other countries to adopt this policy may be doubly wrong, as it will drive practitioners deeper underground.

It is evident in the human sacrifice crisis that it is dangerous to society and the church urgently needs to develop a context that does not compromise the truth, as it may be defended by the church, but should try to reach Africans where they can be reached and find the kind of communication that can reason with Africans in language that conveys the meaning of salvation.

We need a specific approach to understanding the root causes of the current crisis and the Christian church has a role in society to raise people's consciousness of healthy human relations. This means finding preventive measures that protect body and soul from unnecessary harm. The church's obligation is routinely to invoke Christianity in society, to provide spiritual guidance and ultimately to find the capacity to use persuasive language to safeguard its members and eradicate the reccurrence of human self-destruction, which is most significantly visible in false activism today.

Ironically, according to reports cited by the media, church members are some of the victims caught up in fake witchcraft practices, where they are implicated as clients who kill in order to offer human organs in the belief that they will gain protection and wealth. Therefore, Christianity in Africa must not only respond to this current crisis, but go further to heal the past and reconcile the past to the light.

On the other hand, reformers will have to realise that, due to overwhelmingly strong, anti-traditional religious beliefs, sentiment among born-again Christians paints a picture of disillusionment and frustration, which suggests that religious integration is going not to happen tomorrow. This is seen as realistic, in the sense that the problem has not just happened in one day and also suggests that the process of reversing this crisis will be a long one of educating society. When crisis strikes, no one wants to take the blame, but when it falls, everyone wants to take the credit.

The reversal of the bias against traditional religious beliefs requires careful handling with clear understanding. As always, matters concerning beliefs and faith are deep rooted, as they touch people's treasured beliefs and cultural values, so they require more sensitive and delicate handling than might appear on the surface. In this view, it is further argued that sound contextual theological reasoning is require to work hard to develop an inclusive theory of diversity over religious differences in practice to discern authentic and genuine healing practices from fake ones.

The plea is for the church to stop apportioning blame to traditional healers and to start providing more practical help and support for integration and to halt preaching against traditional beliefs. The mission paradigm of a monopoly on truth is criticised heavily today in intellectual circles and is considered to have been used to prejudice local beliefs, but it still poses a challenge for churches to face the truth because the solution isn't simply passing by on the other side.

The old Christian population, having had fear heavily instilled into them, visibly regard traditional beliefs as devilish. Therefore, there is a need for religious dialogue to deal with the resistance to integrating traditional beliefs into church teaching, where each feeds off and reinforces the other, even though they may appear superficially contradictory.

There is no bridging space; instead of the church being a cultural melting pot, it has become a church that does everything possible to maintain the past. The religious dialogue has to address the cynicism about devilish worship, which was functionally analogous to the role of missionary Christianity, which caused tension about releasing people's emotions and expression in worship. It is evident in the order of service in liturgical worship that not only worship, but hymns and the Christian ethos, are still foreign in nature, with negative attitudes towards drums and clapping in church and the preference towards pianos and organs as holier instruments of worship.

The anti-traditional religious beliefs in today's African church must be considered as a thing of the past, even though the trend continues to dominate minds in many African churches' old populations. The integration debate has not yet reached fever pitch, but who knows, a real test for multicultural worship could happen in the future. As a matter of fact, the integration of traditional beliefs in my opinion has to be enforceable in society, as all claims set in every system of belief that requires enforceable rights imply that there must be somebody to enforce the rights of traditional healers, in the "rule of law" and in society.

If the idea of traditional healing is to be one with effect, it will always require the potential for the enforcement of order and safety for public use, not enforced by the owner of the rights (even if at his or her behest or request), but rather by the rule of law. In order to protect the public, it is essential that rights are legitimated and enforced by law.

13.2 Regulating Traditional Healing

The analysis of guidelines for good practice is also a means of encouraging and retaining the confidence of practitioners. Affirming good practice where it exists, means introducing a law to protect the public when it becomes necessary to argue that rules cannot be deduced from values, unless a problematic situation prompts someone to make the deduction. This is why it requires urgent and decisive action to guarantee the freedom of genuine traditional healers and to protect the most vulnerable; otherwise the culture of corruption will continue to breed a more severe crisis. One of the key goals is to regulate by law because the law is a rational, deductive system that controls what the state has granted permission to do, including church self-regulation and traditional healers.

For instance, as far as possible, the environment for healing should be suitable, safe, clean, well-lit, suitably ventilated, with comfortable seating provided and access and facilities available for elderly and disabled people. The whole establishment has to be agreed by the healing practice and parishioners under the guidance of agreed guidelines, based either on religious traditions, or on a cultural basis. A peaceful and reverent atmosphere conducive to healing depends on various factors, but must be recognised by the regulating body.

It is helpful to distinguish between the natural environment and adaptations to the different kinds of places in which the healing ministry is offered; for example, healing rituals taking places in shrines, in church, healing to the sick by hospital chaplaincy at home, healing ministries at open-air services and healing centres. In any circumstance, when administering healing to someone in the home setting, care should be taken to avoid informality slipping into, or appearing to become, inappropriate intimacy. In the context of healing, for instance, at church or at home, it is good practice to avoid healing in privacy and on one's own with persons of the opposite sex, children and adolescents and strictly to avoid discussing individuals' private issues with anyone without consent, in private or in public.

It is advisable to avoid having two or more men ministering to a woman alone; whenever possible a family member should be involved who is the same gender as the person receiving healing care. Church leaders or any other group involved in the healing ministry need to accept standards of conduct for all those involved in the healing. A common understanding of what constitutes good practice must be encouraged and everyone involved should take sensible precautions to safeguard their profession and to protect themselves from any malicious or scandalous allegations and from any possibility of physical attack from sick patients. It is also preferable to avoid late-night visits to people who are not already known, if no one else is around to assist or witness, in case of unexpected behaviour.

This all stems from a view of how to manage good practice, where public values can provide major premises from which specific rules are deduced and conflict minimised between specific groups, with shared or differing interests. At this juncture, there is a realisation that when one section forbids traditional healing practices and another demands them, this then becomes a social conflict. Therefore, the basic principle of state intervention in traditional healing is a principle of public protection, stipulating the legal observance and requirements of all those who are in healing practice following traditional methods. It is arguable that in the longer term, extending education will achieve inclusion and enhance tolerance and stability, ushering in opportunities in society.

I will also conclude that, if missionaries had not meddled in things they did not understand, traditional religious beliefs could have been encouraged to take on a more positive role and there might have been drastic reduction in the existence of dubious traditionalist claims from magicians and witchcraft.

The rapid increase in the number of fake healers is due to the fact that traditional healers still offer the opportunity as a source of hidden culture. Furthermore, when the freedom of individual values is ambiguous and generally interfered with to restrict bad and unacceptable practices, those concerned are more likely to form resistance for their survival. It is under this situation that the rule of law is applicable, when a piece of carefully drawn legislation can promote harmony. Overall, there is a feeling that the system as it currently operates is very arbitrary and should be changed or tightened up in order to effectively manage the service, both in terms of clinical safety and availability to clients.

The lack of guidance or a standardised procedure for eliciting evidence means, not surprisingly, that the conviction of suspects has not been easy because of poor litigation and often irrelevant organisations tampering with evidence and resulting in the information given being irrelevant, as has happened in some incidents. If the emphasis is put on the protection of the public, it will require a sensitive approach to avoid misunderstandings from traditional groups, who should not feel as if the government's regulatory rules are encroaching on their right to existence. In order to maintain a traditional healing service in safety, it requires standards and quality therapeutic intervention and supervision to ensure that the healing service is clinically safe.

The nature of traditional healers' work is such that its input will greatly benefit the public user. In turn, traditional healing clinics must end being secretive, hidden services and operate according to set working hours, like modern Western medical centres. On the other hand, the supporters of traditional healing believe that the use of European medicine and the supernatural are mutually exclusive. In some way, both traditional healers and Christianity seem to agree that since the root cause of sickness is sin and the only cure of sin is spiritual, the cure for sickness is spiritual.

So far, there are beliefs among many Africans that the introduction of European medicine was the missionaries' instrument to defeat traditional healers' practices. Therefore, the idea behind this is to improve traditional healers' management to offer required guidelines to protect the public and provide sufficient information to enable the healing service to be easily available and safe for its users.

Another issue that urgently needs regulatory attention is the lack of a clear legal distinction in definitions of a traditional healer or herbalist, witchdoctor or wizard. It was therefore proposed recently by the Ugandan parliament to ban pornography and for the government to enact a law regulating the activities and practices of traditional healers and herbalists. (New vision, article, by Joyce Namutebi and Catherine Bekunda Friday, 10th April, 2009).

At the same time, civic leadership in African society needs to tighten the control and punishment of those proved guilty of the practice of sacrificing human beings. The theory of knowledge is important and must be put into practise through biblical teaching in order for people to know God well in their own cultures. Firstly, we must keep in mind that the Bible is the self-revelation of God disclosed to people in their own geographical environment, and the urban and rural messages required to be set up in the teaching of Christianity in Africa are the source material for developing great thoughts about God.

In this concluding section, I wish to pay particular attention to safeguarding the public in terms of taking responsibility for all issues relating to vulnerability, especially child protection. Basic preventive measures must be put in place, but advocacy of the African mode of thinking must be encouraged to promote its societal culture, tradition and beliefs which, based on hard evidence, have persisted all these centuries. Therefore, preventive measures are not to prevent the development of the belief, but for full recognition of the contribution it may offer in a healing role in society. If services are regulated and officially granted the freedom to develop in their technique, it will weed out fake pretenders who exploit vulnerable people.

This demands that the government plays a critical role as a regulator of physiology and behaviour. This includes regulatory healing procedures and openness practices. An operational balance in regulatory policy is argued as the right course of action to end the demonisation of African beliefs and healing practice by opposing forces, which seem to have either misunderstood them or to have denied them opportunity for so long. It is therefore under these conditions that it becomes vital to regulate the operation of traditional healing for public safety. In brief, the proposed regularising mechanism for traditional healing falls into three categories:

1. Public protection will mean introducing testing of all traditional healers and those inspiring to become such. The assessment process comprises representatives from various communities in society and must include traditional religious leaders to establish operating guidelines. Also, the

traditional healers need to carry out thorough scrutiny to examine and test the proven authenticity of each aspirant traditional healer. Authenticity need not concern the church, as it is its attitude that remains significant, yet the questions that are posed are questions that really do require answers. The scrutiny must include proof of an element of moral blamelessness, without a devilish mind of any kind.

In the process of approving each traditional healer, some mental element is always necessary and in legal terms this is known as mens rea. In order for the government to protect the public properly, it has to appreciate that it is necessary to distinguish between a number of different possible mental attitudes, which individual healers may have with respect to public safety and healing quality.

The purpose of questioning is to establish the following: (a) intention, (b) stable mind, (c) duty of care and (d) blameless inadvertence. In this case, the selection of traditional healers has to follow some guidelines set by traditionalist religious leaders, guided by the government-appointed body, which likewise needs to fall into line in the selection process of other accredited organisations serving the public, if they are to be trusted in society as genuine healers. Numerous cases of rape and murder have been reported relating to traditional healers' misconduct and the failure to implement a protective policy is seen by many as the government's failure to protect its citizens.

2. Registration of all approved traditional healers is necessary to protect clients who use the service. To build and maintain links with authorities and associations is a measure of inclusion similar to Western medical practitioners' registration, which enables knowledge of who is providing a service and accountable to the public and also requires practitioners to keep visible records of their clients. There is a need to provide general consultancy and advice to a range of traditional healing individuals, or

groups interested in developing healing practices in openness. On this note, I wish to raise another issue, which may sound irrelevant but is important, which is how politicians in society often fail to implement protective measures in order to avoid offending their voters, instead of waiting to respond to crises, which can be prevented before they happen. They put on a show as if they care for public safety and yet do nothing about the root cause of the problem, which arises out of the lack of safeguarding policies.

3. There is a further need to collect and disseminate examples of good practice using a range of formats, to keep records and monitor and evaluate the work undertaken and to provide feedback to the body of traditional healers, who will also need government protection and monitoring based on multidisciplinary approaches, including an independent monitoring body. To access traditional healers' performances, the monitoring body will annually provide a report of performance to relevant authorities; for instance, politicians and other concerned officials, as agreed by the government.

The purpose of these reports is to assess the good or bad conduct of certain traditional healers; those found disregarding the guidelines must be cautioned and if they habitually abuse the code of conduct, the governing body will decide whether to put them under suspension and to forbid them from doing any healing service until they have agreed to reform. Furthermore, their names should be published so that the public is aware of the suspension of their service.

The decision that needs to be reached not only provides a solution to the present crisis, but also establishes guidelines that can be followed in the future. However, if there is evidence of any risk to clients' lives by the service provided by traditional healers or if anyone ignores the guidelines, and if they fail to give sound reasons, then the governing body must do what medical bodies do and strike off from the register of authorised healers.

Some critics may argue that removing them from the register is sanctioning them to operate an underground practice. However, I disagree, because removing them from the register does two important things for the public. Firstly, it informs the public about useless or fake healers who are a danger to clients' lives. Secondly, if anything endangers people's lives or an incident occurs that is related to traditional healers, the police will know where to start with their enquiries. Nevertheless, if the public ignores the warning they have no one to blame but themselves. Also, these guidelines obviate the need to "reinvent the wheel" every time new fake healing techniques are re-discovered by the governing body, which will deny them authorisation.

I therefore agree with the view held by a Ugandan government minister, whose argument was that the absence of a national policy on the operations of traditional healers and herbalists was hampering the fight against the vice. (New Vision, Tuesday, 17th March 2009). He added that in January of that year a murder case linked to human sacrifice was registered, while seven deaths were recorded in February. In the same month, 18 people were reported missing, only five of whom have been found.

Therefore, it is naïve to suggest that if traditional healers and herbal medicine can offer a complementary therapeutic alternative to Western medical healing care, it would be advantageous in a society where there are financial problems to meet the population's demand for more doctors. Of course, traditional healing could simply supplement modern medicine and it may be seen as the best measure to integrate traditional healers into a more specialised system of modern medicine, which should not give any impression of the government reducing the national healthcare budget.

The regulatory system should depend on the usual channels of financial assistance from government. This would allow the government to impose restrictions on all traditional practitioners and require them to register their services for expansion, regardless of how traditional healing individuals choose to channel those services. This would strengthen public safety and traditional healers' rights to develop their skills in an open atmosphere.

It is further argued that the spiritual element can be channelled into psychiatrists and therapists and that religious communities should explore the possibilities of creating a dialogue for constructive debate with all those concerned to harmonise traditional healers' conduct and weed out what are regarded as devilish acts, to nurture what is agreed as acceptable. In actual fact, there are some practices which, when reinforced positively and properly, could help in personal development, especially in worship, but it initially requires the church to acknowledge such practices. It will all depend on the use of historical-critical tools of biblical exegesis to promote a healthy environment for poor and rich alike and for all religious communities to live in diversity. (New Vision, Tuesday, 17 March 2009).

Interestingly, findings have also identified that each tribe or area has its own ritual celebrations, but similar cultural values, as revealed recently when the Mengo government was negotiating with the Busoga to let the Baganda perform their rituals. As stated by Musoke, "We cannot allow people from Busoga to perform rituals on this river." The spokesperson of Buganda went on to explain that the issue of ritual celebration on the river was being handled by the kingdom's culture ministry. He added that the Mengo would identify people eligible to carry out the rituals. Traditional healers in the district, led by Godfrey Najja, alleged that the spirits recently washed away the bridge and caused the death of eight people who were crossing the river in a canoe.

In the view of past misconceptions of society's traditional values, all these incidents were likely to occur and are signs of neglect and the lack of a focused vision to prevent a crisis before it happens. While it challenges Christianity in Africa to sound warnings in the public interest, even if it is a voice in the wilderness, it is the best broad vision of Christianity in Africa to protect society at the same time as saving human lives. This is argued as the mission of Christ's liberation for Christianity in Africa with its immediate needs.

The early church doctrine played up "big factor" religious misconceptions, often associated with local crises in beliefs. It was therefore against this background that inculturation was addressed in the Pope's encyclicals Evangelii Praecones and Fidei Donum, issued on 2nd June 1951 and 21st April 1957, respectively, which increased the local decision making of Catholic missions, many of which became independent dioceses. Pius XII demanded recognition of local cultures as fully equal to European culture. (Audience for the directors of mission activities in 1944 A.A.S., 1944, p. 208; *Evangelii Praecones* p. 56).

Finally, the churches must come together in the midst of the crisis to radically overhaul the past misconceptions of African culture, in order to appreciate people's beliefs, improve decision making and value what is important and good for the church and what is not.

Chapter Fourteen

Conclusion

I have tried to show how the process of the resurgence of ritualistic sacrifice has been built into the abolition of traditional African religious beliefs and, through numerous social changes, has been brought about by both external and internal influences on people's way of thinking, believing and acting.

This final chapter seeks to draw conclusions from the past events of Christian conversion, in order to bring out the meaning and relevance of gospel church teaching today in African society. Thus, it is befitting to conclude with stressing that it was a mistake to distort people's beliefs and abolish their religious traditions, which dispensed with all rituals and beliefs that diverted Africans from their own revelation of God. The diversion, in essence a falsification or distortion, is argued as having had an impact on people in society, which led to the consequence of a resurgence of ritualistic beliefs, as well as the innovation of a newly illegal fake healing culture.

This short chapter will aim to give a brief summary of the main findings of the historical impact of Christianity in Africa, which can be analysed as more than a wish to convert people to Christianity. Its hypothesis is a legitimate goal of making an ideological contribution to the colonising forces examined in sociological research, from an empirical scientific system linked to the abolition of people's cultures and the suppression of their beliefs. All points of human experience gradually faced controversies associated with the unjust changes, which were one-sided in the conversion doctrine in African society.

Finally, there are signs of strained relationships and subsequent developments that have led to social disintegration. This is seen as long-term deviant behaviour which might have affected people's thinking and acting.

The resurgence of ritual sacrifice is a result of such long-term suppression, where there was no room for negotiation between the new belief (Christianity) and traditional beliefs; the imposed culture and ideas lacked development in the long run and wrecked community morality. Furthermore, in a society that is full of an obsession for wealth, people will continue to lose the sense of valuing and caring for one another. It is this crisis, clearly arising out of extreme corruption, which calls for a consciousness of mission, whose purpose is to develop pastoral inclusiveness theoretically and practically.

Firstly, Christianity in Africa needed to free itself from all the continuing influences of the colonial period. Secondly, there was a tendency for missionary Christianity to devalue traditional African culture and especially to dismiss traditional religion as heathen or pagan. This attitude left no room for a sympathetic appreciation of all that there was in African culture, or for the assimilation of traditional ideas and rituals into Christianity.

The root cause common to the entire movement for independence, therefore, may be seen in this one aspect of culture clash. This agrees with D. B. Barrett's observation of the following failures on the part of missionaries: the failure to demonstrate consistently the fullness of the biblical concept of love as sensitive understanding towards others as equals; the failure to study or understand African society, religion and psychology in any depth and the failure to draw an African perspective from the vernacular scriptures. There is an urgent necessity to remedy this situation in order that Christianity might survive on African soil. (Barrett, D. B., 1968, P.156).

This inability to communicate is manifested particularly in certain areas, namely the ancestor cult, magic, illness and sexuality, in which all missionaries failed to appreciate the African point of view. This could be argued as due to the fact that missionaries looked at society with differing beliefs, through European lenses and had no instruction in diversity. Of course, this situation is a challenge to the general and overdue need for the church to change its perception about the exclusivist and pluralist relationship between traditional beliefs and Christianity in African society in general.

In today's pluralistic environment, every religion has the right of expression and propagation of its belief. John Calvin once remarked that true wisdom consists almost entirely of two parts: the knowledge of God and the knowledge of ourselves. He went on to say that "As these are connected together by many ties, it is not easy to determine which of the two proceeds and gives birth to the other."

Following on from this, in the days when missionary change was high on the agenda, the church could probably have disagreed by saying that everyone's salvation is on the line and the converts had to obey the rules. It is also arguable that where religion is concerned, there are many roads up the mountain, but the view from the top is the same.

Traditional believers were under pressure to believe wholeheartedly and the doctrinal use of bias excluded traditional beliefs that constantly undermine Christian principles, the church testimony of tolerance and the greater commandment of love thy neighbour as thy self. In general, the approach to change and conversion in African society meant that traditional beliefs and culture were deemed as unacceptable, looking at it from the Christian point of view. This is why it is argued that the spirit of intolerance departed from the Christian truth that if you don't agree with someone in a particular respect, that does not mean that you must abolish their beliefs or punish them. Thus it was vital to consider a more appropriate approach to conversion to Christianity.

It is argued that the Christian task is always to love thy enemy, even if there is no enemy in the physical sense, or for that matter, the spiritual sense. What existed was only a difference between Christianity and traditional beliefs in the source of revelation and the background of tradition and culture. These differences needed to be examined and allowed to nurture, so that cultural and theological differences could develop and be integrated and protected in a spirit of diversity.

This book has given an analysis of the process by which society has for a long time been engaged in creating a culture that has placed people in a process used to endanger human lives in the form of ritualistic sacrifice.

It seems obvious to me from considerable field experience and observation that this is a very relevant, fertile ground on which the process of corruption and cultural manipulation became entrenched and, in the process, allowed the resurrection of ritualistic murder in the form of fake traditional healing and a trade in human sacrifice.

The book has also criticised the lack of freedom for traditional beliefs to develop and their abolition by Christianity, whose agents cooperated with the colonisers to marginalise local ideas, beliefs and cultures. It has demonstrated aspects of the changes emerging during colonial rule, when missionary conversion in society established structures of conflict between the old beliefs and the new religiosity. It has shown how beliefs and concern for culture were defused, diverted or bluntly ignored and marginalised in a process that was restrictive of cultural development.

To describe missionary conversion as “insensitive” to African society’s ideas, beliefs and culture would be too generous. Most societies’ experience of Christian conversion was that missionaries neglected local beliefs and ignored people’s cultures. The crisis of human sacrifices is intimately associated with these patterns of change. The fact that missionaries underplayed the role of community values and traditional beliefs has been criticised as a mistaken decision today.

This book has extensively argued that the early practices constituted much of the differentiation and have continued to foster a spiral of discontent and mistrust in the relationship between the church and traditional beliefs, to such an extent that the author is doubtful that society will ever restore the old traditional religious beliefs to their former respected place.

The hypothesis has centred on the church’s belief that the fact that traditional ritualistic practices were forced underground is now the source of the search for help to allow genuine traditional healers to seek redress, and that introducing regulatory control of anti-social fake groups’ activities will develop stronger and tougher procedures and allow the perpetrators of ritualistic murder to be punished. No issue is more worrying than achieving a total and uncompromising crackdown on fake behaviour, but it is otherwise essential for the church to be willing to read the sources and evaluate the reasons for the resurgence in rituals, which could easily become a deeper problem for society.

The dilemma, which still poses a danger, is the ineffectual persistence of past missionary teaching, which increasingly shows signs of irrelevance leading to a loss of impact in the church’s message and its relevance and legitimacy in controlling people’s conduct. In the eyes of those who continue to search for help, if their voices were heard, they might argue that condemnation alone is a form of self-defence but not a remedy. They may then seek an alternative solution, when in a sense, the church's condemnation is an admission of society's failure, a condemnation of despair and one from which fake traditional healers are more likely to recoil.

It is against this sobering background of failure and continuing despair that this conclusion sets out the overwhelming factor that runs through the heart of the problem: the paradox that informs and explains so much of the failure of religious institutions to make a rigorous analysis of the source of the ritualistic murder. In these circumstances, a theological model that deals with uncomfortable and contradictory situations is suddenly supposed to become a source of support at a time of crisis, specifically designed to build a social structure through which the Christian message can be made effectively accountable to the wider society. This theology accounts for a lot of the misunderstanding and negative feeling among practitioners of traditional medicine and the victims of ritual practices. So what are the fundamental changes that need to be considered?

It is true that, in the long term, the church has denied validity of traditional religious beliefs in a society where they still draw large numbers of believers or sympathisers into their network. However, to maintain this condemnation does not take away the possibility of concessions, which would allow professional practices to be permitted, but controlled and regulated under a supervisory system.

If the faulty messages of conversion were ill designed for the task, the argument is as follows. The primary function - and indeed the proper function - of the church is to ensure that its proper messages reign and that the church system is restructured and reformed. For any amount of additional improvements to be likely to bring about significant benefit for the targeted communities, permission for access to traditional practice will have to be agreeable. Since time has moved on, traditional beliefs will have to move on too in order to find their rightful place to continue to shape society in the right way. The cutting edge of these functions is delegated to those who still trust and believe in traditional rituals and who need to liaise on a day-to-day basis and look for help, acting as their clients do. In these circumstances, the church has to be realistic and exercise a quasi-mediating function, recognising as a necessity that Christianity accepts the integration of what is essentially regarded as an important culture and identity for people.

Domination ideology was dominant, not total, and Christian conversion signified the practice of many contradictions in the form of different denominations that offered rival versions. On the other hand, it is difficult to deal with some of the traditional beliefs, which had such unpleasant manifestations. It is not surprising that many church leaders find the whole subject very off-putting. However, the view that has to change is that there is nothing good in traditional beliefs; the church is obviously challenged by their presence and persistence and their survival in society for centuries. The church needs to focus on mediation, support and policing function and to be willing to reconcile with and help traditional healers where it can. There are, however, other dimensions of the question of what can be done about the fear of human sacrifice.

Firstly, the church's leadership needs urgently to recognise the constant need to inject fresh ideas and impetus for behavioural change into its ministry, looking to bridge gaps and help individuals cope with an ever-changing society by enabling strategies for spiritual growth. To change human behaviour requires a very strong commitment to learning and development and opportunities that constantly encourage personal growth on a daily basis.

It may be appropriate here to propose that the public needs to hear constantly about state policies that support a high regard for human life, which is vital to create an atmosphere of mutual trust and creates public confidence that the state is in control of responsible behaviour.

Secondly, if institutions in society know the source of the crisis, it does help the public through the provision of high moral principles, which will enable and support the change in human behaviour.

Thirdly, the priority of improving living conditions needs attention, given the fact that signs of moral deterioration have shown that society will never end the corruption culture unless threats to human survival are prevented, which for many is a great concern considering the lack of community care for one another either socially, economically or religiously.

Some research I recently came across shows that the consequences of the deterioration in moral values have significantly altered the delivery of community care to the population in a culture in which corruption is already endemic. It is therefore imperative for society collectively to instil the values that linked communities together in the past. Civic and religious institutions need to work hard to restore a more responsible, supportive network where every citizen realises the duty of good citizenship, rather than merely condemning bad behaviours or hanging offenders.

Finally, without entering into a full-scale discussion of the possible alternatives for how to handle the problem of human sacrifice, the idea is to protect human rights at all costs, as people will always need examples that uphold the sanctity of life. A flexible and innovative society, particularly of individualism obsessed with being wealthier, will not eradicate the corrupt culture where the statutory authorities have failed. Thus, the conclusion suggests that institutions, especially the church, need to coordinate in the process of changing society and consciously and realistically address the question of past bias in three ways.

Firstly, society must restrain from bias and instead engage in dialogue with those who uphold traditional beliefs and cultural practices. Secondly, regulating traditional healing is seen as the right approach to legitimise genuine traditional healers and isolate fake ones. Thirdly, civic institutions should introduce anti-corruption programmes in schools and work places as restraints to corruption.

Finally, there needs to be a regulatory mechanism to enforce tough and strict monitoring of any hidden healing practices, which should be reported by neighbourhood watch methods and through mentoring communities in every functioning organisation, with powers of reporting incidents for arrest. Whereas society actively takes procedures to require proof of corrupt acts, anti-corruption law and the fight for the right kind of culture have to be taken seriously to address the challenge.

Finally, this book has advocated that evil forces have arisen in beliefs for the accumulation of wealth, which have led people into unanticipated dangers. Churches, civic leadership and society at large need to deal collectively with the advance effects of every source of corruption as a way of creating a better social context and tighter obligations. The church needs to be committed to the toleration of divergent beliefs in a spirit of openness to what is largely seen as a moral ideal, where the moral duty of citizenship means treating each other with equal rights, justice, dignity and respect.

Bibliography

Barrett, D. B., 1968, Schism and Renewal in Africa, Analysis of six thousand contemporary religious movement, Oxford.

Bowie, F. (2000). "Ritual Theory, rites of passage and ritual violence". The Anthropology of Religion, Oxford: Basil Blackwell.

Brown, I. C., (1963). "Understanding Other Cultures", Prentice Hall, Inc., Englewood Cliffs, New Jersey.

Boxer, C. R., The Portuguese Seaborne Empire (1415-1825), London Hutchison.

Chrétien, J. P., (1991). 'Presse libre' et Propagande Raciste au Rwanda: Kangura et 'Les 10 Commandements du Hutu, Politique Africaine' 42, pp. 127-129.

Durkheim, Emile, (1915), The Elementary Forms of the Religious Life, London: Allen and Unwin.

Hannerz, U., (1992), Cultural Complexity. Studies in the Social Organisation of Meaning, New York.

Huntington, S., (1996), the Clash of Civilisations and the Remaking of the World Order, New York.

Parrinder, E. G., 1987, Encountering World Religions, Edinburgh, T and T Clack Ltd.

1953, Religion in an African City, London.

Sheppard, D., (1983). Bias to the Poor, London: Hodder and Stoughton.

Shriver, W. D., Woodstock Report, March 1996, No. 45.

Turner, H. W., 1967, History of an African Independent Church, The life and faith of the Church of the Lord (Aladura) vol. 2, London, Oxford, University Press.

Jan Olav Smit, Pope Pius XII, Burns Oates & Washburne, London, Dublin, 1951.

Joseph Metzler, La Congregazione 'de Propaganda Fide' e lo sviluppo delle missioni cattoliche (sec. XVIII al XX), in Anuario de la Historia de la Iglesia, Año/Vol IX, Pamplona, 2000, pp.145–154.

Kolini, Emmanuel, (1995). 'Towards Reconciliation in Rwanda', Transformation, Vol. 12, No2, April/June.

Marx, K.,"A Contribution to the Critique of Hegel's Philosophy of Right: Introduction" in e.g. David McLellan (ed), Karl Marx: Selected Writings, Oxford: OUP, 1977.

Merton, R., (1936). in American Sociological Review 1, pp.894-904.

Nguema, I., The Challenges for Peace Making in Africa, Conflict Resolution, Addis Ababa, Ethiopia, London: International Alert Report, September 1994 p.7.

Levi-Struss, C., (1949); The Elementary Structures of Kinship Boston: Beacon Press.

Wijsen, F., and J. van Slageren, Missiologie-beoefening in Nederland en België, in: Wereld en Zending 27 (1998/4), 25-34.

Electronic Sources

Hubert Jedin, *Kirchengeschichte* Vol. VII, Herder Freiburg, 1988.

Mantienne, Frédéric 1999 Monseigneur Pigneau de Béhaine, Editions Eglises d'Asie, 128 Rue du Bac, Paris, ISSN 12756865 ISBN 2914402201.

Missions étrangères de Paris. 350 ans au service du Christ 2008 Editeurs Malesherbes Publications, Paris ISBN 9782916828107.

http://www.interfaithdialog.org/reading-room/the-problem-mission-and-or-dialogue.html/1/10/09

Les Missions Etrangères. Trois siècles et demi d'histoire et d'aventure en Asie Editions Perrin, 2008, ISBN 9782262025717

hhp://www.mamaafrica.com/article/articleone.php/16/9/2009

http://www.sedos.org/english/liden2.htm/12/8/07

hhp://www.mamaafrica.com/article/articleone.php/16/9/2009

http://colanmc.siu.edu/BAS495/students/chris/ghweb.html9/7/09
http://www.messiahtruth.com/response.html/15/9/09

www.ingramcontent.com/pod-product-compliance
Ingram Content Group UK Ltd.
Pitfield, Milton Keynes, MK11 3LW, UK
UKHW021052270726
13967UKWH00012B/586